Wars of imperial conquest in Africa, 1830–1914

Wars of imperial conquest in Africa, 1830–1914

Bruce Vandervort

Indiana University Press
Bloomington and Indianapolis

First published in North America in 1998 by

Indiana University Press
601 North Morton Street
Bloomington, Indiana 47404

Manufactured in Great Britain

Library of Congress Cataloging-in-Publication Data
A catalog record for this book is available from the Library of Congress.

ISBN 0-253-21178-6 (paper)
ISBN 0-253-33383-0 (cloth)

1 2 3 4 5   02 01 00 99 98

Contents

For my children
Mark, Emily, Lucy and Nick

List of maps

Preface

The aim of this book is to examine the origins and conduct of colonial warfare in Africa in the late nineteenth century, as far as possible from the perspectives both of the European invaders and the African resisters, and in the process to demonstrate the impact, both immediate and long-term, of these wars upon the societies, political structures and military theory and practice of both victors and vanquished.

I have written this book with the student and general reader in mind. Scholarly apparatus has been kept to a minimum. Notes are limited to indicating the sources of direct quotations and of viewpoints on matters about which there is some controversy. The bibliographical entries have been annotated where appropriate in an effort to point students toward the more important works in the field.

For present purposes, Africa is defined as including North Africa and the Horn of Africa as well as the sub-Saharan portion of the continent. There are at least three good reasons for this. First, the French experience in Algeria from 1830 onwards exercised a potent influence upon French military practice and relations with African peoples (especially Muslims) south of the Sahara. Secondly, the events of 1898 in the Sudan, beginning with the suppression of Mahdism at the battle of Omdurman and culminating in the Franco-British confrontation at Fashoda, forced a reappraisal of the aspirations of all the imperial powers in Africa–Belgian, German and Italian as well as British and French. Finally, news of the defeat of an Italian army by the Ethiopians at Adowa in 1896 reverberated throughout the imperial world and served as a beacon of hope, both then and later, for colonized people across Africa and for oppressed people of colour everywhere.

The treatment in the book of European imperial powers and the African peoples who joined with or resisted them is intended to be even-handed. The reader will learn as much about the role of the historical memory of conquest and resistance in the forging of the modern African identity as about that of "Queen Victoria's Little Wars" in fostering popular imperialism in late-nineteenth-century Britain. On the imperial side, coverage is more inclusive than has usually been the case. While the British and French experiences must bulk large in the narrative because of the greater scope of their activity in Africa, the German, Italian, Belgian and Portuguese imperial ventures also receive considerable attention.

Even so, limitations of space have forced me to be selective. The reader will therefore find here only peripheral references to, for example, the French conquest of Dahomey in the early 1890s, the Portuguese campaigns in Angola and Guinea-Bissau in the late nineteenth and early twentieth centuries, the revolts of the Ndebele and Shona peoples against settler rule in Zimbabwe in the 1890s, and the "pacification" of Kenya and Somalia in the years before the First World War. Readers who wish to know more about these episodes will find a number of helpful titles listed in the Notes and Bibliography.

Perhaps the most significant omission concerns the First (1880–1) and Second (1899–1902) Boer Wars. It is my view that these wars, important as they may have been to the future of the British Empire and, indeed, to that of South Africa, still fall only partly within the scope of this book. My overriding concern here is with the wars fought in Africa between Africans and Europeans. The Boer wars, as I see them, were European wars fought in Africa. And, just as the American War of Independence cannot be considered an episode in the American Indian resistance to European invasion, so the Boer wars cannot be seen as part of the saga of African resistance to European encroachments. Nevertheless, both wars are at least of peripheral interest to our story, in that, by way of comparison, they shed further light on warfare elsewhere in Africa during the same period. The two wars will be considered together in this light at the beginning of Chapter Five.

The approach taken here has been inspired by the "New Military History", a way of writing about warfare now some twenty years old (but still hotly contested in some quarters), which agrees with Georges Clemenceau that war is too important to be left to the generals. The "New Military Historians" contend that

> War is more than military operations. Modern war, above all, came to enlist every aspect of life. This enlargement has altered the way historians write about war. Traditional military history has evolved into a

broader and deeper approach to the relationship between war and society.[1]

The "New Military History" is at least as much concerned with the impact of war on society and culture as it is with the strategies and tactics of armies. It seeks to measure the impact upon the rise and decline of states of military establishments and the wars they wage. It is interested in the role of warfare in propagating the myths and legends that bind peoples together or tear them apart. It wants to know how the private soldier fared on the day of battle, as well as the general who commanded him. These concerns will be reflected in this book.

But the older *histoire bataille*, the "guns and drums" history of battles won and lost, of wise and foolish generals, cannot be eschewed altogether. Some of the battles fought in Africa during the colonial wars enjoyed a prominent place in the iconography, literature, and collective memory of peoples on both sides, e.g., Isandlwana, Adowa, Omdurman. Some account must be given of these events which so gripped people both at the time and later. Nor can one dismiss entirely the great commanders of the era, whose deeds not only fired the imagination, but also stoked the fires of patriotism and helped swing votes in elections. Some, indeed, have continued to wield great influence almost down to our own day. Perhaps the best example of this is the great leader of the Mandingo people in their late-nineteenth-century struggle against the French in West Africa, Samori Touré, the "Bonaparte of the Sudan". A claim of descent from Samori contributed to the rise to power of Sekou Touré, the late dictator of Guinea.

But the tone and content of this book have also been influenced by the new approaches to the history of the African resistance to conquest that began to manifest themselves in Anglo-American academic circles in the 1960s and 1970s. As readers will surmise, while I have generally embraced the outlook and findings of this new school of interpretation, my relationship to it remains conflictual on some points.

A historiographical revolution

The momentum towards decolonization in the years after the Second World War prompted anxious European historians to depart somewhat from their earlier preoccupation with the purely European dynamics of the nineteenth-century "Scramble" to divide up Africa, and to take a more searching look at the African response to European invasion and conquest. The mainstream standpoint which now emerged in Anglo-American circles, most prominently represented by the scholarly duo of Roland Oliver & John Fage, jettisoned earlier tendencies to explain European triumph in the African wars as a result of "moral" or racial superiority and, instead, stressed the overwhelming military superiority of the Europeans. It was further argued, in the words of Oliver and Fage, that, for Africans facing the European juggernaut, "nothing was to be gained by resistance and much by negotiation".[2] Those who had resisted imperial conquest arms in hand were dismissed as "romantic reactionaries" or premature nationalists, who had risen up in a gallant but doomed defence of state systems and ways of life that the arrival of the Europeans had rendered anachronistic. Of more interest to this group of historians were those seemingly more rational African leaders who had bowed to the verdict of history and who had wisely decided to collaborate with the invader and thus shore up their own authority and enhance the well-being of their people. These astute precursors, it was hoped, had left a usable legacy of good sense and co-operative spirit to the leaders of the newly-independent African nations.

New directions in the Anglo-Saxon historiography of the African wars began to make their presence felt in the 1960s, and by the 1970s could be said to have constituted themselves as a new orthodoxy. Briefly, two new points of departure set off this approach from what had been written before.

One was the tendency to see Europeans responding to events in Africa rather than the other way around. This was to a large extent a by-product of the path-breaking research of Ronald Robinson & John Gallagher on the "New Imperialism". In their seminal book, *Africa and the Victorians: the official mind of imperialism*, Robinson & Gallagher argued that, if British imperialism in the 1880s and 1890s was "new" at all, it wasn't in the sense that it suddenly turned aggressive and acquisitive, but because it faced "new" challenges at the periphery that forced it to attack and occupy.[3] Their two main cases in point were the invasion of Egypt in 1882 and the Second Boer War (1899–1902), both undertaken to stifle flux at the periphery and thus safeguard the lifeline to India. Robinson later made this argument even more explicit in shorter pieces, going so far as to state that

> European economic and strategic expansion took imperial form when these two components operated at cross-purposes with a third and non-European component – that of indigenous collaboration and resistance. The missing key to a more historical theory [of imperialism] perhaps is to be found in this third element.[4]

What made this argument important for writers of African colonial military history was that, for the first time, it put African flux and African agency at the centre of events in the years of the "Scramble", rather than initiatives to divide up Africa taken in European capitals for largely European reasons.

The second fresh point of departure essentially followed on from the first. It featured a much more intense focus on African resistance than had been the case earlier. To begin with, the new generation of Anglo-American historians found that African resistance to conquest was much more intensive and widespread than was earlier reported. The Ghanaian historian A. Adu Boahen, for example, contended that "an overwhelming majority of the Africans adopted the military option, either in isolation or in combination with diplomacy".[5] As Boahen's phrase suggests, recent historians of the imperial wars in Africa have taken issue with the earlier division by Oliver & Fage of the African objects of conquest into "romantic reactionaries" who fought back and "rational realists" who negotiated. John Hargreaves wrote that

> In West Africa, as in East and Central Africa, it cannot be said that those who opted for resistance were less far-sighted or forward-looking than the "collaborators". In fact they were often the same men.[6]

The historians whose work began to appear in the 1960s and 1970s also called into question the older notion that African resistance had ended with the battlefield Armageddon. Focusing mainly on East and Central Africa, Terence Ranger posited a much more sophisticated model of resistance, seeing it as a continuum beginning with the phase of armed or "primary" resistance, continuing through a "post-pacification" phase in which resistance was manifested in ways ranging from protest and non-compliance to revolt, and ending in the emergence of movements of national liberation in the post-Second World War era.

Ranger was also in the forefront of those who challenged the earlier contention that armed resistance was futile. He showed that in Tanganyika and Southern Rhodesia, for example, African armed resistance forced the imperial powers to take the resisters seriously or, at the very least, not take them for granted in the post-pacification era.[7] But, for Ranger and others, perhaps the greatest value of resistance lay in its meaning for the African future. Hargreaves, once again, observed that

> It is hardly profound to conclude that the most important element making for the survival of African politics under colonial rule was simply a strong sense of ethnic or political identity – the attachment of their subjects to what has been called the "national cause". This sense

of identity tended to be strengthened when the rulers who represented it could point to some record of resistance to imperialism.[8]

These early revisionists also provided us with much new information on the physical and spiritual capacities of the Africans for effective resistance, on their strategies and tactics, and on the qualities of their leaders and the troops they led.

By the 1970s the revisionist viewpoint on African resistance to European conquest had acquired the trappings of a new orthodoxy. John M. O'Sullivan was surely guilty of understatement in 1978 when he wrote that "presentations of historical African resistance [are] in considerable vogue now." After several decades of playing down African resistance as minimal or futile, historians in some cases appeared to have gone to the other extreme. "The dead horse of African passivity to European conquest has been so thoroughly laid to rest," wrote O'Sullivan, "that various authors strive to prove that their people fought the longest war or the hardest war or produced the most European casualties."[9]

Criticism also emerged of the claims of Terence Ranger and others that direct links could be established between the resistance movements of the nineteenth century and the nationalist movements which took control of independent Africa in the 1960s. For example, Donald Denoon and Adam Kuper, in their article, "Nationalist historians in search of a nation: the 'new historiography' in Dar-es-Salaam",[10] attacked Ranger et al. for forcing the evidence to fashion an historical pedigree for modern nationalist movements such as Julius Nyerere's Tanganyika African National Union.

Even more problematical than this "inflation" of the impact of African resistance on the European invaders or on twentieth-century African nationalism, was the attempt to recast the meaning of resistance. Whereas earlier generations of historians generally understood resistance to mean *armed* opposition, writers beginning in the 1960s broadened the definition to embrace a host of other reactions. "Although primarily thought of as martial," wrote two prominent commentators on African resistance in 1970, "resistance was equally political, and in many areas a resistance of the mind rather than of the hands."[11]

There are two problems with this formulation. First, it harks back to the kind of "compartmentalization" of African responses to imperial conquest that John Hargreaves took to task earlier on, namely, that it seems to assume that "martial" resisters will eschew politics, and vice-versa, and that they must choose between an opposition of "the mind" and one of "the hands." The second and perhaps most important problem is that this all-inclusive approach risks stretching the definition of resistance so far that the word becomes meaningless.

It is to be hoped that I have not given the impression that all of the important work in recent years on the wars of imperial conquest in Africa has been done in the Anglo-Saxon world. As the notes and bibliography to this book should demonstrate, I have profited enormously from the recent work done by scholars writing in other languages, and by African historians working in English and French. Among the monuments of non-English-language scholarship on the African colonial wars – in many cases studies of their subjects unmatched elsewhere – there is room for only the following here.

Non-English-language sources

Among the large number of books on the subject published in French in recent years, pride of place must go to the late Yves Person's massive, three-volume biography of the West African resistance leader, Samori Touré, entitled *Samori: une révolution dyula* (Dakar: Institut Fondamental de l'Afrique Noire, 1971). Among the most helpful books published recently on France's colonial army is Jean-Charles Jauffret's sprawling doctoral dissertation, *Parlement, gouvernement, commandement: l'armée de métier sous la 3e République, 1871–1914* (Vincennes: Service historique de l'armée de terre, 1987).[12]

Italian historical writing on that nation's colonial wars has undergone a revolution in the last three decades. The bellwether of change, after decades of domination of the field by pro-Fascist accounts, was the appearance in the late 1970s and 1980s of Angelo del Boca's monumental revisionist history of Italian imperialism, which covers not only Ethiopia and Libya but Somalia as well: *Gli italiani in Africa orientale*, 4 vols (Rome-Bari: Laterza, 1976–84), and *Gli italiani in Libia,* 2 vols (Rome-Bari: Laterza, 1986–88). Then in 1993, Nicola Labanca published his *In marcia verso Adua* (Turin: Einaudi, 1993), to my knowledge the first study of the social composition and *mentalité* of a European expeditionary force in Africa, in this case that of Italy in Eritrea and Ethiopia in the 1880s and 1890s. It is to be hoped that Labanca has launched a trend and that works of this kind on other European expeditionary forces are forthcoming.

The historiography of Portugal's "effective occupation" of its African domains in the late nineteenth century and the resistance it engendered is dominated by the works of a Frenchman, the extraordinarily prolific René

Pélissier. His military history of Portuguese Africa from the mid-nineteenth century down to pacification in the interwar era was completed in 1989 with publication of *Naissance de la Guiné: Portugais et Africains en Senegambie (1841–1936).* The series began with the publication in 1977 of *Les guerres grises: résistance et révoltes en Angola (1845–1941),* and continued with the appearance of the two-volume *Naissance de Mozambique: résistance et révoltes anticoloniales (1854–1918)* in 1984. As the titles of his books indicate, Pélissier tends to approach his subject from the standpoint of the resistance. This has not stopped him from documenting every conceivable Portuguese incursion into the African interior during the period covered, from major expeditions to platoon-sized raids.[13] The outstanding work on the nineteenth-century African colonial wars in Portuguese in recent years has been Antonio José Telo's *Economia e imperio no Portugal contemporaneo* (Lisbon: Edições Cosmos, 1994), which places Portugal's wars firmly in the context of the Portuguese political economy as it evolved from the early years of the century. Telo's book also provides one of the best demonstrations of the role of the new military technology of the nineteenth century in securing victory in the colonial wars.

Conclusion

The book which follows takes as its point of departure the belief that we have now reached a point in our understanding of the military history of the partition of Africa where it is possible to begin to draw some meaningful general conclusions. Evidence from the European side has been plentiful for generations and continues to accumulate. The intense focus on the African resistance in the 1960s and 1970s has produced a substantial harvest of monographs and articles. This abundant and varied data makes it possible for the first time, it seems to me, to write a military history of the late-nineteenth-century European conquest of Africa that has a good chance of presenting a full and reasonably accurate account of these events from both sides of the battle line.

But perhaps the time is now ripe for historians to cast their nets even more widely than I have suggested. To the merging of data from European and African perspectives they could usefully add the insights that have emerged as a result of research in neighbouring areas, especially multi-disciplinary studies of the European conquest and colonization of North America, Asia and the South Pacific. The most readily applicable of these books are the valuable comparative studies emanating from the Centre for the History of European Expansion at the University of Leiden: e.g., H.L. Wesseling (ed.), *Expansion and reaction* (Leiden University Press, 1978) and J.A. De Moor and H.L. Wesseling (eds), *Imperialism and war: essays on colonial war in Asia and Africa* (Leiden University Press, 1989). Also useful have been recent studies of colonial warfare in Asia, e.g. C. Fourniau, *Annam-Tonkin, 1885–1896: lettrés et paysans vietnamiens face à la conquête coloniale* (Paris: L'Harmattan, 1989), M. Kuitenbrouwer, *The Netherlands and the rise of modern imperialism: colonies and foreign policy* (Oxford: Berg, 1991), David Omissi, *The sepoy and the raj: the Indian Army, 1860–1940* (London: Macmillan, 1994) and, especially, James Belich's path-breaking study, *The New Zealand wars and the Victorian interpretation of racial conflict* (Auckland: Auckland University Press, 1986). Of methodological value to historians of the colonial wars in Africa are the ethno-historically-informed studies of Francis Jennings and James Axtell on the resistance of the North American woodland Indians to European and American incursions,[14] and Ian Steele's similarly-enriched military history of this drama, *Warpaths: invasions of North America* (New York: Oxford University Press, 1994).

What we do not have enough of yet, however, is the kind of cross-cultural comparative study done by James O. Gump in his fascinating study, *The dust rose like smoke: the subjugation of the Zulus and the Sioux* (Lincoln: University of Nebraska Press, 1994). Perhaps this is the most important task for the immediate future.

Acknowledgements

Many people have helped me with the preparation of this book and I can only hope that none of them have been omitted here.

First, I wish to thank Dr. Jeremy Black, Chair of the Department of History & Archaeology at the University of Exeter and Director of the "Warfare and History" series at the University College London Press, for inviting me to contribute this volume. Publisher, Steven Gerrard, Commissioning Editor, Aisling Ryan and the editorial team at UCL Press have been unfailingly patient and supportive.

I wish to thank the authorities of the Virginia Military Institute for granting me a Wachtmeister Sabbatical Leave for the first half of the 1996–7 academic year, during which time most of this book was written. That part of the task was helped along enormously by the wizardry of Jan Holly and Elizabeth Hostetter of VMI's Preston Library in locating the books I needed through inter-library loan. Funding from VMI's Summer Research

Program enabled me to undertake research in the archives of the Royal Marines' Museum in Southsea, Hampshire. My all too brief visit to that remarkable institution was made pleasant and fruitful by the assistance of the Museum's archivist, Mr. M.G. Little.

A number of individual scholars helped in the elaboration of this book by offering inspiration and advice. First place on the list belongs to my colleague and friend, Dr. Blair Turner, chair of the VMI History Department, whose encouragement and interest have done much to assist my scholarly endeavours over the years. I have also profited greatly from the support of Dr. Henry Bausum, editor of the *Journal of Military History*. Still on this side of the water, I would like to acknowledge special debts to Joe Smaldone, Doug Porch, Alberto Sbacchi, Woodruff Smith, Douglas Wheeler, and Brian Sullivan in the USA, and Cornelius Jaenen in Canada. In Britain, Brian Bond, Tony Clayton, Malyn Newitt and Bruce Collins offered useful advice, as did Jean-Charles Jauffret and René Pélissier in France and Jean Stengers and Col. Louis-François Vanderstraeten in Belgium. I owe a great deal to Antonio José Telo in Lisbon. Of all the historical fraternities in Europe, I have found none to be warmer or more generous than the Italian. Nicola Labanca, Angelo del Boca and Giorgio Rochat went beyond the bounds of the usual scholarly solidarity in rendering assistance, and I am very grateful for it. Bahru Zewde and Richard Pankhurst in Addis Ababa offered valuable insights into the Ethiopian fight against Italian imperialism. Finally, a special word of thanks goes to my son, Mark Cottingham, in Geneva, Switzerland, who provided invaluable help with a crucial German source.

My only regret about the book is that it so often took me away from my family. I hope my wife, Wendy, and my children, Lucy, Nick, Emily and Mark, will let me make it up to them once this book is safely between two covers.

Bruce Vandervort
Lexington, Virginia
February 1998

1. Africa before the Scramble: indigenous and alien powers in 1876

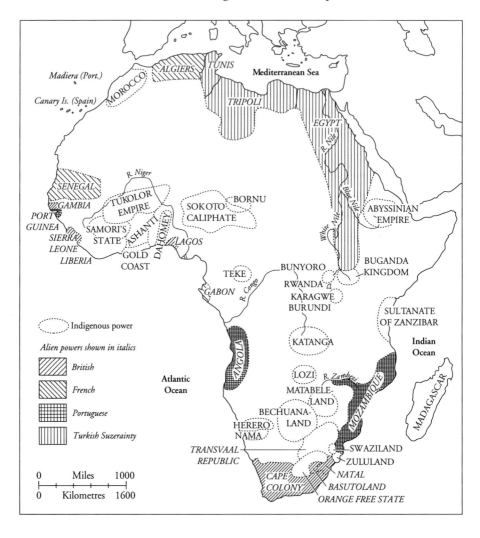

Chapter One

Lords of the land: Africa on the eve of conquest

Introduction

Despite the three-centuries-long slave trade which sent some twelve million Africans into servitude in the Americas, relations between black Africans and Europeans were carried on largely at arm's length until the 1850s. The interior of Africa was still mainly in the hands of African peoples, whose hostility, combined with the rigors of tropical diseases, kept European penetration to a minimum. It was still a time when African princes could think themselves magnanimous in according European newcomers the title of "masters of the water", secure in the knowledge that they retained the vastly more important title of "lords of the land".

The main exceptions to this were a series of wars that raged at the more or less temperate extremities of the African continent. The best known of these was the two-decade-long struggle by the French to "pacify" Algeria. But there were also the so-called "Kaffir Wars" between Britain and the Xhosa people, which troubled the eastern frontier of Cape Province in South Africa from the Napoleonic era down to the eve of the Zulu War of 1879.[1] Still, as late as 1876 less than ten per cent of the continent had fallen into European hands, and most of that was accounted for by France's Algerian colony.[2]

Change in pre-colonial Africa

The European soldiers and statesmen who engineered the conquest of most of Africa in the late nineteenth century liked to think of themselves as

1

ambassadors of innovation and progress to a continent mired in timeless savagery. Succeeding generations of Europeans saw modern Africa as the more or less exclusive product of initiatives undertaken by white colonizers. Most of today's historians of Africa do not share that view. Their research has demonstrated that, far from being static and impervious to change, the societies and polities of much of Africa were constantly in flux, and that at no time was this more so than on the eve of the European invasions. Indeed, it has lately been shown that these European incursions quite often occurred in response to economic or political changes within Africa that Europeans found threatening to their interests and believed it necessary to stop.[3]

Recent historians have stressed the trends toward a greater economic integration of Africa on the eve of European conquest, and further suggest that the continent may also have been undergoing social change. New commercial classes, a sort of African equivalent to the dynamic bourgeoisie of nineteenth-century Europe, are seen as rising to challenge the traditional establishment for social dominance. African states, particularly the larger entities, have also been described as undertaking significant modernization programs, including ones in the military sphere.[4] This internally-generated change, in the view of some historians, would have opened up a distinctly African path to modernity, but the process was brought to a halt as a result of European conquest and the imposition of European priorities under imperial rule.[5]

Most important, recent histories of nineteenth-century Africa have described the pre-colonial years of the century as a time of movement toward a greater centralization of power: in larger polities such as the Zulu empire that emerged from the "crushing" of neighbouring tribes or "*Mfecane*" as it was known in Zulu; the jihad states of al-Hajj Umar, Ahmadu Seku and Samori in West Africa; the Mahdist theocratic state in the Sudan; the rejuvenated Solomonic empire of Ethiopia; the Sokoto empire of northern Nigeria; and the Ashanti empire of present-day Ghana. It must be remembered, writes Philip Curtin, that in Africa "the empire-building of the pre-colonial century had been mainly African . . ."[6] Until fairly recently, historians have tended to view this efflorescence of African empires as a largely positive development, foreshadowing and in some cases linking forward to the nation-building of the post-independence era. As we will see below, there was sometimes a negative side as well to the ebb and flow of state-building in Africa, one that frequently had disastrous consequences for the African peoples involved.

While the characterizations of trends in late pre-colonial Africa outlined above continue to be the subjects of debate, what cannot be contested is that, as a result of this tremendous burst of empire-building and an equally remarkable explosion of religious crusading, wars in Africa during the first three-quarters of the nineteenth century, prior to the European invasions, tended to occur more often, last longer and lead to greater bloodshed.

The implications of this more or less constant upheaval for the political, economic and social history of the continent, while certainly not ignored, have nonetheless not been sufficiently addressed in African history textbooks to date. In a military history such as this one, the impact of this unprecedented flux must, of course, occupy a central place.

Pre-colonial African armies

Types of armies and their evolution

Armies reflect the societies from which they spring, but their composition and ways of waging war are determined perhaps even more by geography. Horsebreeding has prospered in the grasslands north of the Sahara desert and in the western and central Sudan south of it. These wide-open spaces also permit the kind of manoeuvre warfare that is not possible in the rain forests of the African tropical zone. Thus, it will come as no surprise to learn that, on the plains north and south of the Sahara, armies from very early on tended to rely upon the mobility and shock power of cavalry. Two different kinds of horsemen evolved. Light cavalry, which used the small, wiry horses bred locally throughout the region, excelled at scouting, raiding and flank attacks. The shock arm of these armies, however, was the heavy cavalry, and for this the Arab "chargers" raised by specialist breeders in North Africa were required. In western and central Sudan, heavy cavalry mounts of this type had to be imported from north of the Sahara at great cost. Harness and maintenance also came dear. This virtually guaranteed that the Sudan military, and much else in the region besides, would be dominated by the landed aristocracy, the only social class that could afford to buy and maintain such formidable steeds. The anthropologist Jack Goody has tried to erect a general principle upon this fact: arguing that cavalry states tend to be autocratic, while infantry states tend toward democracy.[7]

There are problems with this attractive thesis, however. One is the fact that the savannah armies also enrolled large contingents of infantry – archers and spearmen in particular – and that these foot soldiers often provided the winning margin in wars. "Cavalry may win a battle, but infantry are needed to win a war", remarks Robert S. Smith, historian of Africa's pre-colonial wars.[8]

3

Outside North Africa and the savannah regions, armies were composed almost entirely of infantry. This had much to do with the pervasiveness of trypanosomiasis, or sleeping sickness, a disease spread by the tsetse fly. Sleeping sickness was fatal to most domestic animals, including horses. As a result, horses were largely unknown in the areas where the tsetse fly flourished, such as the forest zone of West and Central Africa and East Africa south of the sudd marshes of the southern Sudan. In southern Africa, the more temperate climate, abundant grazing land and relative absence of the tsetse fly once again favoured horse-raising. Here, horses arrived with the first white invaders, the Dutch, who occupied Cape Province in the seventeenth century. In time, this region also produced some formidable horsemen, especially the Boer mounted infantry of South Africa and their counterparts among the the Nama of South West Africa (present-day Namibia). Perhaps surprisingly, the various branches of the Nguni people (the Zulus, Swazis and Ndebele), Southern Africa's most storied warrior peoples, never took to the horse. This appears to have been for largely cultural reasons. The highly-structured Nguni military systems, built around an infantry primed for hand-to-hand combat, rejected all innovations that might threaten their integrity (and the monarchical political structures they kept in place), ultimately including firearms.

Generally speaking, military organization in pre-colonial Africa usually took one of four different forms. First, in some kingdoms soldiers were raised locally and fought as bands from their home areas under territorial chiefs, in the fashion of feudal Europe. This was probably the most common form of military organization in Africa. Its most famous examples probably would have been the armies of Ethiopia and the Ashanti empire in present-day Ghana.

Secondly, in other states soldiers were amalgamated and then divided up in some way – for example, in regiments. This was the structure adopted by the various Nguni peoples of southeastern Africa: the Zulus, certainly, but also the Swazis of Swaziland, the Ndebele of Zimbabwe and the Gaza Nguni of southern Mozambique.

Thirdly, in some states "citizen armies" emerged to take up arms when needed. This was the system which predominated in much of West Africa until relatively modern times. Here, all free adult males capable of bearing arms could be called up in time of war. Finally, while professional standing armies existed in Africa, they were rare until fairly late in the nineteenth century. Even then, in many armies the only units functioning on a full-time basis were specialized formations such as musketeers or, later, riflemen and cannoneers. These kinds of unit tended to be formed in states where efforts were being made to adapt western technology to local needs, such as Abd el-Kader's Algeria, Samori's West African empire, and the Mahdist theocracy in the Sudan.[9]

Social composition of African armies

As we have seen, in many African societies military service was an obligation falling upon all able-bodied free adult males. Almost everywhere in Africa, however, the type of military service rendered depended upon one's social status. In the states of the Western and Central Sudan, as in Europe under the *Ancien Régime*, the cavalry was the aristocratic arm *par excellence*, while less fortunate members of society inevitably ended up in the infantry.

There was one interesting exception to this, however. In the Muslim empire of Masina (1818–62), near the bend of the Niger River, the state controlled the supply of warhorses and made all able-bodied males eligible to serve as cavalrymen.

> The cavalry of Masina was not an aristocratic institution: the state gave horsemen an allowance for weapons and harness, provided rations for men and horses and gave an allowance of food to cavalrymen's families.[10]

Outside the savannah regions, the absence of cavalry meant that the upper classes had to content themselves with ordering foot soldiers about. In many forest zone states they did tend to reserve the higher ranks of the officer corps for themselves. In others, however, command devolved upon men who had acquired reputations for bravery or martial skill, regardless of their social origins.

Women played a much more important role in warfare in Africa than anywhere else during the nineteenth century. The so-called "Amazons" of Dahomey, a West African kingdom located between the Gold Coast and Nigeria, were the world's only all-female combat unit during this period. The "Amazons", who, as one might imagine, aroused a great deal of interest in Europe, started out as a royal bodyguard, but evolved into the Dahomean army's elite contingent by the late 1800s. About 3,000 strong, they first saw combat in the 1840s and

> soon became the most warlike, and the most feared, of all the Dahomean troops. It was they who bore the brunt of the fighting in

5

a number of the most important of the nineteenth-century Dahomean wars. . . . During the most desperately fought of all [these] wars, the struggle against the French [1890–94], their losses were so severe that as a fighting force they were completely destroyed.[11]

In the nineteenth century fascinated Victorian observers tried to explain the "unfeminine" nature of the "Amazons" as the result of repressed sexual desire. The "Amazons" were royal wives and were allowed to have sex only with the king. This Victorian theory has persisted into the twentieth century. An expert on the wars of the Dahomey kingdom wrote recently that the "Amazons' enforced state of chastity does a good deal towards explaining their ferocity".[12] Interestingly, Victorians offered the same explanation for the battlefield prowess of Zulu males, who were only allowed to marry after retirement from military service around the age of 40. In a famous statement, Sir Bartle Frere, Britain's commander-in-chief in South Africa at the beginning of the Anglo-Zulu War of 1879, referred to the Zulus as "celibate manslaying gladiators".[13]

African women also played important non-combat roles. In West Africa particularly, military campaigns were often family affairs. Frequently accompanied by their children, women followed their soldier husbands into the field, carrying food and cooking utensils and sometimes military gear as well. Their main job was to cook meals for their families, but sometimes also for bachelor soldiers in the army. In the Congo, African soldiers' wives carried earthenware pots containing lighted tinder on their heads, to speed up the process of cooking meals for their husbands when the day's march was over.[14] This pattern of family participation in warfare was continued in the West African units created by the Europeans in the late 1800s. Although European officers thought that too much of this sort of "domestication" was likely to dampen the martial ardour of their black soldiers, they had no choice but to go along with it. Attempts by the French to ban family members from the columns of their Senegalese light infantry led to threats of mutiny.[15] The British faced similar experiences with troops of their West African Frontier Force.

The military obligations of Africa's large slave population, meanwhile, varied from society to society. In some, slaves were exempt from bearing arms, while in others they represented a significant proportion, sometimes even a majority, of the armed forces. This seems to have been particularly common in the kingdoms of the Western and Central Sudan, in Bornu and the Sokoto Caliphate, for example. Here much of the infantry tended to be unfree, a situation which persisted in some cases down to the late nineteenth century.

Armament

Although firearms made their first appearance in Africa not long after their debut in Europe, the evolution in armament from bows and arrows and lances and spears to guns proceeded more slowly and unevenly in Africa. Indeed, some of the most warlike societies in Africa never took up the gun at all. The reasons for this rather remarkable refusal are instructive and will be dealt with below.

Firearms first appeared in sub-Saharan Africa in the late fifteenth century, surfacing within a few years of each other on the Atlantic and Indian Ocean coasts of Africa, where they arrived in the baggage of the first Portuguese explorers, and among the kingdoms of the Central Sudan, where they were brought as presents from fellow potentates in North Africa. The first record of the actual use of firearms in combat in sub-Saharan Africa, however, dates from a century later. In the late sixteenth century, the king of Bornu in the Central Sudan acquired a stand of muskets and a squad of trained musketeers from the Ottoman Turks in Libya. The king's action seems to have been inspired by one of the signal events of the African Middle Ages: the overthrow in 1591 of the powerful Songhai empire in the Western Sudan by a small Moroccan army equipped with muskets. After this early exposure to firearms, there followed, with one or two notable exceptions, a long hiatus in which guns in Africa were more likely to be found in royal armouries than on the battlefield.

Apart from North Africa, where firearms were introduced early and almost immediately became indispensable weapons, the only areas where guns acquired a leading role in warfare were Ethiopia and certain slave-trading states of West Africa.

Next door, in the Western Sudan, the cavalry states around the bend of the Niger River were slow to acquire firearms. It was only in the early nineteenth century that muskets began to be used in the region and it was only at mid-century that they became an important factor in warfare. After that, however, the use of firearms grew apace. The jihad army of the Tukolor ruler, al-Hajj Umar, in the 1850s and 1860s and, especially, the army of Samori Touré in Guinea in the 1880s and 1890s relied heavily on firearms. Both armies employed trained corps of riflemen, many of whom were slaves, called *sofas*. Umar's army occupied a transitional position between the cavalry-dominated force so long characteristic of the region and a more modern, European-style force built around artillery and infantry firepower. Samori's army, on the other hand, trusted in the firepower of its infantry and only used cavalry for raiding and scouting, as did most European armies.

That firearms did not "catch on" to a greater extent than they did in the Central Sudan, despite their early introduction there, may have had something to do with

> a prevailing feeling that there was something underhand about fighting with guns or, indeed, with missile or projectile weapons in general. Manly and heroic combat, as many Hausa sayings have it, was engaged in by mounted warriors using lance and sword.[16]

Although firearms only reached the inland forest states of West Africa in the seventeenth century, they very quickly assumed an important role in regional warfare. By 1700 the Ashantis, for example, were well-equipped with muskets. In fact,

> it was their comparative strength in firearms which largely enabled them both to dominate their neighbours [in the savannah] to the north, especially the Dagomba, and to initiate their drive to the coast with its trading opportunities – especially of obtaining more guns and powder.[17]

The peoples of Eastern Africa were slower to take up the gun than their West African counterparts. The cattle-herding Maasai, for example, "disdained to use firearms for many years, despite their easy availability through the slave and ivory caravans which regularly passed through Maasai territory in the late nineteenth century".[18] Maasai hesitation derived from the same basic source as that of the Zulu: fear that adoption of this new weapon would upset their highly-organized military system, built around the spear, and, by extension, their social and political structure. The major exception to this tendency in East Africa were the so-called "Congo Arabs", migrants from the Swahili coast who relied heavily on firearms to cow local peoples and carve out new states for themselves in the eastern Congo basin.

The reception of guns was also mixed in Southern Africa. The peoples of what would become South West Africa – the Hereros and Namas – readily embraced firearms, as did the Xhosas of the Cape Province frontier and the Sotho and Pedi of the high veldt. The various Nguni peoples, the Ndebele, Swazis and Zulus, however, did not.

Instead of adopting firearms, the Nguni peoples carried through a military revolution of their own which found new uses for old weapons and devised new tactics in order to maximize their battlefield effectiveness. Legend credits the great Zulu king Shaka (1787–1828) with launching this revolution. A veteran soldier himself, Shaka was not impressed with the weapons and tactics of the local African armies of his day, his own Zulu troops included. Accordingly, he replaced the throwing assegai or javelin, a spindly six-foot shaft with a six-inch blade, with a shorter stabbing assegai featuring a heavy broad blade, eighteen inches long. This was a thrusting weapon and could be used only if the warrior carrying it closed with the enemy. Shaka called the new stabbing spear *iKlwa*, after the sucking sound it supposedly made when it was withdrawn from the victim's flesh. Shaka also transformed the oxhide shield of his warriors into an offensive weapon. Hooking its left edge over the left edge of his opponent's shield, the Zulu warrior could spin a foe to the right with a powerful backhand sweep. His own left would remain covered, while his opponent, off balance and hampered by his shield, which had been dragged across his front, would not be able to find an opening for his spear. The hooked shield would pull the foe's left arm over with it and expose his left armpit to an assegai thrust. Finally, there was the business of footwear. Earlier, Zulu warriors had worn oxhide sandals into battle. Shaka thought the sandals reduced speed and mobility and so ordered his men to go barefoot. Zulu warriors in Shaka's day and after were capable of almost unbelievable speed and manoeuvrability. How much this was owed to the abandonment of sandals is unclear.

Logistics

Logistics was the weak spot for all the armies that campaigned in Africa, indigenous and European alike. Keeping the troops fed in the field was a never-ending problem. African troops in the forest zone whose wives did not accompany them were expected to carry their own rations, which were made up for them at home. Yoruba soldiers on campaign in southern Nigeria dined on parched beans and hardtack made from beans and maize flour, while Dahomean soldiers ate toasted grains and bean cake. When these rations ran out, which they soon did, the troops had to forage for food.

Zulu warriors might take with them into the field "a skin bag, tied to their waist-belts and containing a cooked calf's liver and a handful of roasted mealies [ears of maize], but these could scarcely contain them for long". When these scant rations were gone, Zulu fighters were obliged to forage for their food. This could have devastating effects. When the fighting was on Zulu soil, as it was in the Anglo-Zulu War of 1879, whole areas of the homeland could be plucked clean of grain and livestock by foragers. Even then, hunger often stalked the Zulu armies. After the Zulu defeat at Kambula in March 1879, British soldiers "found a number of Zulu dead, who had overrun part of the camp, with their mouths stuffed full of porridge which they had just then looted from abandoned cooking pots".[19]

The African army that probably had the hardest time keeping its troops in the field was the Ethiopian. This was because of its greater size: the Ethiopian army that fought the Italians in 1896 numbered at least 100,000 men. Inability to provide food and forage for the army often forced Ethiopian generals to terminate sieges or call off campaigns. An Ethiopian army without food was like a plague of locusts. It was not unusual for the army to have to fight angry peasants as well as enemy soldiers.[20]

Strategy and tactics

For Africans as for Europeans, strategy was understood to mean the use of military force to achieve long-term objectives of paramount importance to the state or community. Tactics, on the other hand, referred to the military means used to achieve shorter-term goals, such as battlefield victories, on the way to the realization of the larger objective.

Strategy

The pursuit of strategic goals is easier to follow in the histories of the larger polities in Africa, which is not to say that smaller states or stateless peoples, for that matter, did not think in strategic terms. One of the most obvious examples of the pursuit of a strategic design by African states was the effort by some West African forest kingdoms, beginning in the seventeenth century, to break out of their isolation and establish themselves as Atlantic coast powers. The original motivation for this was a desire to participate in the lucrative trans-Atlantic slave trade, but the lure of the coast persisted long after the slave trade had died out. The interior states of Oyo, Dahomey and Ashanti are prime examples of this phenomenon.

In the 1600s the powerful state of Oyo, based in the savannah on the northern edge of the Nigerian forest zone, pushed south into the so-called "Dahomey gap" in the forest and on to the sea. The "Dahomey gap" was a strip of grassland that extended southwest from northern Nigeria all the way to the Atlantic; Oyo's strength lay in its cavalry, and its ability to deploy its horsemen in the "Dahomey gap" assured its control over that particular strip of the coast for the next two centuries. In the early 1700s the kingdom of Dahomey just to the west of the "gap" also pushed its way to the sea, overwhelming the coastal city-state of Whydah. Dahomey and Oyo both grew wealthy from participation in the international slave trade.[21]

The Ashanti state's expansion strategy looms even larger in African history because of its long duration and dramatic consequences. The Ashanti *Drang nach Suden*, as one author has called it, began in the early 1700s and involved the Ashantis in a seemingly interminable series of wars with the Fante people, whose lands lay between them and the sea. The southward thrust in the eighteenth century was motivated by a desire to sell its slaves directly to European buyers in the Atlantic slave trade. In the next century, however, even after the slave trade was abolished, there was no let-up in pressure. The Ashanti army had in the meantime converted to firearms and it was now considered imperative to have direct access to European suppliers of weapons and gunpowder on the coast. Although the Ashantis' strategy was ultimately frustrated by the British in the Anglo-Ashanti War of 1873–4, nonetheless "the Ashanti command's strategic concept and the skill and persistence with which this was implemented were certainly outstanding in West Africa".[22]

Tactics

In the forest zones south of the savannah and north of the South African veldt, the environment dictated the tactics of the armies of foot soldiers that predominated there. The dense vegetation restricted the movement of troops, often obliging them to march in single file. The surroundings also tended to rule out the kind of tactical deployment possible on the northern and southern plains. Pitched battles could occur in areas where the rain forest gave way to savannah, such as the southern Gold Coast, where the Ashanti armies roamed, but for the most part, fighting among forest peoples – the Yorubas of southern Nigeria or the Zande of the northern Congo are good examples – was characterized by ambushes and hand-to-hand combat. And, whereas the lance and spear were the classic weapons of Sudanic warfare, as the assegai was of warfare in Southern Africa, forest zone soldiers tended to favour clubs and swords, although bows and crossbows were also used.

On the South African veldt, it was possible to conduct the kind of manoeuvre warfare practised on the plains of the Central Sudan. But here the instrument of manoeuvre warfare was infantry, not cavalry, albeit one of the most mobile infantries in the history of warfare: the Zulu *impi*. Although its antecedents lie elsewhere, the *impi* came into its own, like so much else in the Zulu military system, during the reign of Shaka Zulu. Up to the late eighteenth century or so, warfare among the Nguni and other African peoples of the region had been largely ritualistic, a show of force designed to convince the enemy to give up and offer tribute. To Shaka, however, wars were fought to annihilate the enemy, were waged hand-to-hand with deadly intensity, and when the enemy broke, pursuit was relentless. Tactically, this mission of destruction was entrusted to the famous Zulu "cow horns" formation, composed of four sections of infantry of equal size. The front line was made up of three sections, with a fourth in reserve. The job of the centre section or "chest" of the formation was to hit the enemy head-on and pin him in place. Meanwhile, the two wings or "horns" were to race out and encircle him, joining hands in his rear area, and driving him into the "chest". Stationed nearby with backs turned to the battle to curb excitement, the reserve section would be used when necessary to reinforce encirclement or to pursue those enemies who tried to escape.

The Zulu attack formation was not, however, without parallels elsewhere in Africa. The kind of envelopment the Zulus sought to achieve was also the tactical objective of, among others, the Mahdists in the Sudan, whose battle formation was an elongated crescent. The wings of the crescent were intended to enfold the enemy army, cut off retreat and crush it. Other African armies, the Ashanti, for example, relied on flanking movements to defeat enemy forces. At the battle of Amoafo against the British in 1874, the Ashanti army tried to work its way around the enemy's left flank in order to get into its rear area to disrupt supplies and choke off retreat.

African leadership

Just as the composition of indigenous armies varied greatly across pre-colonial Africa, so did command structures. Among stateless peoples and in the smaller polities, where the whole community was called upon to take part in wars, leadership generally devolved upon the individual who had the greatest reputation as a fighter or hunter. In these situations, therefore, leadership was the province of gifted amateurs. In somewhat larger polities, command in wartime was usually exercised either by the chief himself or by a war chief designated by him or his council of advisors. In either case, command was exercised by someone who could be considered more or less professional.

In the larger states – kingdoms or empires, for example – a more elaborate command structure existed, as might be imagined. Here the head of state, the king or emperor, only rarely ventured on to the battlefield, leaving command of his troops almost completely in the hands of a staff of professional military men, or at least of notables who saw warfare as their vocation, in the manner of the European *Ancien Régime*.

Some degree of specialization could exist in these situations. In armies where attempts were made to train and field troops organized on the European model, officers with some experience of European-style warfare might be set over them. This was the arrangement made in the Sudan, for instance, when a corps of riflemen was formed within the Mahdist army in the 1880s. A Sudanese officer, who knew how Egypt's westernized army fought, was put in command of the new rifle unit. And in those rare African armies that had them, specialists were given command of artillery batteries. This was the case with the Tukolor army of al-Hajj Umar in the western Sudan in the 1850s, where Samba N'Diaye, an indigenous officer who had learned his trade among the French, was made Master of Artillery.

Not all heads of state made way for the specialists, however. The Ethiopian emperors continued to lead their troops in the field right into the twentieth century. The Emperor Yohannes died at the head of his troops in battle against the Mahdists in 1889. The Ethiopian army fought the battle of Adowa against the Italians in 1896 under the personal command of Emperor Menelik; his fiery, nationalistic wife, the Empress Taytu, is said to have appeared on the field of Adowa wielding a great parasol like a sword to urge on the troops. Samori, the professional soldier who forged an empire in Guinea in the 1870s and 1880s also led his troops in combat. Although he amassed a staff of competent officers, to whom he delegated considerable authority, Samori made all the major strategic and tactical decisions personally.

Four African armies

Introduction

The armies described below are broadly representative of the kinds of armed forces Africans fielded against their European opponents. Two of these, the Ashantis of West Africa and the Ethiopians of the Horn of Africa, were mass armies whose leaders had made an effort to forestall European conquest by adopting European weaponry and ways of war.

The Ashantis, dogged by deep political divisions within their ruling elite and, to some extent, within the populace as well, were the less successful of the two in resisting the Europeans. However, to compare the two states is perhaps unfair. Ethiopia possessed advantages shared by almost no other African country. In addition to a stronger sense of cultural and political unity than existed in most African states, the Ethiopians as fellow-Christians enjoyed greater respect among European nations than did most African peoples. Alone among African states of the time, Ethiopia could count on European allies to supply them with the latest firearms, and even to send troops to assist them against other European powers.

The other two armies, those of the Sokoto Caliphate of the Central Sudan and the Zulus of Southern Africa, made sporadic attempts to modernize, but proved incapable of giving up their traditional ways of waging war. The military systems of both Sokoto and the Zulus appear to have been so closely intertwined with traditional social and political structures that to have transformed them would have posed the threat of fundamental change. Both states paid dearly for their attachment to tradition, and both nonetheless found themselves forced to accept profound changes in every aspect of their way of life, the Zulus more so than the peoples of Northern Nigeria.

Ashanti army

The Ashanti state took shape in the interior rain forest of what is today Ghana around 1680, under the leadership of King (Asantehene) Osei Tutu. Originally a small polity centered around the city of Kumasi and its environs, Ashanti had become a major regional power by 1700, following its defeat of the rival state of Denkyera to the southwest.

> Ashanti was fundamentally a military union which aimed at economic expansion. This policy of military expansion was so successful that by the end of the eighteenth century Ashanti was in control of a territory much larger than modern Ghana.[23]

Maintaining unity within this vast empire was a challenge, however, that the kings of Ashanti never entirely succeeded in meeting. From the beginning of its existence down to its final absorption into the British empire in 1900, Ashanti faced continual rebellions by subject peoples. Osei Tutu had tried at the very outset to overcome this tendency to particularism by introducing the idea of the "golden stool" as a symbol of national unity. Each of the district governors of Ashanti boasted a ceremonial stool of office, which embodied the ties of kinship that bound together the people of his area. Now an all-embracing golden stool existed, which sought in the same way to bind all of the peoples of all the districts into one unit. The state also sought to instil a sense of nationalism into its subjects through songs and rituals that stressed the idea of a common origin. Another even more potent unifying instrument was the national army.

The Ashanti army served two basic aims of imperial policy. First, it was assigned the traditional task of defending and expanding the imperial frontiers. Secondly, the army functioned as a powerful instrument of "national" unity, tying together the disparate and potentially fractious parts of the empire, much as the army was supposed to do in contemporary Italy (and still does in Switzerland).

The Ashanti army was not a regular army like the British expeditionary force it faced in 1873–4, although a small trained cadre stationed in the capital formed its nucleus. Beyond this, the Ashanti army most closely resembled the feudal levies of the European Middle Ages, in that most of its manpower was assembled at the outbreak of war from troops raised by provincial warlords. Finally, in cases of great urgency, the king was empowered to mobilize the entire able-bodied male population. At full strength, the Ashanti army was said to number around 100,000 men, which would have made it one of the largest armies in Africa, on a par with Ethiopia's. Most armies that took the field were not as large as this, however. The force that fought the British in 1873–4 was only about 40,000 strong. That the Ashanti army could have been kept together long enough to fight a battle, much less become the kind of empire-binding, disciplined fighting instrument it actually was, may seem just short of miraculous. Many of the provinces supplying soldiers had only recently been added to the empire, and so were unlikely to share the enthusiasms of Kumasi. Also, many of the common soldiers were slaves. Nonetheless, while the army's "great successes came in part from its advantages in firearms . . . more important [were] its remarkable organization and the exceptional discipline and bravery of its officers and men."[24]

The positive elements that held the army together were a reasonably effective command structure centered on the king, his privy council and the army general staff, and the ability to convince soldiers of varying backgrounds that they had a share in the glorious military traditions of Ashanti. Negative forces also played a role. There were severe penalties for failure to report for duty, desertion and cowardice in battle. Military police armed with swords and whips were stationed behind the lines to encourage the troops to remain at their posts.

It seems to have become customary for scholars who write about the Ashanti army to observe that its marching order was modelled on that of the army ants, "who march in several columns before joining at the crucial moment".[25] This method of approaching the battlefield was not as exotic as it sounds, whatever its actual origins. It was, to begin with, vintage Napoleon and, in fact, was employed by the British commander, Sir Garnet Wolseley, during the 1873–4 war. A typical Ashanti column on the march comprised a body of scouts, an advance guard, the main body, a rearguard and left and right wings. Alone among African armies the Ashanti army boasted a corps of medical orderlies who accompanied it into battle, looking after the wounded and removing the dead from the field.

The Ashanti army was made up entirely of infantry. The threat of sleeping sickness, spread by the tsetse fly, made it impossible to maintain cavalry in the forest zone. Most Ashanti infantrymen were equipped with standard European trade muskets, known on the West African coast as "Long Danes". This weapon, which measured six feet in length and weighed nearly 20 lb, could hardly have been more unsuited for warfare in the rain forests. "Long Danes" were, however, almost the only shoulder arms available to African armies on the Gold Coast in the 1870s and, in any case, were good enough for fighting similarly armed African opponents.[26]

In any case, up to then, they had also been good enough to enable the Ashantis to hold their own against European opponents. As the US anthropologist-historian R.B. Edgerton has observed,

> From 1807 to 1900, Asante armies fought numerous small and large battles against the British. In several of these they were the clear victors, the only West African army to defeat a European army in more than one engagement.[27]

The army of the Sokoto Caliphate

West Africa's largest single state in the nineteenth century, the Sokoto Caliphate of Northern Nigeria, was the product of a series of Muslim crusades or jihads in the early 1800s. Their guiding force was Usuman dan Fodio, a devout tutor to the sons of the king of the Hausa state of Gobir. Usuman's family belonged to the Fulani tribe, a largely pastoral people who had migrated to the Central Sudan from Senegal some decades before. In Usuman's day, the Fulani were a numerous but oppressed minority in the Hausa lands.

Usuman dan Fodio is among the more plebeian of the Muslim state-builders to be discussed in this book. Although his father was a respectable religious teacher, Usuman sprang from a persecuted underclass. The Muslim leaders of the next generation, the Algerian resistance chief, Abd el-Kader, and the Tukolor empire builder, al-Hajj Umar, for example, were members of clerical elites. Nor had Usuman gone on pilgrimage to Mecca, as Abd el-Kader and Umar, once again, had done. Finally, although he was a learned man, Usuman was largely self-taught. He had not been able to travel to the great centres of Islamic learning and sit at the feet of the great Islamic scholars, as the younger men were able to do.

Usuman's main aim in launching his crusade was to convert to Islam the large number of his fellow Fulani who were still animists, and to bring the Hausa rulers to a more orthodox brand of Islam. Saintly reformer that he was, however, Usuman withdrew from the fray in 1812, before the jihads had ended. The political result of his labours was the creation of the Sokoto Caliphate. Covering over 400,000 square kilometres, the new state stretched from the source of the Benue River in the east to the bend of the Niger River in the west. Its capital was the new city of Sokoto, the seat of the caliph who, in this orthodox Muslim state, was at once its political head and spiritual guide. The jihad armies which defeated the Hausas and imposed the rule of the Fulani reformers were a new phenomenon in the Central Sudan. Where the traditional armies of the region relied heavily on cavalry, Usuman dan Fodio's forces were composed entirely of light infantry, at least at the outset of the struggle. Although highly mobile, this jihadi infantry was at a disadvantage against cavalry on open ground – that is, until, probably without intending to, they found a tactical formation that would neutralize the enemy horsemen. The first great jihadi victory, at the battle of Tabkin Kwotto in 1804, saw Usuman's men form up in a square, which spewed forth devastating fire from Fulani archers, driving the enemy cavalry and more numerous infantry from the field. Accident or not, the jihadis quickly saw the value of the square formation and used it to good effect on later occasions.

But as the jihad progressed, captured horses and new allies made possible the development by the insurgents of a cavalry arm. This greatly altered their military organization and technology. In the long term, however, it can be seen to have had a regressive effect on the new Sokoto polity and its armed forces. As Joseph Smaldone observes, the development of cavalry warfare in the emergent Sokoto Caliphate ensured the perpetuation of the classical pattern of Sudanic army organization and state structure. Although the Hausa states were over-thrown, the essential elements of the Sudanic war complex were reconstituted in the Sokoto Caliphate. [T]his ancient war complex survived the introduction of firearms in the late nineteenth century and remained remarkably intact until the British conquest [in the first years of the twentieth century].[28]

Smaldone's inference is clear: had the Fulani not laid aside their bows to become aristocratic cavalrymen, the caliphate might have been more recep-tive to the introduction of modern weaponry, such as breechloading rifles and artillery. As it was, this reversion to the Hausa warrior ideal not only meant that the caliphate's armed forces would be largely impervious to change, but also underscored the perpetuation of a highly stratified society and a reactionary state apparatus. It also ensured that slave raiding would continue on a large scale along the frontiers of the caliphate, and that much of its labour force would be unfree when the British descended upon it at the dawn of the twentieth century.

It can be seen at a glance how very conservative this revolution was, at least in terms of its long-range results. Politically, the desire of the revolutionary leadership seems to have been to return to a Golden Age in the past. And just as the promising military innovations of Tabkin Kwotto succumbed before the entrenched aristocratic ethos of the cavalry-man, so the leadership of the Fulani insurgents broke its ties with the peasant masses, and constituted itself as a new nobility. Perhaps, in the end, the only difference was that the newcomers, largely because of their more scrupulous observance of Islamic law, proved to be less corrupt than their predecessors.

Nonetheless, the Sokoto Caliphate was immensely important for the history of Africa in the nineteenth century. Its political structure and military system exercised a great influence on the Western Sudan, for example. The Tukolor empire, founded in the 1850s and 1860s in the Western Sudan to the west of the Sokoto Caliphate, was the product of a jihad modelled upon that of Usuman dan Fodio. Its architect, al-Hajj Umar, was a great admirer and emulator of Usuman and a close associate of Muhammad Bello, Usuman's son and caliph in Sokoto. His own son, Ahmadu Seku, would marry into the caliphate's royal family and would spend his last days there in exile. Nor should we be surprised to learn that the armies of the Tukolor jihad were led by an elite on horseback, albeit one supported by an artillery arm that was rare for its time and place.

The Zulu army

Although Shaka Zulu clearly played a crucial role in the forging of the Zulu empire and in the creation of its powerful army, his accomplishments in these areas were probably less sweeping and original than his admirers have claimed. Some credit for the reorganization of the Zulu army must go to Dingiswayo, Shaka's commander and predecessor as king. "Dingiswayo played Philip to Shaka's Alexander", in E.A. Ritter's apt phrase.[29] It was during the reign of the older man, for example, that the Nguni peoples (of whom the Zulus were only one chiefdom) abandoned the ritual of male circumcision, which had deprived the army of needed fighters for long periods, and restructured their armies on an age-grade basis. Under this system, which may have been borrowed from neighboring Sotho peoples, young men who had reached the age of initiation were organized by the king into regiments with their own distinctive names and accoutrements. These regiments were not constituted on a territorial basis, as British regiments were, or placed under the command of powerful lords, as Ashanti regiments were. Instead, they were assigned to one of the royal households, strategically located around the country. This practice assured cohesion through centralized control, and also promoted the cause of "national" unity. Young men from different parts of the realm were brought together and taught to give their first loyalty to their regiment and thus to the king, who was their commander-in-chief. The age-grade regimental system also facilitated the integration of conquered peoples into the Zulu state. Young men of the newly-absorbed groups were divided up according to age and assigned to regiments where they would serve alongside recruits of their own age from other parts of the realm, learning, once again, regimental loyalty and fidelity to their new king.

What made the Zulu army such a fearsome tactical instrument was the superb physical condition and iron discipline of its warriors. Tall, muscular, and toughened by outdoor living, they were more than a physical match for the European soldiers they faced. They also knew their home terrain intimately and were skilled in handling weapons through hunting for game from an early age. Military discipline was imposed on Zulu youths early in life. At around the age of puberty young men were inducted into age-grade regiments, which were housed in barracks at various places around the country. During their years of regimental life, they were subjected to intense discipline, which, as we have seen, included restrictions on their contact with women.

Command at the company and regimental levels of the *impi* was in the hands of *indunas* or officers drawn from older age groups. Training followed prescribed lines, warriors being drilled in combining to form the *impi* fighting formation, then reverting back to their original groupings. Zulus did not march into battle; they jog-trotted. They could habitually cover 50 miles a day over trackless country, and then go straight into action: their mobility has rarely been equalled among foot soldiers. *En route* to the battle of Isandlwana in January 1879, where they annihilated a British force, the Zulu *impi* covered 50 miles in three days, without food for the last two; on the day of battle, they advanced at a run for five miles, then plunged straight into the attack. The reserve of this *impi* ran another twelve miles that same day to Rorke's Drift and, once there, fought without let-up for some ten hours – albeit in a lost cause.[30]

One of Shaka's main contributions to the edification of this military juggernaut was to turn the age-grade regiments into a standing army. Under Dingiswayo, the regiments had only been called into being when war actually broke out. In Shaka's time, newly-formed regiments were housed in special military settlements, where the soldiers spent their time between wars, drilling and parading and tilling the king's lands, until, at the age of 40, they were discharged. Ian Knight sees in Shaka's system of permanent mobilization the creation of a "fully-fledged national army".[31]

When Shaka became king of the Zulus in 1816, the Zulu "nation" numbered only around 1,500 people and could field a fighting force of no more than 400 men. Shaka's transformation of the tiny army he inherited into a formidable war machine launched the Zulus on the road to power. By 1828, when the increasingly despotic Shaka was assassinated, the Zulu kingdom between the Drakensbergs and the Indian Ocean had swallowed up all of the other Nguni peoples or, at least, all of the Nguni peoples who had not succeeded in escaping the Zulu armies. For many did escape, fleeing eastward into neighboring Mozambique and thence on to present-day Malawi and Tanzania; northward into modern-day Zambia and Zimbabwe; and to the west along the coast into the lands of the Xhosa peoples. This massive upheaval, known as the *Mfecane*, uprooted hundreds of thousands of people in southeastern Africa and altered the lives of hundreds of thousands more to the north and east as they came under the sway of militarized refugees from the Zulu onslaught.

How did the Zulus come to wreak such havoc on their neighbours? How can one explain the *Mfecane*? Although Donald Morris, in his widely-read, popular study, *The washing of the spears*, does note other contributing factors, he gives the distinct impression that "the crushing" to which the Zulus' neighbours were subjected was a result of the bloody-mindedness of Shaka. He would have us believe that the king's thirst for blood and conquest was fed by a massive Oedipus complex and sexual impotency.[32] Be that as it may, it must be stressed that there were also powerful impersonal forces operating during Shaka's reign which helped predispose his people to war. There was, for example, increasing population pressure on the lands between the Drakensberg Mountains and the sea, pressure made worse by droughts in 1800–7 and 1820–3. The ever more numerous Zulus needed additional land for their growing herds and, with new weapons and battle tactics developed during the reign of Shaka and his predecessor, Dingiswayo, were able to take the land they needed from their neighbours.

To return to the Zulu way of war – what makes it so interesting to observers is that it owes almost nothing to outside influences. It was not, as many early white observers believed, based on European examples. Theophilus Shepstone, the longstanding Native Affairs Commissioner of Natal and a presumed "expert" on the Zulus, believed that Dingiswayo had got the idea of how to organize the Zulu armies by watching a British unit at drill in Cape Town. Apart from the fact that there is no record of the Zulu leader ever visiting Cape Town, this is really beside the point. Apparently, it was difficult for Shepstone and other whites of his day to believe that an African people could have developed such a highly-disciplined, efficient fighting force without help or at least inspiration from a "higher" civilization. But there was very little contact with Europeans before Shaka's time. Up to the late 1700s, in fact, Zulus believed that whites came from the bottom of the sea where they had been bleached by the salt water. This was because shipwrecked sailors were the only whites most Zulus had seen up to that point.

The state of permanent war inaugurated under Shaka's rule produced many glorious victories, promoted a sense of Zulu nationhood, and enriched the Zulu people. But the strain of constant warfare and Shaka's increasingly autocratic rule also alienated many of his followers, including members of the royal entourage. When in 1828 he overstretched his army by sending it off on two successive wide-ranging campaigns in opposite directions, while himself staying at home in the royal kraal, his enemies decided to act. On 24 September 1828, in a scene reminiscent of the demise of Julius Caesar, Shaka was stabbed to death by his two half-brothers. The Zulu kingdom did not die with the autocrat, however, but continued to function as a regional power in southeastern Africa until the 1880s.

It is difficult to take a measured view of Shaka and his career, since historians' assessments of him differ so greatly. Some have portrayed him as basically an agent of destruction, a bloodthirsty tyrant who ruled his own people through fear and used his fearsome *impis* to destroy fellow Africans or drive them into exile. Others, on the contrary, have described Shaka as an heroic figure, fierce and uncompromising in his demands upon his people perhaps, but not tyrannical; a giant figure whose deeds ennoble all Africans. If there is anything the two sides in this debate are able to agree on, it is that Shaka was endowed with remarkable talents as both a military leader and state-builder. John Keegan observes that

> Fanciful commentators called him [Shaka] the Black Napoleon, and allowing for different societies and customs, the comparison is apt. Shaka is without doubt the greatest commander to come out of Africa.[33]

Ethiopia

A process of political centralization was clearly underway in Ethiopia on the eve of European penetration. To be more precise, what was being attempted, beginning with the reign of Emperor Tewodros II (1855–68), was a restoration of the Solomonic empire of the early Christian era. Ancient Ethiopia, centred on the holy city of Axum in the northern province of Tigray, its civilization a fertile blend of pre-Muslim South Arabian, Hebraic and Hellenistic influences, its Christianized emperors claiming descent from King Solomon and the Queen of Sheba, had been a major regional political and military power and a key participant in the three-cornered trading network linking India, East Africa and the Mediterranean basin. Over the succeeding centuries, however, the rising tide of Islam had forced the empire to retreat into the more remote central and southern portions of the Ethiopian highlands. Already in the seventh century, Eritrea was overrun by Muslim tribes from the north, a loss which would never really be made good and which today appears to be permanent.

From many points of view, Ethiopia in the early 1800s

> was [a weak] state with serious internal problems and little visible cohesion. It was not, however, like many other areas of Africa, the home of a mere conglomeration of more or less closely affiliated tribes. The many centuries of settled agricultural life in the Ethiopian highlands, the long history of the Ethiopian monarchy and the Christian church in the area, had weakened tribal structures in favor of a more regionally organized society.[34]

Tewodros II, the former bandit chieftain who fought his way to the imperial throne in 1855, was the first emperor since the 1600s who seems to have possessed the will to restore Ethiopia to its former greatness and territorial integrity. Ironically, it was this will to greatness which led the emperor

22

down the road to domestic discord and to Ethiopia's first confrontation with a European imperial power, in the shape of a British expeditionary force from India in 1867–8.

Tewodros seems to have believed that his country could be safe from its many threatening neighbours, only if it succeeded in adopting Western statecraft and technology, especially Western weapons and military organization. To this end, he began importing Western arms and technicians and launched a domestic weapons industry. This proved to be unpopular with the Ethiopian peasantry, whose taxes were increased to pay for these innovations. Worse trouble arose when Tewodros took steps to transform the country's feudal levies, controlled by the local princes, into a national army under his direction. Ethiopia was in a state of virtual civil war when the British expeditionary force landed on its shores in 1867, on a mission to force the emperor to release the British consul and other assorted European hostages. Tewodros had apparently imprisoned the Europeans in a last desperate attempt to convince the British government to take seriously his pleas for support in his crusade against ever-encroaching Islam.[35]

The Ethiopians suffered a shattering defeat at the hands of the British expeditionary force. At the battle of Aroge, which secured British victory, the Ethiopians got their first taste of volley-firing from breechloading rifles. The enemy invasion, although it resulted in the emperor's death and the destruction of his capital, did surprisingly little to disrupt the drive for greater national unity. It brought to the imperial throne the king of Tigre province, who had backed the British against Tewodros, and who now took the title Yohannes IV. Bolstered by a generous £500,000 worth of military equipment left behind by the British, Yohannes proved to be a great warrior, defeating the Egyptians, who sought to conquer his country from the Red Sea enclaves they had taken over from the Turks earlier in the century, and bending the provincial rulers to his will.[36]

In 1875 and again in 1876, Ethiopian troops under the command of Yohannes routed sizeable Egyptian armies trained and officered by European mercenaries and veterans of the US Civil War and equipped with Remington rifles, Krupp artillery, Gatling guns and rocket tubes.

The Ethiopians came away from these engagements not only richer in battlefield experience, but also in military hardware. In addition to a large stock of Remington rolling-block rifles, which became the firearm of choice for the Ethiopian infantry, Yohannes's army also took possession of the enemy's artillery park. With the big guns came captured Egyptian gunners to teach the Ethiopians how to use them.

It was also Yohannes who first had to contend with the Italians as an expansionist power in the region. His great general, Ras Alula, inflicted a crushing defeat on an Italian force at Dogali in 1887. The next year, the emperor died in battle against an even more threatening foe, the Mahdists of the Sudan, and the throne passed to his rival, Menelik, king of Shoa province and the greatest centralizer of them all.

By the 1890s the Ethiopian army had evolved into a formidable fighting machine. To begin with, it was capable of putting huge numbers of reasonably well-equipped men on to the battlefield. Around 100,000 Ethiopian troops fought at Adowa. About 70,000 of them carried modern repeating rifles, some of which were superior in rate of fire to the weapons carried by their Italian counterparts. Also, they knew how to use them.

In addition, the Ethiopians were the only Africans to employ artillery to any extent during the colonial wars. Indeed, their quick-firing Hotchkiss artillery forced the surrender of an Italian fort in the run-up to the battle of Adowa and actually outgunned an Italian battery at a crucial point during the battle itself.

Finally, as has been suggested, this was not an army that adopted modern rifles and artillery as appendages to an otherwise traditional fighting force. Since the introduction of firearms into Ethiopia in the 1500s, Ethiopian monarchs had devoted great efforts to obtaining the most modern weapons and, beginning in the mid-nineteenth century, to manufacturing them domestically, including artillery pieces. Thus, riflemen were the core of the nineteeth-century Ethiopian army, not a palace guard or a sharpshooting elite. Ethiopian infantry also knew how to manoeuvre so as to maximize the impact of their weapons and to minimize their exposure to the enemy's firepower. This knowledge had not been acquired on the drill field or in training exercises, but as the result of experience. For, of all the African armies of the late nineteenth century, the Ethiopian army, as we have seen, had amassed the greatest experience of modern warfare.

By the time the Italians arrived on the scene in the mid-1880s, the Ethiopian army had reached a point in its development where it was nearly the equivalent in firepower and military science of European armies.

> Taken all together, the Ethiopian Army was formidable by any standards. Its tough fighting men were masters of both skirmish, or ambush warfare, and shock action. A rare combination by African standards, and one that often caused an unpleasant surprise for Ethiopia's enemies.[37]

But the Ethiopian army also had weaknesses that European armies usually did not, weaknesses that might have been exploited to greater effect by the Italians. Like so many other African armies, their big weakness was in logistics. Ethiopian armies lived off the land and, given their large size, could quickly decimate whole regions by their demands for supplies. This logistical weakness plus a shortage of heavy artillery led to the other major shortcoming of the Ethiopian army: an inability to prosecute sieges. Had the Italians remained on the defensive in their campaigns in Ethiopia, waiting out the enemy behind the formidable chain of fortresses they had constructed on the Eritrean frontier, the Ethiopian army would probably have been forced from the field through the lack of food and fodder.[38] As it was, the Ethiopian army on the eve of the battle of Adowa was just a day or two away from disintegration for lack of food, when the Italians saved them from ignominious retreat by taking the offensive.[39]

Chapter Two

Masters of the water: the European invaders

Introduction

Up to the late nineteenth century, Europeans came to Africa largely to trade. Their presence on the continent was, for the most part, limited to a small number of trading enclaves along the west and east African coasts.

Just as in Asia in the early modern era, European trading posts along the African coast were maintained and kept alive well into the nineteenth century by the benevolence or avarice of local potentates in good times, and in bad times by European sea-power. Many early modern African rulers would have agreed with Bahadur Shah, the sixteenth-century king of Gujarat in India, that "wars by sea are merchants' affairs and of no concern to the prestige of kings".[1] As late as 1854, al-Hajj Umar, the *khalifa* of the Tukolor empire in the Western Sudan, could still say of the French, two centuries after their first appearance on the Senegal coast:

> The whites are only traders. As long as they bring me merchandise in their ships, as long as they pay me a good tribute when I'm master of the blacks, I will live in peace with them. But they are not to build any more forts or to send warships up the [Senegal] river.[2]

The British were regarded no differently. In the 1600s English traders on the Guinea coast came "not as masters but seeking barter, never sure of their welcome, dependent on the Negroes' good will".[3] Two centuries later, little had changed. Henry Meredith, a British official on the Gold Coast, wrote in 1812 that Europeans in that part of Africa could "claim no right of conquest [for they] pay ground-rent and water custom at most of their settlements. The [African] people are regulated by their own laws and will not submit" to those of the Europeans.[4]

26

The lack of European penetration of the African interior at this juncture is often explained in terms of a deadly "war against nature". Diseases such as malaria and yellow fever, along with noxious insects, burning heat and high humidity, combined to make West Africa a "white man's grave". A sixteenth-century Portuguese chronicler wrote

> It seems that for our sins or for some inscrutable judgement of God, in all the entrances of this great Ethiopia that we navigate along, He has placed a striking angel with a flaming sword of deadly fevers who prevents us from penetrating into the interior to the springs of this garden, whence proceed these rivers of gold that flow to the sea. . . .[5]

British government statistics in the early nineteenth century, while certainly less poetic, offer a no less dire picture of the fate of white interlopers on the African shore. In the period 1819–36, for example, British military deaths at the Sierra Leone station in West Africa, due almost entirely to disease, averaged an incredible 483 per 1,000.[6]

There is an important but often unspoken assumption behind the evocation of "wars against nature": an assumption that, had these natural barriers not existed, Western technological superiority would have assured European expansion into the interior, perhaps even as early as the late fifteenth century, the age of Vasco da Gama. But, upon closer examination, it would seem that, in the early modern period at least, Europe's technological edge was seldom very great, or important, except perhaps at sea. Indigenous peoples were quick to catch up with European innovations. The "gunpowder revolution" which enabled the Moroccans to drive the Portuguese out of North Africa by 1550 quickly spread south across the Sahara. Imported Turkish muskets and musketeers soon were helping to make Bornu the dynamic force of the Central Sudan, while guns purchased with proceeds from the Atlantic slave trade powered Ashanti to dominance of the Gold Coast.[7]

What is clear almost from the beginning of European contact with Africans is that technological superiority was far less important than the ability of the Europeans to profit from the disarray of their enemies, who "were often riven by internal or distracted by external rivalries, which prevented them from uniting effectively". The Portuguese led the way in taking advantage of such disputes to ensconce themselves on the African coasts and, in some cases, to divide and conquer their enemies. For example, "the long-standing rivalry betweem Mombasa and Malindi in East Africa enabled the Portuguese to establish their power on the Swahili coast by allying themselves with the latter".[8] The other European powers who followed the Portuguese into Africa would not be slow to profit from their example. Changing political fortunes in the African interior also provided the vastly overstretched Portuguese with a desperately-needed fighting force for imperial defence. The collapse of the West African empire of Mali in the fifteenth century freed up large numbers of the "redoubtable" Mandingo slave warriors of Guinea for Portuguese service. Prized more highly by their new owners than the "famous Swiss mercenaries", the Guineans became a kind of Portuguese imperial fire brigade, fighting in the breach during the defence of Ormuz castle in the Persian Gulf in 1622, and playing a major role in the repulse of a Dutch attack on Macao in China in the same year.[9] The Portuguese practice of shoring up imperial defenses with indigenous fighting forces was soon emulated by other European powers and set a pattern that would persist well into the twentieth century.

The scramble for Africa

Three hundred years later, however, the wheel had turned. The nineteenth century was the European century. From the defeat of Napoleon in 1815 to the outbreak of the First World War in 1914, most of the earth's surface passed under the control of one or another of the European powers. This was the century in which Britain opened up China for European exploitation in the Opium Wars of the 1850s. It was the century in which the USA opened up Japan once again. And it was also the century when not even the most inaccessible Pacific island could escape the attentions of the European powers.

Africa seems to have been the part of the world most completely over-whelmed by European occupation and conquest. In 1876, more than 90 per cent of the continent was still ruled by Africans. By 1914, all but a tiny fraction of Africa was in the hands of the European powers. Only Liberia and Ethiopia had managed to stay independent. What had happened to upset the balance of centuries past so completely?

In the half century between the French invasion of Algeria in 1830 and the Anglo-Zulu War in South Africa in 1879, the power relationship that had existed between Africans and their European adversaries since the earliest contacts had begun to shift. Much attention has been given recently to the technological changes in the power equation between Africans and Europeans during this period, among which were the many spectacular advances in communications. The perfection of the technology of submarine telegraphy in the 1860s, for example, made possible almost instantaneous communication between capitals and ships at sea and troops in the field. Just how revolution-ary this new means of communication was can be seen in its potential for Portugal's East African colony of Mozambique, whose towns were linked to each other and to Europe by submarine cable in 1879. In 1833, when Zulu raiders sacked the southern Mozambique port city of Lourenço Marques, "the authorities at [the colonial capital of Mozambique City] did not hear of the happening until a year later, by way of Rio de Janeiro".[10]

European penetration of Africa also benefited from new developments in transportation, particularly on the water. The marriage of steam propulsion and metal ship construction, resulting in the iron steamboat, the standard ship of the Western world by the 1850s, had a particularly profound impact on shipping in the tropics. Largely immune to tropical parasites, less likely to catch fire or break up on rocks, iron ships were also lighter and stronger than wooden ones and thus could be built to greater sizes, cutting down on the number of ships needed to move troops and supplies to the wars in Africa.[11]

Weapons technology was transformed by the so-called "breechloader revolution" of the 1860s. This innovation, which allowed soldiers to feed cartridges one after another into the chambers of their rifles rather than laboriously reload powder and ball at the muzzle end after each shot, greatly increased the infantry's rate of fire. An arms race was launched among European powers, with gun designs changing every few years. This was an arms race from which Africans were largely excluded. Often at parity with European troops in the age of the muzzle-loader, they fell behind with the coming of the "breechloader revolution" and with few exceptions never caught up.

What needs to be kept in mind, however, is that these and other technological changes, important though they might have been, did not confer anything like instant superiority upon the European invaders of Africa. To begin with, there was a considerable lag between the availability of the new technologies and their actual appearance on African battlefields. In some cases, they never arrived at all, at least not in our era. Also, even when the new technologies were present on the battlefield, success was far from automatic, as the British disaster at Isandlwana during the Anglo-Zulu War of 1879 and the Italian debacle at Adowa in 1896 clearly demonstrate.

A major argument of this book will be that there is a more reliable explanation of European success in the African colonial wars than the thesis of triumphant technology: the ability of Europeans to recruit large armies of African troops. In this regard, remarkably little had changed since the early modern era. Just as Portugal and the Netherlands, both with populations of some two million, had been forced to rely on indigenous troops to keep their imperial holdings together in the 1600s, so nineteenth-century European armies, faced with pressing commitments elsewhere and still fearful of "the white man's grave", turned to indigenous soldiers to wage war on their behalf in Africa.

The availability of these African soldiers, it should be pointed out, was largely the result of the extraordinary flux which beset internal African politics in the nineteenth century, as empires expanded and retracted and smaller states rose and fell. The "peripheral flux" that stemmed from the decline of African states (and sometimes also their growth, as in the case of Samori's empire in Guinea) gave the European invaders the opportunity to insert themselves into local political disputes and, ultimately, to divide and conquer. But the benefit to the newcomers was even more direct than this. From out of the upheaval and civil war that afflicted African states they were able to draw the manpower they needed to build their armies.

European motives for expansion

Historians have by now abandoned the search for the philosopher's stone that will reveal the identity of the universal motivation that underlay European imperialism. If little else about that contentious subject has been agreed, it has at least been accepted that the motives for participation in the imperial venture were multiple and complex and varied considerably among nations. For example, whereas tacit agreement seems to have been reached on the principle that Britain's wars of imperial conquest were as often the result of metropolitan responses to events in Africa or Asia as of metropolitan calculation, the same cannot generally be said of the other participants in the rush to divide up Africa.

Britain

Before the 1870s British imperialists practised what Ronald Robinson and John Gallagher have called "the imperialism of free trade".

> From the 1820s to the '70s, in what might be termed the external or informal stage of industrial imperialism, Europe attempted to lever Afro-Asian regimes into collaboration from outside and to reshape their institutions through commerce. Naval and diplomatic power forced their rulers to abolish commercial monopolies, lower tariffs and open their doors to the "Imperialism of Free Trade". Later, in return for loans, or under the muzzles of high-velocity guns, they were bundled into liberalising their traditional political, legal and fiscal institutions to make elbowroom for their "productive" classes in commercial collaboration with Europe, to take over power.[12]

30

This attitude to empire began to alter somewhat in the 1870s, under pressure from Conservative expansionist rhetoric and jingoistic public opinion. That matters went no further than they did at this point, however, had much to do with the presence in office during much of the period of William Ewart Gladstone and his Liberal party. Still largely wedded to "free-trade imperialism", the Liberals refused to add Ashanti or Zululand to the empire after British victories over their indigenous rulers in the wars of 1873–4 and 1879.

Britain's adoption of a more aggressive policy in Africa in the 1880s has been convincingly explained as a response to challenges to the security of her lifeline to India. Hence: the occupation in 1882 of Egypt, site of the Suez Canal, a key link in the lifeline; the conquest in 1898 of the Anglo-Egyptian Sudan, guardian of the Red Sea flank of the lifeline and conduit of the Nile River, source of Egyptian prosperity; and the decision a year later to go to war with the Boers in South Africa, rivals for control of the flank of yet another vital route to India.

In conclusion, it might be useful to emphasize the point that, for a nation whose empire spanned the globe to an extent that no other came close to doing, Britain's imperial policy during this period of headlong expansion seems strangely "other-directed". British statesmen acquired territory in Africa for the most part only reluctantly, when the instability of certain African states seemed to have become so great as to threaten the empire's most important strategic interests. A.S. Kanya-Forstner has drawn a useful contrast between "the dynamism, self-confidence and expansiveness of mid-Victorian Britain, and the pessimistic, frightened, neurotic men like Salisbury who presided over the end of an era".[13] There is an equally instructive comparison to be made between the statesmen in London and the generals who did their bidding: Wolseley, Kitchener, Lugard, Roberts. Salisbury and company may have been "pessimistic, frightened, neurotic", but their generals were not.

France

It is difficult to show that France was drawn deeper into Africa because of threats to her vital interests from African instability. A partial case might be made for this concerning the frantic drive to the Niger in the 1880s, prompted to some extent by fears that the decline of the Tukolor empire might encourage British expansion into the Western Sudan. But it could also be argued that French fears had nothing to do with African "instability", and that the French were just as paranoid about British designs on the region when the Tukolor empire was strong as when it was weak.

It has been argued that French expansionism in Africa (and Asia as well, for that matter) was prompted by a desire to win back through overseas conquest the prestige that was lost in Europe as a result of defeat in the Franco-Prussian War. The late Henri Brunschwig wrote that

> a nationalism common to all elements of the population after the defeat of 1871 orientated towards colonial expansion governments which were confronted neither by demographic pressure nor by imperative needs for raw materials or markets.[14]

Not all historians have been happy with Brunschwig's sweeping assertion. Careful archival research has uncovered a significant influence on French imperial policy of representatives of what might be called "municipal imperialism". These people, who spoke for companies with extensive interests in African trade from, for example, Marseilles or Bordeaux, often had the ear of important decision-makers in Paris, and sometimes even of French commanders in the field. They appear to have been influential in promoting French expansion in both West and Equatorial Africa.[15]

The nationalistic and commercial urges to empire coexisted with another form of expansionism that was more or less peculiar to France: the phenomenon Kanya-Forstner has called "military imperialism". Thus, the *officiers soudanais* of the French marine corps, a tightly-knit guild of junior officers with powerful protectors in the Paris military establishment, between 1880 and 1900 carved out an empire in the Western Sudan that official France at least had not sought and that unofficial France was not certain she wanted. They had conquered this vast territory, the marine officers said, for the greater glory of France and to spite the British, but those who knew them were aware that they had also done it for promotions and medals and out of contempt for their civilian superiors.[16]

Italy

Nor does Italian expansion in Africa appear to have been prompted by "flux" at the periphery. Again, nationalism is held to have played an important role. Having finally achieved national unity in 1870, Italy moved to take her place among the great powers of Europe. But acceptance by her presumed peers did not come easily. "Rome had been won, but ingloriously; the Risorgimento had succeeded, but after too many lost battles; Italy had a large army, but other Europeans did not take it seriously".[17] The main goal of Italian foreign policy and military planners in the late nineteenth century thus became the acknowledgement of the new nation's status as a great power. In the late nineteenth century such a position seemed to demand possession of an empire, and Italy almost immediately after achieving nationhood set out to find one. The frantic quest for "prestige", writes Nicola Labanca, "was at the bottom of all Italian foreign policy problems and initiatives" in the 1880s and 1890s, including imperial undertakings.[18]

But, Italy was also impelled along the expansionist path by land hunger. Lacking in natural resources, heavily overpopulated, especially in the *Mezzogiorno*, her still-feudal southland, Italy, alone among the imperial nations, sought foreign conquests not for gold or glory or strategic advantage alone, but as land on which to settle her surplus population. By the time the Italians entered the imperial sweepstakes in Africa, however, most of the good available farmland had already been taken. Consequently, the Italian expansionists were reduced to pretending that there was sufficient land to accommodate the land-hungry peasants of the *Mezzogiorno* in the temperate inland hills of Eritrea on the Red Sea coast of Ethiopia, and in Cyrenaica, the fertile strip of land in Libya along the Mediterranean shore. But the peasants were not impressed; few went to Eritrea or Libya. Instead, they emigrated in huge numbers to the cities of the USA and Argentina.

Germany

The other newcomer to the colonial game was Germany, newly-united and eager, like Italy, to establish herself as a *bona fide* Great Power. The German chancellor, Otto von Bismarck, had been converted to a pro-imperial stance late in his career, largely in response to domestic political concerns. He knew that there was strong public sentiment in favor of colonies, on the grounds that Germany could not be a Great Power without them. There is also reason to believe that Bismarck wanted to tap into the patriotic fervour aroused by imperial rivalry in order to wean German workers away from socialism and trade unionism. There was also pressure from trading firms in port cities like Hamburg and Bremen for state help in securing captive sources of tropical products. The parallels here with French "municipal imperialism" are striking. One thing seems certain about German imperial ventures in Africa: they were not provoked by "peripheral flux". "Where could one find [African] traditional interests and protonationalistic movements influencing German overseas policy at the time when German imperialism began?" asked German historian Hans-Ulrich Wehler. "To the contrary, the fundamental point is that German imperialism must be seen primarily as a result of endogenous socioeconomic and political forces and not as a reaction to exogenous pressures or circumstances abroad".[19]

Portugal

Portugal's wars in Africa in the nineteenth and early twentieth centuries differ fundamentally from those of the other European imperial powers. These other powers fought, in some cases, to expand footholds won in Africa during the wars of the Old Regime or the Revolutionary and Napoleonic eras, or, in other cases, to carve out wholly new domains. Portugal, on the other hand, had been in possession, however precariously, of a substantial African empire since the 1500s. It was to occupy and develop that empire effectively and thus keep it out of the hands of more powerful rivals that the Portuguese waged war in Africa in the late-nineteenth and early-twentieth centuries.

But this was only the means to a more important end. By the 1880s Portuguese politicians, civil servants and soldiers saw "pacification" of the African peoples of Angola, Guinea-Bissau and Mozambique as the vital first step toward the development of these colonies into more lucrative sources of income for the Portuguese state and as protected markets for the products of Portuguese domestic industry. Many of these same leaders came to believe that it was only by transforming her African empire into a "second Brazil" that weak, unstable, dependent Portugal could save her national honor and, perhaps, even herself.[20]

Portuguese plans for imperial revival received a rude shock in January 1890, when the British prime minister, Lord Salisbury, under pressure from missionary and commercial interests, demanded that Portugal withdraw its troops from Nyasaland and abandon its claims to territory lying between Angola and Mozambique. To enforce the ultimatum, British warships were sent to blockade Mozambique and similar action was threatened against Portugal itself. Although the Portuguese government eventually was forced to give in to the British demands, the ultimatum provoked riots in Portugal and sparked the rise of a powerful movement for colonial regeneration, known as the Generation of 1895, among the nation's army officers.

Leopold II of Belgium

The present-day state of Congo (until recently Zaire) was a Belgian colony from 1908 to 1960. It had an area of over 900,000 sq. miles, while Belgium measured a mere 12,000. But if this seems like a classic case of the tail wagging the dog, the situation was even more remarkable before the

Belgians took over in 1908. Prior to this, the whole vast area was the personal property of one man, the Belgian king, Leopold II. Leopold proved that individuals can make history. His vast Congo Free State is perhaps the last example in history of a one-man feudal domain.

In the 1870s the Belgian king had founded a philanthropic and scientific organization called the International Association which, among other things, sponsored humanitarian and exploratory missions to Africa. After Henry M. Stanley, the Anglo-American newspaperman-turned-African-explorer, succeeded in trekking from the east coast of Africa across the Congo to the Atlantic coast in 1877, the first European to do so, Leopold hired him to map out the contours of a state in the Congo basin. Leopold's International Association quickly established a "Committee for Study of the Upper Congo", whose purpose was to promote the idea of a federal state to unite the peoples of the Congo and to bring them the blessings of European civilization.

At the Berlin West Africa Conference in 1884–5, which was called to try to instil some order into what looked to be an impending "scramble" to divide up Africa (see below), the Great Powers were persuaded to turn over management of the vast Congo region to Leopold's International Association. By this time, it should be noted, all of the other partners in the Association had been bought out by the very wealthy Belgian king. Thus, the new Congo Free State, as it was named in 1886, became Leopold's very own personal domain.

There is some evidence that Leopold's Congo venture was not motivated entirely by personal greed. The Belgian historian Jean Stengers, while agreeing that Leopold's undertaking can be seen as "simply 'pillage' of the most old-fashioned kind", feels compelled to add that the king never intended to keep all the loot for himself. Leopold believed that "Belgium, having gained its political independence in 1830, had to be economically 'completed' by overseas possession". He was determined to give his people the advantage of colonies whether they wanted them or not.[21]

Conference of Berlin (1884–5)

Before the 1870s, European penetration of sub-Saharan Africa had been limited to Portugal's precarious coastal holdings in Angola, Guinea-Bissau and Mozambique, British commercial ventures in the so-called Oil Rivers region of what is today Nigeria, and French expansion up the Senegal River in the direction of the Western Sudan.

During the 1870s and 1880s, these British and French initiatives in the area of the Niger River had produced a series of acrimonious territorial disputes, with, as it turned out, profound implications for international relations as a whole. Although competition for control of the Niger valley never led to hostilities between the European powers involved, the threat of violence was sufficient to bring the two sides to the negotiating table in the mid-1880s to seek a settlement that would divide West Africa between them. France was to get control of the coastal area from Senegal to the Gold Coast as well as the hinterland behind it. Britain, meanwhile, was to profit from a similar arrangement from the Gold Coast south to Gabon.

This division of the spoils was never to come to pass, however. For other European powers refused to stand idly by while Britain and France divided West Africa between them. Two newcomers to imperial affairs were particularly insistent on receiving their share of the booty.

The first newcomer was not a state, but an individual: Leopold II, King of the Belgians. By 1884, as we have seen, the Belgian monarch had worked out a scheme to establish a personal commercial monopoly over the vast region of the Congo basin.

The second newcomer *was* a state, in fact the most powerful state on the European continent, Imperial Germany. The German chancellor, the redoubtable Otto von Bismarck, had not been a notable friend of imperialism up to this point. He believed that colonies were expensive to acquire and almost never paid off. Besides, rivalry over colonies added unnecessarily to international tension. But Bismarck knew that the intensely nationalistic German public was wild about empire. Wasn't Germany a Great Power? And didn't all Great Powers have empires, they asked?

Always an astute politician, Bismarck realized he would have to make some concessions to the public enthusiasm for colonies. This would require immediate action, before the British and French had managed to seize everything in Africa that wasn't already spoken for. Accordingly, in 1884 he called an international conference in Berlin to try to introduce some order into the looming scramble to carve up Africa. This meant, among other things, ensuring that there would be some of Africa left to grab for newcomers like his own country.

The measures agreed by the Berlin West Africa Conference included the following:

(a) Leopold was given the green light to establish a commercial monopoly over the Congo region; eventually, the area would be known as the Congo Free State. In return, the king promised to make the Congo a free trade zone, to open its rivers to all comers, to fight the slave trade and to save the indigenous population from the evils of drink.

(b) The French and British positions in West Africa were frozen; no new coastal areas were to be acquired and no deals to exchange territories were to be struck.

(c) Germany received title to Togo and Cameroon in West Africa, and South West Africa in southern Africa.

(d) The participants in the conference agreed that henceforth claims for control over territories lying inland from European coastal possessions could not be accepted unless they were buttressed by evidence of what was called "effective occupation". It would have to be shown, for example, that officials of the European claimant were resident in the interior and that indigenous peoples of the region recognized their authority. This principle was presumably directed against Britain, whose claim of "paramountcy" over areas of West Africa such as present-day Nigeria had long been resented by other European powers, but the country that felt most threatened by it was Portugal. The weakest of the European imperial powers, Portugal exercized almost no control over the interior regions of Angola, Guinea-Bissau and Mozambique. The remainder of the century would be consumed in a desperate but ultimately successful attempt by the Portuguese to achieve "effective occupation" of these areas, just ahead of bullying efforts by the British and Germans to prise them away.

The ostensible goal of the conference – to ease international tensions arising from the impending scramble for Africa – was achieved, at least for the moment. There would be further crises resulting from rivalries over African territories, some far more serious than the confrontation of 1884. The Fashoda Incident of 1898, setting France against Britain, and the Moroccan Crises of 1905 and 1911, setting France against Germany, brought the nations involved to the brink of war. But, for the crucial decade and a half from 1884 to 1898, the Berlin formula kept the European powers from treading too heavily on each other's toes.

The instruments of imperial conquest

The thin red line

Compared to the armies deployed in Europe during the Napoleonic wars at the beginning of the nineteenth century and, especially, those that manned the trenches in Europe during the First World War, the European forces that took part in the conquest of most of Africa in the second half of the 1800s seem absurdly small. In retrospect, it may seem incredible that Portugal, whose entire standing army (some 24,000 men) was about the same size as the force Kitchener led to Omdurman in 1898, and of which only a few thousand ever saw overseas duty, should have been able to exercize control over areas of the African continent many times the size of the *métropole*. Or that, while Germany's armed forces totalled some 524,000 men in 1900, only 2,871 of them were on duty at that time in her main African colonies: Tanganyika, South West Africa and Cameroon.[22]

Writers in 1900 would probably have been less surprised at the lilliputian scale of these armies than we are today. After all, it was a staple of the late-nineteenth-century Western ethos that the disparity in military organization and technology between European and African armies was so great that large forces were not required to conquer and hold African territories. European confidence on this score appears to have been boundless. Lieutenant-Colonel Paul-Louis Monteil of the French marine infantry, back from a trek across the Sahara by way of Lake Chad, boasted in 1895 that "with ten armed men you can go all the way across Africa."[23] Today, however, with the benefit of hindsight and somewhat greater detachment, it is possible to see that there were other important factors militating against the commitment of large European armies to Africa, apart from the view that the superiority of European firepower rendered them superfluous.

The first and foremost constraint on the employment of European troops in Africa was the continuously high level of demand for their services elsewhere. The tensions existing among the continental European powers in the years 1870 to 1914 precluded the dispatch of more than small numbers of French, German and Italian soldiers to Africa during this period.[24] Pressures for the retention of troops in Europe became particularly acute during the general heightening of tension following the Franco-Russian alliance of 1894, when the Germans began to make plans to cope with the apparent necessity of waging a two-front war in the event of a general conflict. It was no coincidence that the Germans consistently fielded the smallest colonial army in Africa and relied more heavily than anyone, with the possible exception of the Portuguese, on African troops.

Britain's situation was somewhat different. Her army during the Victorian era was an all-volunteer force. Its heart was the Regular Army, based in England but available for service wherever British interests might require its presence. During the last quarter of the nineteenth century, in fact, about a third of the Regular Army, which fielded some 212,000 men in 1897, was stationed in India. During the Victorian era, with no continental commitment until after 1904, the defence of India against Russian invasion was Britain's overriding imperial concern. This placed limits on the number of British troops available for service in Africa, as did fears of vulnerability to attack across the English Channel and the constant threat of upheaval in Ireland. The only alternative source of troops for Africa was the Indian Army, and, whereas help was received from that quarter from time to time, it was always done grudgingly. Consequently, the main burden of fulfilling the requirements for Africa fell upon the Regular Army in Britain. It was a matter of no little concern that British manpower needs in the Second Boer War in 1899–1902 left the country largely deprived of troops for defence against invasion and for manning the garrisons in Ireland.

It was not continental commitments, however, that kept the colonial forces of Portugal and the Congo Free State small. Portugal simply could not afford a large military establishment and was continually hard-pressed to maintain more than a symbolic presence in her colonies. In this respect the Congo Free State was, as in so many others, a case apart. Because it was technically not a Belgian colony but the private preserve of the Belgian monarch, Leopold II, there were domestic constraints upon the employment of Belgian soldiers in the Congo Free State army, the *Force Publique*. Belgian officers and NCOs who served in the Congo were obliged to contract out to the Free State government through something called the Military Cartographical Institute in Brussels.[25] In any case, there were few Belgian troops to spare for African service, since neutral Belgium maintained only a skeletal military establishment.

Secondly, the scale of warfare in Africa in modern times has been modest compared to other continents. Even if there had not been a technological gap between African and European armies or a pressing need for European troops elsewhere, it would rarely have been necessary to send large armies to Africa. The "savage hordes" of popular lore seldom materialized on African battlefields. Because of its "exceptionally hostile . . . environment", its "ancient rocks, poor soils, fickle rainfall, abundant insects, and unique prevalence of disease", Africa remained "an underpopulated continent until the late twentieth century".[26] Few African states in the late nineteenth century were capable of fielding armies even remotely as large as those routinely assembled for war in Europe, and the same conditions that kept African populations small also militated against the deployment of large European armies in Africa. As one British military historian has put it, there were "no agricultural revolutions here [in Africa] to allow large-scale requisitioning".[27]

Thus, battles on the scale of Königgrätz/Sadowa (1866), during the German wars of unification, pitting some 300,000 Prussians against an only slightly smaller number of Austrians, were unthinkable in the African context. The battle that most closely approximates to the Victorian nightmare of "savage hordes" descending upon a brave little band of Europeans is Adowa, the 1896 triumph of some 100,000 Ethiopians over a much smaller Italian force. Unhappily for the Italians, Ethiopia was probably the only African state in the nineteenth century whose size, combined with a strong sense of religious and cultural community, if not nationhood, made possible the mobilization of an army as large as this. More typical of African–European engagements of the era was the battle of Marrecuene (2 February 1895) in Mozambique in which some 3,000 Tonga warriors were repulsed by 812 Portuguese and African soldiers.[28]

The white man's grave

Fears of susceptibility to tropical diseases and a hostile climate also kept European armies in Africa small, even after medical and other improvements had dramatically reduced levels of morbidity. Early in the nineteenth century the susceptibility of European soldiers to tropical diseases such as malaria and yellow fever "meant a death rate at least twice that of soldiers who stayed home, and possibly much higher." Starting about mid-century, medical advances such as the widespread use of quinine to combat malaria, the discovery of the causes of cholera and the stricter enforcement of hygiene regulations among troops began to reduce the health risks to European soldiers in the tropics. Between 1820–30 and 1914 average annual death rates for European military personnel in these regions fell by 85–95 per cent.[29]

That progress in this area came slowly, that it had more impact on troops in barracks than those in the field, and was probably most dramatic at the latter end of the 1820–1914 period, is borne out by the fate of a British Royal Marine detachment on the Gold Coast at the outset of the Ashanti War of 1873–4. In June 1873, 110 Royal Marines had arrived on the Gold Coast express from England to shore up defences against an invading Ashanti army until such time as a British expeditionary force could be sent out. The marine detachment was composed of men between the ages of 20 and 30, which, in the opinion of the naval surgeon present, "is the most likely age to resist the African climate". Nevertheless, by August 1873, most of the marines had been taken off duty, suffering from heat exhaustion or sunstroke, or invalided out with illnesses ranging from diarrhoea to malaria. Part of the problem was judged to be poor diet. The marines were "constantly fed on pork, which is the very worst food for the African climate, and is poison to men suffering from diarrhoea". The marines' difficulties with the heat had begun with their arrival in Africa: "the first time they were landed, they were marched, some of them 22 miles and others 18 miles, which is quite equal to double that distance in a temperate climate."[30] Their vulnerability had been enhanced, however, by a lack of sun helmets, which by this time were part of the normal kit of army troops on tropical service but not that of marines or sailors.[31] Following complaints, sun helmets were eventually sent out to the Gold Coast for the marines but, because of a lack of supply personnel, were never distributed. The unused helmets were sold at the end of the war at an auction of surplus British stores.[32]

With developments such as these, and the slow circulation of "good news" about the fight against tropical disease, it is not surprising that the general public in Europe continued to view the tropics as "the white man's grave". Accordingly, there was no relaxation in countries with conscription, such as France and Germany, of curbs on the deployment of conscripts to tropical areas. Nor were military men generally moved by reports of reduced health risks to propose the dispatch of more European troops to Africa. "Anyone who recommends using a force composed entirely of European soldiers in Central Africa is just betraying his complete inexperience," wrote the German explorer, soldier and colonial administrator, Hermann von Wissmann.[33]

Also of continuing concern were the difficulties posed for the European soldier by the hot and humid African climate. Even though by the 1890s most European troops in Africa had been issued with sun helmets and lighter, looser fitting uniforms, they still functioned poorly in most parts of the continent. In 1901, however, Captain J.S. Herron of the US Second Cavalry informed his superiors in Washington that British colonial troops had found a way of dealing with this problem:

> In spite of their long tours of tropical service the British troops succeed in resisting the effects of the climate without excessive losses. This result is achieved by the system . . . of keeping the soldier a fighting man and, for all labor which is fatiguing, unhealthy or repugnant, employing natives paid by the state. In the field the British troops are accompanied by numerous drivers, packers, laborers, etc. . . . it often happens that noncombatants are more numerous than the combatants.[34]

African colonial troops

Although the British approach was also followed to some extent by most other European armies in Africa, it was not deemed a particularly satisfactory solution to the climate problem. A more practical – and cheaper – answer was increased recourse to African troops. Although their numbers and the nature of their employment varied from one colonial army to another, large numbers of African soldiers were employed by each of the European colonial powers. In their wars of conquest in Africa indeed, David Killingray exaggerates only slightly when he asserts that

> European empires in Africa were gained principally by African mercenary armies, occasionally supported by white or other colonial troops. In what Kipling described as "savage wars of peace" the bulk of the fighting was done by black soldiers whose disciplined firepower and organization invariably defeated numerically superior African armies.[35]

Of the European powers involved in Africa, the French probably used the largest number of African troops, even though the African percentage of overall French troop strength in West Africa was lower than in the admittedly smaller *Schutztruppe* in German East Africa or *Force Publique* in the Congo Free State. From 1857, when the first battalion of Senegalese light infantry (*Tirailleurs Sénégalais*) was raised, up to the First World War, the part played by African soldiers in the French forces in West Africa grew steadily. In 1910 Marine Colonel (later General) Charles Mangin wrote:

> Today a force of 12,500 [Tirailleurs Sénégalais] guards the whole of our possessions in West Africa and the Congo-Chad region, for, in all of this area, larger than Europe, there is now only a single European unit, a battalion of three companies (450 men) of colonial infantry, stationed at Dakar to defend the main [South Atlantic] base of our fleet.[36]

Already in the mid–1880s most of the fighting in the French campaigns in the Western Sudan was being done by the Tirailleurs Sénégalais. The commander of French forces in the region in 1886–8, Lieutenant-Colonel Joseph-Simon Galliéni, confirmed the assumption by African troops of the primary role in the French conquest of West Africa:

> The Senegalese light infantry are the real soldiers of the Sudan. By turns engineers, gunners, couriers, porters, always ready, always loyal, it is because of them that we are able to hold the vast territory [from the Senegal River] to the Niger River.[37]

It might also be noted that the force which set out with French Marine Captain Jean-Baptiste Marchand on his celebrated trek from Gabon across central Africa to confront Kitchener at Fashoda in 1898 was composed of seven Frenchmen and 150 Senegalese riflemen.[38]

The French made no secret of why they relied increasingly on black troops to do their fighting in Africa. "Their susceptibility to tropical diseases is four to five times less than that of Europeans and, moreover, their needs are less complex," said Lieutenant-Colonel Albert Ditte in 1905. "[With African troops] you can put more combatants in the field, you have fewer sick, and there is less gear to drag around."[39] And African soldiers were much cheaper. In 1900, it cost 2,127–2,540 francs a year to maintain a French marine infantryman in West Africa, but only 980.35 francs a year to maintain a *Tirailleur Sénégalais*.[40]

British forces in tropical Africa also relied heavily on African troops. The 11,500 soldiers serving under the Union Jack in West Africa, East and Central Africa and Northern Nigeria in 1902 included no more than 300 white officers and NCOs.[41] Most of these troops were in the ranks of the West African Frontier Force (WAFF), founded in 1897 and composed of regiments from the Gambia, Gold Coast, Northern and Southern Nigeria and Sierra Leone, or the King's African Rifles (KAR), founded in 1902 through the merger of pre-existing chartered company regiments in Central Africa, Kenya and Uganda.[42]

Except for South West Africa, where the occupation forces were comprised exclusively of white mounted infantry, the Germans relied heavily upon African soldiers (*askaris*) to do their fighting in Africa. In 1912 German forces outside South West Africa included 226 whites, of whom 108 were officers and physicians, and 2,664 Africans.[43]

The Italian army in East Africa boasted a large contingent of Eritrean *ascaris*, almost all of whom were Muslims. The Italian victory over the Sudanese Mahdists at Agordat on the Ethiopian frontier in 1893 was won by a force of 75 Italian officers and NCOs and 2,106 *ascaris*.[44] General Oreste Baratieri's defeat of the 19,000 Tigrayans of Ras Mengesha at Coatit in Ethiopia in 1895 was the work of 171 Italian officers and NCOs and 3,729 *ascaris*.[45] And when Baratieri led the Italian army to its epic demise at Adowa the next year, about half of his command of 20,000 men were Eritrean *ascaris* and Tigrayan irregulars. This was despite the fact that his army had been heavily reinforced by regulars sent express from Italy.

Portugal, the smallest of the imperial powers in Africa but also the oldest, had through the centuries used large numbers of African troops in its campaigns in Angola, Mozambique and Guinea-Bissau. Although the Portuguese war against the Gaza Nguni and their Tonga allies in Mozambique in 1895 was waged largely by white regulars, this was done for specifically ideological reasons, as we will see. Much more typical was the Portuguese force which in 1902 invaded the kingdom of Barue in Mozambique's Zambezi river valley under the command of local governor João de Azevedo Coutinho. Only 477 of its 15,000 men were Portuguese.[46]

The *Force Publique*, the private army which conquered the Congo Free State for Belgian king, Leopold II in the 1880s and 1890s, had a strength of about 6,000 regulars in 1900. Only its 200 officers and an undisclosed number of NCOs were European.[47]

Specialized colonial armies

Despite the growing reliance upon African troops to do the bulk of the fighting in tropical regions, discussion continued in most capitals about the desirability of creating specialized European armies for colonial service. The French, who were the only ones eventually to create such a body, the *Armée coloniale* (1900), had been debating the issue since the aftermath of the Franco-Prussian War. Proponents of a tropical equivalent of the *Armée d'Afrique*, which was based permanently in Algeria, argued that African troops could not in the final analysis be trusted to stand fast in tight situations and thus required "stiffening" by white troops. There was also doubt about the ultimate loyalty of African troops. It was felt that they needed to be flanked by white troops who could get them to see where their duty lay if they began to waver. The objections to a colonial army for the tropics mainly concerned its all-volunteer nature (under law, French conscripts could not be forced to serve outside Europe). The French Left tended to equate conscription with democracy and saw volunteer armies as potential praetorian guards. It was also felt that armies based far from home with their own command structures might be difficult to control. This was not an unreasonable fear.

The *Armée coloniale* finally agreed upon was, in essence, the old French marine corps, which had been serving very largely in that capacity in West Africa since Bonaparte's time. The marines were shifted from the naval to the war ministry for the occasion.[48] One of the models French parliamentarians had studied in the 1880s in trying to decide the shape of their colonial army was the Italian *Corpo Speciale per l'Africa*. This force had been created in 1887 after a long debate on the issue in Italian government and military circles. The Italian debate had featured many of the same arguments raised in France over the creation of the *Armée coloniale*, but Italian critics had also charged that forming a special colonial army would draw troops away from Europe, where Italy was already having a hard time meeting its defence obligations. Some soldiers also contended that this new army would become a kind of elite. Since it would be in combat frequently, promotions would come more rapidly in the colonial army than in the metropolitan forces, and the colonials would also have a monopoly on decorations. Although, not surprisingly, younger officers lobbied hard for an independent colonial army, what the *Corpo Speciale* eventually agreed upon was basically an expeditionary force. It had no command structure of its own and was composed of volunteers from the regular army. Based in Italy, the *Corpo Speciale* only served abroad in emergencies.[49]

Although some British soldiers and politicians recognized the need for a force especially trained and equipped for colonial service, none was ever organized.[50] Equally fruitless discussions were held about the usefulness of a large, permanent amphibious force. The nucleus of such a formation (or of a specialized colonial army, for that matter) existed in the Royal Marines, but efforts to increase their numbers or to give them a mission beyond that of auxiliaries to gunboat diplomacy met with little success.[51] Although the major obstacle to the creation of special forces of this type in Britain seems to have been budgetary, there were also questions about how troops would be chosen for service in such a force, and the kind of command structure it would require.

After the Herero–Nama War of 1904–7 had revealed deficiencies in the German army's capacity to wage war in Africa, the General Staff proposed the creation of a separate colonial army, especially equipped and trained for African service.[52] No action was taken on this in the short period preceding the First World War, however, and after 1914, of course, the issue became a dead letter.

European military leadership

Africa was a providential land for European professional soldiers. Many a subaltern who might have languished in career-long obscurity in the garrisons of Europe took advantage of the colonial wars in Africa to win decorations, promotions and glory on African battlefields. Colonial officers were also able to turn their hands to administration, ruling over thousands of "natives" and, in some areas, white settlers as well. And since the African wars of imperial conquest coincided with the rise of mass circulation newspapers, colonial soldiers had a chance to become popular heroes back home, and more than a few did.

For those European officers who found themselves at odds with the democratization of politics and society taking place at home – and they were numerous – the African colonial wars offered a new lease of life. The desire to escape to a safe haven in the colonies is thought to have been particularly rife in the French army.

> In a dark world of French civil-military relations, the colonial army provided a shaft of light. The suspicion, the hesitation, the latent mistrust which separated republicans and soldiers at home was not transported to the colonies. Soldiers who were distrusted, spied upon and humiliated in France were pampered, promoted and decorated abroad. Overseas, the army was largely immune from close government scrutiny, free to impose its order and ideology upon the native population which fell under its control and to carve out an area of influence which stretched from Tonkin to Timbuktu, from Pondicherry to the Palais Bourbon.[53]

The sense of alienation which drove so many French officers into the colonial forces was perhaps felt most acutely by members of the aristocracy, who often had difficulty accepting the republic imposed in France following the Franco-Prussian War of 1870 and the Paris Commune. But we should not exaggerate: the boredom of garrison life and the long nineteenth-century European peace was no respecter of social class. So, for every frustrated aristocrat in the French colonial officer corps, for every Bugeaud or Lyautey, there was an equally frustrated bourgeois, a Faidherbe or Galliéni.

Indeed, the tendency of aristocrats in Germany, Italy and Portugal to flock into the officer corps of their country's colonial armies was much more pronounced than in France. In part this was due to the simple fact that officers in these countries tended to come from the aristocracy, but other factors also came into play. All three countries experienced social and political upheavals in the course of the nineteenth century that served to reduce the power and prestige of their upper classes. It was disappointment with this trend, as much as boredom with garrison life and peacetime service, that convinced German, Italian and Portuguese nobles to take commissions in the colonial armies. The officer corps of the

Schutztruppe, Germany's colonial army, was heavily aristocratic. Of 21 Schutztruppe commanders in Africa down to 1914, 15 were noblemen. All those in Tanganyika were aristocrats, as were five of seven in South West Africa; only in the Cameroons, "the least desirable colony of the four", did commoners outnumber noblemen (four of six commanders). Further, a high percentage of these aristocratic *Schutztruppe* officers came from eastern Germany, a region of big rural estates and small towns. "Like his opposite number in the British colonial units, his [*Schutztruppe* officer's] ethos tended to be rural, and he often had little knowledge of – and less sympathy with – the problems of industrial development".[54]

In nineteenth-century Italy the army remained very much under the control of the king. This meant that its officer corps was dominated by the Piedmontese nobility, with its almost familial ties to the royal family, the House of Savoy. It was no secret that northerners rose through the ranks much faster than their southern compatriots. "If an officer wanted to reach the General Staff, it was said, he should be noble, blond and in the artillery".[55] All four of the brigade commanders who served under General Baratieri in Ethiopia in the 1890s – Generals Albertone, Arimondi, Dabormida and Ellena – were Piedmontese.

The Generation of 1895, the dominant clique in the Portuguese colonial army in the era of the imperial wars, was made up almost entirely of aristocratic officers. Its leading figure, Captain Joaquim Augusto Mousinho de Albuquerque, claimed descent from a royal bastard. He looked as if he had "dropped, booted and spurred, off a medieval tapestry", wrote René Pélissier.[56]

All of the officers of the nineteenth-century British army, save two, could be described as "gentlemen". This term, which tends to confuse Continental Europeans (and Americans), does not necessarily denote membership of the aristocracy. Thus, while some of Britain's colonial officers, like Lord Roberts, were genuine bluebloods, many others, like Frederick Lugard, whose father was an impecunious clergyman, came from more modest, if still "gentle", backgrounds. The two celebrated exceptions to the rule were Sir William "Wully" Robertson, who began life as the son of a tailor and ended up as head of the Imperial General Staff during the First World War, and General Hector MacDonald, who worked his way up from the ranks of the Gordon Highlanders. "Fighting Mac", veteran of Majuba Hill, hero of Omdurman, ended badly, however. Accused of a homosexual relationship with a boy in Ceylon, he was recalled to England to face charges, but then shot himself in a hotel room in Paris *en route* back to the sub-continent.

Weaponry

Shoulder arms

The French were the first to equip their troops, both in Europe and in Africa, with magazine rifles. In fact, this weapon, the 1884 model Gras-Kropatschek rifle (most often simply referred to as the "Kropatschek"), was first issued to the marine infantry in West Africa in 1885, on the insistence of their new commander, Lieutenant-Colonel Galliéni. As would be the case in all the colonial armies, the new rifles went first to the white troops. In the 1890s most of the *Tirailleurs Sénégalais* were still carrying the Gras single-shot breechloader which had been the standard French infantry weapon prior to 1885. The Kropatschek, which had the great advantage for African warfare of being relatively short (1.32 m long) and light (4.5 kg) but still hardhitting, also became the standard infantry weapon of the Portuguese colonial army in the 1890s.[57] By this time, however, French soldiers were already discarding their Kropatscheks for a new magazine rifle, the Model 1886 Lebel, "the first smallbore and smokeless powder rifle to be adopted by a major world power".[58]

British troops in Africa were a bit slower than some others to equip themselves with the new weaponry spawned by the "breechloader revolution" of the 1860s. The Martini-Henry single-shot breechloader, adopted by the British army in 1869 and first issued in 1871, would see its initial service in Africa against the Zulus in 1879. "It was capable of killing an opponent at up to 1,000 yards, if handled by an expert, but prone to jam and apt to bruise a marksman's shoulder or even cause his nose to bleed because of the rifle's terrific kickback".[59] The Martini-Henry's replacement in 1889, the Lee-Metford magazine rifle, which fired a smokeless-powder cartridge, was initially issued only to European troops. At the battle of Omdurman in 1898, the Egyptian and Sudanese troops, who made up the major part of Kitchener's force, carried Martini-Henrys.

The story was the same in the other European armies in Africa. The small white contingent in the *Schutztruppe* in German East Africa began receiving the Mauser Mark 98 magazine rifle shortly after its adoption by the German army in 1885, while African askaris were still carrying single-shot, black-powder Mauser breechloaders when the First World War broke out. Italian soldiers at the battle of Adowa in 1896 carried Swiss-made Model 1887 Vetterli magazine rifles, while the Eritrean *ascaris* who fought alongside them were equipped with single-shot Model 1870 Vetterli breechloaders. In 1891, the African troops of the *Force Publique* in the Congo Free State began receiving the single-shot Albini breechloading rifle formerly in use in the

Belgian army. The force's European officers and NCOs, meanwhile, were issued with Mauser magazine rifles. Lastly, the Portuguese army in the late 1880s began replacing its standard infantry weapon, the single-shot Castro Guedes breechloader, an adaptation of the British Martini-Henry, with the French Kropatschek. The new French magazine rifles went first to the metropolitan army, and its old single-shot breechloaders were shipped off to the colonies. By 1895, however, many of Portugal's colonial troops were also carrying Kropatscheks.

Machine guns

Gann and Duignan are mistaken in stating that "The development of the machine gun was relatively neglected in the British army", at least as insofar as the years of imperial conquest in Africa are concerned.[60] Rather, the British would appear to have been in the forefront in introducing machine guns in African land warfare. The first recorded use of the Gatling gun by European troops in Africa was by the British army during the Ashanti war of 1873–4 (not in the Zulu war of 1879, as Gann and Duignan, once again, would have it).[61] This was well in advance of the employment of automatic weapons by other imperial powers. But if machine guns can be said to have played a major role in British campaigns in Africa, they played almost none in the imperial conquests of the French. Indeed, the French, who seem to go through spasms of aversion to adding foreign weapons to their arsenal, only began to issue machine guns to their metropolitan army in the early years of the twentieth century, when they were able to employ a French-made gun, the Hotchkiss Model 1897.

Although a few machine guns had been used on French naval vessels in Africa in the last quarter of the nineteenth century, the weapon only came into general use with French troops in Africa on the eve of the First World War.[62] The Germans, usually quick to embrace new technology, also proved surprisingly slow to adopt the machine gun. The big impediment here was the General Staff's indifference to the new weapon, which they considered irrelevant to modern European warfare and wasteful of ammunition to boot. It was thought that machine guns might be useful for terrorizing Africans, however, and so a few were sent out to the colonies, where they were instrumental in putting down the mass rebellions of 1904–7 in German South West Africa and Tanganyika. The Germans began manufacturing the Maxim machine gun under license in 1894, but far and away the biggest customer for the weapons was the German navy; the army placed its first important order for Maxims only in 1899.[63] The Italians, the first Europeans to adopt the Maxim machine gun officially, followed the same route in 1887. The first Maxims went to the Italian navy, although the Italian army subsequently used large numbers of them in its campaigns in East and North Africa.

It might be worth pointing out here that almost everywhere in Europe navies were much quicker than armies to adopt the machine gun. Carting the heavy weapons around wasn't as much of a problem for navies as it was for armies, and ships provided a solid, fixed platform to fire from.

King Leopold II's *Force Publique*, meanwhile, used machine guns to protect forts but not as a field weapon during its Congo wars in the 1890s. The Portuguese, who had followed the British use of the Gatling gun in the Zulu war with great interest, generally had, however, unhappy experiences with machine guns during their own wars in Mozambique in the 1890s. Two jammed Nordenfelt machine guns nearly opened up a Portuguese square to enemy penetration at the battle of Magul in 1895.[64]

Artillery

Attitudes which developed during the imperial wars in Africa have been blamed for the neglect of the artillery arm in European armies on the eve of the First World War. Soldiers in Africa learned to get along without artillery in large measure because the big guns proved exceedingly difficult to transport across the trackless savannah or through the dense rain forests. The British experience on the plains of Northern Nigeria in the campaign of 1903 offers insight into the problem.

> The 75-mm gun . . . required a carrier party numbering, with reliefs, thirty-two in all. One man carried all the spare parts, four carried the gun slung on a pole, two a wheel each, one the axle, four more the cradle, and another four the trail, both of which were slung on poles as well. The trail, the cradle, and the gun each weighed over 200 pounds.[65]

Another factor militating against the use of artillery was the lack of targets sufficiently important to justify the expenditure of manpower and effort described above. There were very few defensive obstacles like the walled cities of the Western Sudan which the French were obliged to reduce in their campaigns in the 1880s and 1890s, or the forts or *bomas* the *Force*

Publique levelled with artillery barrages during the Arab War in the Congo in 1891–4. And, apart from the Boers, few opponents in the African wars fought from trenches or other prepared positions that required bombardment. Finally, accounts of the wars of imperial conquest in Africa offer numerous examples of the ineffectiveness of artillery against loose enemy attack formations. The uselessness of British artillery against the Zulus at the battle of Isandlwana makes the point.

> It was easier for [the attacking Zulus] to avoid the shells from the seven-pounders than the rifle volleys. When they saw the gunners stand clear, they either fell down or parted ranks, allowing the shot to pass as harmlessly as wind, and leaving the British unsure as to whether their fire had taken effect or not. They took this evasive action with no hurry or confusion, as if they had been drilled to it.[66]

The colonial experience was not entirely negative, however. The African campaigns did speed up the development of mountain artillery light enough to be packed on draft animals. Africa also provided a testing ground for the new quick-firing artillery being produced by, among others, Krupp in Germany and Hotchkiss in France, and for a new family of high explosive shells. The Western Sudan was the venue for the debut of the French high explosive melinite in 1890, while Britain's lyddite was first tried out against the Mahdists at Omdurman in 1898.

Navies

The lament of Royal Navy historian Sir William Laird Clowes that the contribution of the navy to British victory in the Boer War has been insufficiently appreciated,[67] could easily be applied to the whole European imperial experience in Africa at the end of the nineteenth century. Since the wars of imperial conquest involved no ship-to-ship engagements and not much more in the way of ship-to-shore bombardment, the tendency has been to downplay the naval contribution to the European penetration of Africa. Yet, from beginning to end, naval support was crucial to European military success in the African wars, including many conflicts that took place a considerable distance from the sea.

The success of Britain's "free-trade imperialism" along portions of the West African coast in the early nineteenth century owed much to the presence of the Royal Navy. Its anti-slavery patrols during these years "immeasurably strengthened Britain's influence in those regions, added several useful naval bases to the Empire and confirmed the impressions of European and native rulers that an 'informal rule' actually existed".[68]

In addition to maintaining coastal patrols and transporting troops and supplies to the African wars, the Royal Navy also contributed substantially to the firepower of British land forces. For example, it operated armoured steamboats equipped with cannon and machine guns on the Nile in support of Kitchener in 1898. But, most important, because of its longer experience with machine guns and its traditional expertise with heavy artillery, the navy was frequently called upon to provide special brigades of bluejackets to accompany the army into action. Naval brigades often ended up serving deep in the African interior during the colonial wars. Sailors fired off rockets at Ashantis in 1873–4, manned machine guns against the "Fuzzy-Wuzzies" in the Sudan in the 1880s, and operated big guns against the Boers in 1899–1902. These naval brigades, which also saw action as infantry, sometimes in tandem with the Royal Marines, were probably as close as Britain ever came to forming an amphibious strike force during the Victorian era.

The French navy had been a vigorous proponent of empire ever since its formal launching by Colbert in the seventeenth century. In the nineteenth century,

> the relationship between the navy and the colonial movement was closer than in any other European state. Naval officers were among the most ardent supporters of colonialism. Even after the colonial administration was finally separated from the Ministry of Marine in 1893, the navy retained sole responsibility for colonial defense.[69]

Naval officers had almost singlehandedly got France involved in Indochina under the Second Empire, and during the years of the Third Republic the navy was equally at the forefront in promoting expansion in Africa. This connection was particularly close during the 1880s, when Admiral Hyacinthe-Laurent-Théophile Aube was at the head of the navy. Aube, who is perhaps best known to history as one of the founders of the *Jeune École* approach to naval warfare, which stressed commerce-destruction rather than big ship engagements, was also a colonial fanatic. He had spent almost all of his career in the colonies and, to top it all, had married the niece of the great French proconsul in Senegal, General Louis Faidherbe.

> Aube's military ideas were based on the premise that the navy had but one function: the defense of the colonial empire against England. This was to be accomplished by ruthless commerce-destroying and by coastal defenses.[70]

Critics have charged that the French navy's colonial obsession had a negative impact upon its ability to defend France in Europe. The fleet and its armament were for the most part geared to colonial warfare, not operations in the Channel or the Mediterranean. Most of its budget was spent on colonial expansion, a large part of it surreptitiously.[71]

Nonetheless, the navy's contribution to France's conquest of West Africa was enormous. In addition to transporting troops and supplies along the coasts and up the rivers of the region, naval vessels provided firepower to assist the progress of land columns. Symbolic evidence of the French navy's prime role in the African colonial wars was the fact that the first French fighting men to enter the fabled desert city of Timbuktu, the ultimate goal of France's Western Sudan adventure, were sailors (see Chapter Four).

The German navy played a major role in the establishment of German colonies in Africa. Its light cruisers and gunboats enforced the establishment of German protectorates in Cameroon and Tanganyika and provided firepower to assist in the repression of a revolt against German rule in Tanganyika in 1888. This was precisely the limited role Bismarck had foreseen for the German fleet in the 1880s: to open up business opportunities and protect commerce. This orientation would go by the board after Bismarck's departure from office in 1890. Under Kaiser Wilhelm II and his naval secretary, Admiral Alfred von Tirpitz, the navy was transformed into a High Seas Fleet intended to contest the Royal Navy's maritime dominance.

The German marines also played an important part in the expansion in Africa. At the outset they were almost the only metropolitan infantry available for duty in the various German protectorates. Later, they served as a rapid intervention force to aid the *Schutztruppe* in repressing revolts, fulfilling this function in both the Herero–Nama and Maji–Maji wars in 1904–7. Although the marines were said to have played only a minor part in these campaigns "without, under unfamiliar conditions, gaining particular distinction", they were lionized by the Kaiser. "Kaiser Wilhelm, for all his colonial ambitions, preferred his smart *Marineinfanterie* to the hard-working *Schutztruppe*".[72]

Perhaps no imperial power profited as much from naval power, however, as did the master of the Congo, the Belgian king, Leopold II. His control over the vast region he had persuaded the other, greater powers to allot him rested narrowly on the dominance of its complex river system. This his administrators achieved through the development of a large fleet of river-going steamboats, whose ability to move troops around quickly was the deciding factor in the Arab War of the 1890s, the greatest challenge to Leopold's rule.

Conclusion

Africa on the eve of conquest remained a "Dark Continent" to many Europeans despite an increase in exploration in the early 1800s, but Europeans were not at a complete loss to know how to deal with the peoples they would find there. British and French armies came already equipped with considerable experience in treating with and fighting peoples of less technologically advanced cultures that could be applied in Africa:

(a) They had developed relevant diplomatic and fighting skills in two centuries of contact with the forest Indians of North America and the various peoples encountered in Asia.

(b) These same experiences had also taught them how to recruit, train and employ local levies.

(c) Europeans had plentiful experience of informal warfare, both as a result of bush fighting in their colonial possessions and their wars with each other in Europe.

(d) Europeans had developed a logistics capability that enabled them to mount expeditions and gather supplies from the far corners of their domains and bring them to bear with fairly precise and often devastating effect.

(e) Europeans had reached a level of expertise in combined operations that enabled them to supply their troops and outflank their enemies by the use of river and coastal shipping.

However impressive these European capabilities may have been, what many historians, revisionist and traditional alike, have chosen to single out as the key to the European conquest of Africa was the revolutionary progress in military technology in the latter half of the 1800s. For the Ghanaian historian of the imperial wars, A. Adu Boahen,

> There is no doubt that the most crucial [European advantage] was military . . . Above all, technologically and logistically, African armies were at a great disadvantage in comparison with their invaders . . . Nor did any of them have a navy. What chance would such an army have against a well-trained, professional one armed with cannons and repeater rifles [and] maxim guns and enjoying naval and logistic support?[73]

Again, we believe that the importance of military hardware in the conquest of Africa has been exaggerated, and, as we see here, not only by Western technological determinists. There is a note of fatalism in views like those of African historians such as Boahen that is not justified. To argue that Western martial prowess was invincible enables African historians to excuse or play down serious shortcomings on the African side that contributed at least as much to the African defeat as did superior European firepower. These shortcomings included the inability to bury old tribal enmities long enough to forge alliances against the European enemy; the unwillingness to rethink strategies and tactics that had proved ineffective against European methods of warfare; the refusal to abandon hierarchical and inegalitarian social structures that inhibited African peoples from presenting a united front against the invader.

In any case, the opening shots in the European invasion of Africa were already fired well before the European revolution in military hardware took place. European penetration had begun with the French seizure of the Mediterranean coast of Algeria in 1830. As will be noted in greater detail in Chapter Three, although this invasion progressed fitfully in areas beyond the Mediterranean littoral, it would be heavy with consequences not only for Algerians and other North Africans but for black Africans across the Sahara as well.

Chapter Three

A shifting balance, 1830–80

Algeria

Introduction

The military history of the European conquest of Africa in the nineteenth century begins north of the Sahara, in Algeria, long before the onset of the Scramble. The long and brutal campaign by France to "pacify" Algeria from 1830 to 1847 saw the emergence for the first time of many of the features we associate with the European wars of conquest and with the resistance they met from indigenous peoples. To begin with, it was in Algeria during this time that some of the best known institutional symbols and most enduring imagery of European colonial warfare first took shape. In the 1830s the French government took the first steps toward creating a separate force, the *Armée d'Afrique*, to fight its wars in North Africa. Eventually garrisoned permanently in Algeria, the *Armée d'Afrique* would include some of the more colourful units in colonial military history: the *Zouaves*, European infantry decked out in the baggy pants and embroidered tunics of the Berber peoples of the Algerian mountains; the *Spahis*, Arab cavalry in flowing burnooses; and the *Turcos*, the Algerian light infantry who would go on to serve with such distinction in both world wars and in Indochina. The other famous military unit created during this time was, of course, the French Foreign Legion, formed in 1831 to siphon off the less desirable elements among France's large foreign population. The Legion fought some of its first battles in Algeria and would eventually establish its home base at Sidi Bel Abbès, near Oran.

It was also in Algeria that European soldiers first began to work out and apply the politico-military strategies and tactics that would enable them to cope with the particularities of warfare in Africa: great distances, a hostile landscape, a scarcity of traditional military targets, an elusive and anonymous enemy. In the process of confronting these challenges, the soldiers rediscovered the importance to military success of a grasp of indigenous politics, which would enable them to turn ethnic groups and religious factions against each other, in effect to divide and conquer. These were skills that European governments and soldiers had cultivated for centuries in relations with domestic minorities and indigenous peoples in Asia and North America.

Warfare in Algeria in the 1830s and 1840s also highlighted the kinds of logistical problems that would plague European armies in Africa throughout the wars of conquest, such as the difficulty of securing transport for supplies over long distances and providing drinkable water and edible rations for long campaigns. The kinds of medical problems that would dog European armies in Africa were particularly rampant in Algeria. The range of afflictions faced by the *Armée d'Afrique* in Algeria during this time was certainly broader than that experienced by troops in Africa later in the century. Cholera, which ceased to be a threat by the second half of the century, killed thousands of soldiers and civilians in France and North Africa in the 1830s. Malaria stalked soldiers and peasants on Algeria's coastal plains. And Algeria was one of the few African battle zones where soldiers risked freezing to death, as many did in the campaigns in the 1840s to subdue the Berber tribes in the Kabylia, the mountainous area just behind the Algerian coast.[1]

Finally, the deterioration in civil-military relations that became such a characteristic feature of the wars of imperial conquest had its beginnings in Algeria. "Here," explains A.S. Kanya-Forstner, "the French Army first demonstrated its full potential as an independent force. From the start, the Algerian High Command set out to free itself from metropolitan control by systematically disregarding its instructions." This tendency to insubordination, and the contempt for civilians and civilian institutions it engendered, were encouraged by the French government's decision in 1834 to entrust to the army not only the war in Algeria but also Algerian colonial administration. Consequently, the army "monopolized the sources of political power, deliberately excluding civilian colonists from any effective participation in political affairs. For forty years its mastery over Algeria was virtually absolute."[2] This was long enough to give shape to a distinctively "military" brand of imperialism, which, while it achieved its greatest notoriety during the employment of the French colonial forces, also had its champions in other colonial armies.

Resistance movement

The Algerian war also brings into relief many of the essential features of African resistance movements in the nineteenth century. First, the Algerian conflict demonstrates the powerful integrative function of religion in resistance struggles, a phenomenon largely undervalued by historians until fairly recently. The coupling of religious and secular authority in the person of the Algerian resistance leader, the Amir Abd el-Kader (1807–83), gave the movement an exceptionally broad appeal. This, together with the amir's charismatic leadership, goes far towards explaining how the Algerians were able to hold the field for nearly two decades against a European expeditionary force superior in firepower and often in numbers as well.

Secondly, the Algerian drama shows why it was important for resistance movements to cultivate the arts of diplomacy along with those of war. Abd el-Kader's negotiated truces with the French twice gave the Algerian resistance movement the breathing space it needed at crucial junctures in the war. The amir's alliance with the ruler of neighboring Morocco and his diplomatic feelers to the British at Tangier and Gibraltar also helped keep the French off balance.

Thirdly, the Algerian resistance demonstrated a capacity for adapting Western military technology that would later also characterize other prominent resistance movements. With help from European mercenaries and prisoners of war, the amir's staff organized and trained infantry units along Western lines, equipped them with modern European firearms, and operated workshops for manufacturing and repairing weapons, including artillery pieces.[3]

Fourthly, the French invasion of Algeria fostered a reaction among the populace, fearful of the loss of its Arab and Muslim identity, that bordered on nationalism. Abd el-Kader was able to build on that sentiment to create a new political structure in insurgent Algeria which, if "not yet a nation-state", nonetheless represented "a major departure from the state-building efforts of North Africa's past and a sign that important segments of Algerian society were ready for a new, more unified social and political order".[4] Although the Algerians may have moved further along this path than most other African peoples at this early stage, theirs was not the only nineteenth-century African resistance movement to give rise to proto-nationalist sentiments.

Finally, although Abd el-Kader is today remembered as the greatest of the early fighters for Algerian independence and nationhood, the ultimate demise of the amir and his resistance movement should remind us that there were definite limits to the solidarity or "national feeling" of African indigenous peoples in the face of European invasion in the nineteenth century. Ethnic divisions, tribal rivalries, religious differences and conflicts between town and countryside all played into the hands of the Europeans, and contributed greatly to the defeat of the resistance in Algeria and elsewhere.

Before the deluge, 1830–40

The French seizure of Algiers in 1830 from its nominal Turkish overlords was not intended to be permanent, much less the prelude to a conquest of the interior of the country. Rather, it was a last-ditch effort by the unloved Bourbon monarchy in France to avert revolution by winning glory for the country abroad. Even so, the expedition was a substantial undertaking, whose scale gives an early indication of the kind of strategic and logistical advantage the European powers would enjoy in their wars in Africa. Some 675 ships were assembled at the Toulon naval base near Marseille to transport the troops and baggage of the 37,000-man assault force across the sea to Algiers and to blockade the Algerian coast in case the Turks decided to attempt a rescue.[5]

The Algerian diversion proved politically futile, as the Revolution of 1830 overthrew the Bourbons, but French troops remained in North Africa. And in 1834 the new regime of King Louis-Philippe, believing that the public wanted it and national prestige demanded it, decided that France should retain not only Algiers but the rest of the Algerian seaboard as well. A desire to twist the tail of the British lion, the would-be lord of the Mediterranean, played a major role in this aspect of the decision.

Historians have seized upon the absence of economic claims in the government's brief for Algerian occupation as yet another proof of the limited part played by the profit motive in imperial conquest. There was, however, a definite economic dimension to French designs on Algeria. French soldiers gave vent to one of the more basic economic motives in their frenzied looting of the Algiers Casbah in 1830. Put simply, Algeria, for a long time a stronghold of the Barbary pirates, was thought to be home to a treasure-trove of gold and jewels. Marseille's merchants offered a more serious economic rationale for hanging on to Algeria. They wanted to divert its foreign trade, which was thought to have considerable potential, from Italian and Spanish hands into their own.[6]

In addition, optimistic estimates of the amount of fertile land in Algeria gave rise to a movement for French colonization. The government's enthusiasm for this scheme was heightened by fears of an impending crisis in France's cities, where the restiveness of large numbers of dispossessed peasants and unemployed artisans threatened social peace. As would be the case in Italy later in the century, France in the 1830s looked to settlement in Africa as a safety valve for the easing of domestic social tensions.

Finally, attempts were made to justify the French presence in Algeria on the grounds that it would bring the advantages of France's superior civilization to the indigenous population. The "natives" in time would become Europeanized and could then be "assimilated" into French culture. It should be emphasized, however, that this early appeal to France's *mission civilisatrice* was less strident than it or the corresponding Anglo-Saxon evocation of the "White Man's Burden" would be later in the century.

The jihad of Abd el-Kader

The French presence in Algeria almost immediately led to conflict with the indigenous population, as Arab peoples in the interior, under the leadership of the Amir Abd el-Kader, began to mobilize to expel the invader. Abd el-Kader came from a powerful aristocratic family in the Mascara region of western Algeria, which claimed descent from the Prophet. The family had migrated to North Africa from the holy city of Medina in Arabia and had arrived in Algeria by way of Morocco, with which it continued to maintain close ties. The family's "Moroccan connection" would stand Abd el-Kader in good stead during his war against the French. His father, Muhyi al-Din, was the head of the *Mukhtariyya* branch of Algeria's largest and most influential Sufi brotherhood, the *Qadiriyya*.[7] The Sufi brotherhoods, of whom there were several throughout the Muslim world, were groups of mystics who, by offering the faithful a more intimate relationship with God than traditional practice allowed, won a large following among the general population. In North and West Africa, their popularity often propelled the Sufis into the leadership of movements to revitalize or spread the faith, or to resist the encroachments of the infidel.

Intensely devout, even puritanical, a poet and close student of the Koran, it was as a *marabout* or spiritual leader, not a warrior, that Abd el-Kader presided over the Algerian resistance movement. But whereas the only official title he ever held was *amir el-mu'minin*, "commander of the faithful," the amir also held supreme political power, which meant that he oversaw the administration of justice, the collection of taxes, and, most important, the creation of a modern, "national" military force.

Abd el-Kader took what may seem like a surprising interest in the military side of his mandate. Charles-André Julien is right to call him a "warrior-monk."[8] His goal was not to drive the French into the sea – since he lacked a navy, he believed he had no authority over the coastal zone – but to contain them in the port cities they already controlled: Algiers, Oran, Bone.[9] In 1832 Abd el-Kader pronounced a jihad against the Christian invaders of Algeria, declaring:

> We have assumed this important charge [the office of commander of the faithful] hoping that it may be the means of uniting the great body of Muslims and preventing dissensions among them, of affording general security to all dwellers in the land and of driving back the enemy who had invaded our country with a view to placing his yoke upon our necks.[10]

But the amir knew that success in this task would require a more highly-centralized and homogeneous state than had ever existed before in Algeria. This new state would cut across the complex lineage institutions that had been at the heart of the old order; tribal autonomy would have to be curbed, along with that of the powerful regional nobility.

It is difficult to know what sort of state Abd el-Kader envisioned in the long term, since almost all we know of his plans comes from hostile or uninformed French sources. What is clear is that the immediate goal of the amir's reforms was to create a political infrastructure that could enforce unity among the Arab population of the interior and make possible extensive and prolonged military resistance to the French.

Abd el-Kader faced enormous challenges in his struggle against the encroachments of the French. To begin with, despite his great spiritual and political authority, the amir failed to contain important centrifugal forces in the Algerian population: local leaders who resented their loss of autonomy; Berber tribes that feared their Muslim Arab neighbours more than the infidel foreigner; and rival religious organizations, such as the second largest Sufi brotherhood in Algeria, the *Tijaniyya*. Because of an earlier dispute with Abd el-Kader's order, the *Qadiriyya*, the *Tijaniyya* brotherhood not only refused to support the amir, but actually rallied to the French.[11] So did most of the coastal urban population.[12] The French profited from these divisions to force Abd el-Kader on to the defensive.

The amir also had to contend with an enemy that appeared ready to spare no cost to secure his defeat. It was rare in African colonial warfare for European invaders to outnumber their indigenous opponents. Algeria in the 1840s was one of the most striking exceptions. By 1847, on the eve of Abd el-Kader's surrender, there were 108,000 French troops in Algeria, a third of the entire French army and the largest European force to serve in Africa prior to the second Boer War in 1899–1902.[13] By contrast, the amir was never able to field an army larger than some 50,000, and most of these were brave but poorly armed and undisciplined irregulars.

To wage war against the French, Abd el-Kader set about building a modern army, trained in the European fashion and armed with modern weapons. A force of some 10,000 regulars (mostly infantry) was formed and equipped with muskets obtained from the French and British. The results, however, proved disappointing. The amir's first test of his regulars in pitched battle against the French, an 1836 engagement on the river Sikkak against his future nemesis, General Bugeaud, ended in defeat.[14]

After the repulse on the Sikkak, the amir's army engaged almost exclusively in hit-and-run warfare. The result was a half-decade of desultory conflict, in which the Arabs succeeded in confining the French to the hinterlands of the coastal cities. French troops which ventured outside the coastal zone manoeuvred across the landscape in dense, heavily-protected, presumably self-sufficient columns. Tied to long baggage trains, encumbered by heavy artillery, they were no match for Abd el-Kader's forces. Extremely mobile, intimately familiar with the terrain, the amir's men were able to strike French columns with impunity and melt away into the hills or desert before a pursuit could be organized. Attempts to "occupy" territory outside the coastal areas involved the construction of isolated forts, where small garrisons sweated and sickened without exercising the least control over the surrounding peoples.[15]

The Bugeaud era, 1841–7

France's Algerian army was in a parlous state by 1840, when it came under the command of General Thomas-Robert Bugeaud (1784–1849), a Napoleonic veteran who was made both civilian and military ruler in Algeria. Constant failures in the field had combined with appalling sanitary conditions and poor logistical support to reduce morale to a disastrously low ebb. It was not uncommon, for instance, for ill or wounded soldiers to commit suicide rather than undergo treatment in the army's ramshackle hospitals.[16]

Bugeaud's appointment brought reforms that not only succeeded in "pacifying" Algeria by 1847 but created precedents and generated principles that would characterize and influence colonial warfare in Africa ever after. The conflict in Algeria in the 1830s and 1840s has long been viewed as the seedbed of French colonial military theory and practice. "Whether for good or evil," wrote Georges Hardy, a former French colonial official, "the mark of Algeria's colonisation is to be found on all parts of the French domain."[17]

Writers on the subject have traced a direct line of descent from Marshal Bugeaud through General Louis Léon César Faidherbe, architect of the French conquests in Senegal and the Western Sudan that began in the 1850s and 1860s, and Marshal Joseph-Simon Galliéni, commander in the Western Sudan and proconsul in Indochina and Madagascar in the 1880s and 1890s, to Marshal Hubert Louis Lyautey, conqueror and governor of Morocco in the early part of this century.[18] While this line of descent is less direct than is often claimed, as we will see, there is no doubt that, in some elements and certainly in mythic impact, the Algerian experience was fundamental in shaping what some would profess to see as the French colonial military art. What is not such an established fact is the influence on other colonial armies of the French experience in North Africa. Comparison of the writings of colonial field officers and military theorists in a number of countries, however, provides eloquent testimony to that impact. Perhaps surprisingly, nowhere is this more evident than in the work of a British officer, Colonel Charles Callwell's *Small wars*, first published in 1896 and subsequently the Anglo-Saxon world's classic primer on colonial warfare. Callwell's pages abound with "lessons" gleaned from the Algerian campaigns, which he ranks alongside those learned from the Indian Mutiny of 1857 as the most important for European soldiers engaged in the colonial warfare of his day. Bugeaud, he writes, was "one of the greatest of masters of irregular warfare."[19]

The changes Bugeaud initiated after 1840 were largely the fruit of his own experiences fighting irregulars in Spain during the Napoleonic wars, and tested on the ground in his brief stint in Algeria in 1836. Indeed, one observer has commented that "perhaps Bugeaud's principal contribution to military doctrine was his insistence that tactics used successfully in guerrilla warfare be incorporated more fully into conventional military doctrine".[20]

Bugeaud had seen immediately that the main advantage of Abd el-Kader's troops was mobility, and the first initiative he undertook was to restore mobility to the French army. To start with, the big guns went back to the artillery park and the long wagon trains that had accompanied the French columns were retired. The load of the individual infantryman was lightened. No longer would French troops go into combat weighed down like beasts of burden, toting a week's rations, large amounts of ammunition, extra shoes, and cooking gear. The bulk of this equipment would henceforth be transported by the army's new mule corps. Soldiers would carry little more than their weapons and a limited amount of ammunition, and they would live off the land, not off supplies carried by wagon. Food now came from the seizure of enemy flocks and herds or from hunting. These changes enabled Bugeaud to field light, mobile columns that could pursue the enemy deep into his territory and harry him until he was forced to give battle or submit.[21]

Bugeaud is largely responsible for the emergence of the light infantry as France's Queen of Battles in the African colonial wars. There were more than purely utilitarian reasons for this. Bugeaud was, after all, an infantry general. He disliked the artillery because its officer corps was too "theoretical," composed, as it largely was, of bourgeois graduates of the Ècole Polytechnique. The cavalry, Bugeaud felt, remained useful for scouting and raiding – indeed, he made great use of mounted infantry – but was doomed as a shock weapon by the massed firepower of modern infantry.

Despite Bugeaud's indifference, however, the cavalry also emerged from the Algerian wars with an enhanced reputation. This was due largely to an exploit in 1843 by a unit of the European cavalry, the Chasseurs d'Afrique, under the command of the Duc d'Aumale, one of Louis-Philippe's sons. The French army had burned Abd el-Kader's capital at Tagdempt, and the amir and his entourage were obliged to conduct government from an itinerant tent city. On 14 May 1843, the amir's caravan was surprised on the march by the Duc's cavalry and, although heavily outnumbered, the French-men came away with 3,000 prisoners and the amir's treasury. Abd el-Kader, who was elsewhere at the time, eluded capture. This feat, carried off as it was under the command of a prince of the blood, did much to restore the glorious image of the cavalry as wielder of the arme blanche, one of the more dubious legacies of the colonial wars.[22]

Bugeaud has also been credited with giving a new lease on life to that most venerable of infantry formations, the square. Considered outmoded in Europe because of its vulnerability to artillery, the square found a new home in Africa, first of all in Algeria in the 1830s and 1840s, and then virtually everywhere where European and African armies faced each other. We must be careful, however, in attributing the revival of the square to Bugeaud. For while it is true that Bugeaud speculated a great deal about the structure of the square and its proper functioning in combat, it should be emphasized that he saw it as a formation to be employed only on those rare occasions when his troops found themselves under assault by massive numbers of enemy cavalry. In fact, for most fire actions he favoured the two-rank line and even "recommended [using] a three-rank line rather than a square" against most cavalry attacks.[23] The key to his preference for the line over the square was the greater ease with which it could be transformed into an offensive instrument. Loyal to his former master, Napoleon, in this respect at least, Bugeaud distrusted the defensive and believed "every good defensive strategy must be capable of instantaneous transformation into an offensive one".[24]

Legacy of "Père" Bugeaud

For all his ability to adapt to new situations, Bugeaud seems like a man from a bygone age. Descended from an impoverished aristocratic family, he spent his formative years on the family estate deep in the countryside of the Dordogne. Mentally and psychologically, he seems never to have left this bucolic environment. The marshal who liked to describe himself as a "soldier-peasant" had no difficulty ingratiating himself with the other ranks in his overwhelmingly peasant army. On the other hand, his barnyard humour and rustic manners shocked some of his officers, particularly graduates of the *École Polytechnique* such as generals Louis Christophe La Moricière and Louis Eugène Cavaignac. The marshal had no time for the "smart alecks" of the *École* and tried to keep them as far from the limelight as possible, but, "soldier-peasant" that he was, he reserved his greatest contempt for the urban working classes, whose aspirations he never understood and whom he repressed with a will in the uprisings of 1834 and 1848. It was this participation of the colonial generals, the "*Algériens*" as they were popularly known, and sometimes colonial troops, in the repression of domestic insurrections that did more than anything else to alienate the French lower classes from France's colonial ventures.

Obedient to orders when it came to crushing worker revolts in Paris, Bugeaud took quite another view of government oversight when campaigning abroad. It is probably unfair to charge the marshal with originating the tradition of military insubordination that plagued the French Third Republic in the nineteenth century and would eventually lead to the military "putsch" in Algeria in 1958. Nevertheless, as Kanya-Forstner has observed, "During the Governorship [in Algeria] of General Bugeaud (1840–47), military insubordination was raised to the level of an art".[25] Bugeaud's response to a directive from the Minister of War, ordering him not to launch an offensive, is a classic in the genre:

> I received your message. It's too late. My troops are already on the march. If we succeed, the government and France will gain honor from it. If we fail, the entire responsibility will fall on my shoulders. I accept it willingly.[26]

This kind of truculence led eventually to Bugeaud's recall, but, as we shall see, this did not stop officers later in the century, especially junior officers in the Western Sudan like Colonel Louis Archinard, from emulating him.

Not even his most severe critics, however, could deny that, in the words of one of them, Charles-André Julien, Bugeaud was "an ideal moulder of men."[27] For "Père Bugeaud," as the common soldiers called him, led from the front. He dressed like a ranker and lived like one on campaign. Although he was over sixty by the time he left Algeria in 1847, Bugeaud often marched on foot alongside his men. And when the day was done, he liked talking to them until late in the evening around the campfire. Said one of his admiring younger officers, a future marshal and hero of the Franco-Prussian War, General François Canrobert:

> Perhaps never before has an army commander been able, by his benevolence and moral authority, to get as much out of his soldiers. [Bugeaud] could have led them to the end of the earth, or made them throw themselves on to the fire.[28]

Bugeaud did not believe that the moral authority required to make men throw themselves on to a fire could be taught at St. Cyr or the École Polytechnique. Moral authority was something which came naturally to those destined to lead; it could not be learned. And it came most naturally to men of his social class, country squires whose vocation it was to play father figure to peasant tenants on their estates. Nor did Bugeaud believe that the kind of men who would jump into a fire if ordered to do so were likely to be found in the annual intake of conscripts. The marshal, whose experience of Napoleonic warfare consisted largely of small-unit actions against partisans, not monster battles like Wagram or Waterloo, contended that quality – small, highly-motivated armies of professionals, led from the front – would always prevail over quantity on the battlefield. This conviction survived Algeria, where, although he commanded a mass conscript army, Bugeaud defined victory in terms of the *élan* and punch of his stripped-down flying columns. This vision of a small army of inspired professional soldiers, led by men born to command, taking the offensive and winning against the savage hordes of Africa (or the conscript hordes of Germany), was perhaps Bugeaud's most significant legacy to the colonial (and metropolitan) soldiers of the next generation. The vision, later amplified in the writings of his widely-read disciples Ardant du Picq and Louis Jules Trochu, proved particularly appealing to young men of the upper classes. It pointed them in the direction of a field of honour where their values, not the bourgeois values of the Third Republic, still reigned supreme and where glory and prestige could still be won by force of arms. Hubert Louis Lyautey, son of an old aristocratic family and a monarchist in politics, is perhaps the best example of a young officer drawn into colonial military service in this way.[29] But it would be a mistake to assume that only sons of the aristocracy were seduced by Bugeaud's vision. Junior officers of all backgrounds, faced with the prospect of long years of garrison duty and glacially slow promotion, were thus encouraged to apply for postings in the *Armée d'Afrique* in Algeria or the marine infantry in West Africa. This is the origin of the group of officers which corresponds most closely to the Bugeaud type, the *officiers soudanais*, the captains, majors and colonels who, largely on their own initiative, conquered the Western Sudan for France in the 1880s and 1890s.

In the context of late-nineteenth-century French national politics, of course, Bugeaud's patronage of the concept of a professional army ran counter to mainstream opinion, which favoured reliance on a conscript army to defend France. After all, Prussian conscripts had defeated France's professional army in 1870. But, if Bugeaud's ideas were out of step as far as the metropolitan army was concerned, they ultimately prevailed in the colonial sphere. Here, because public opinion resisted sending French conscripts to serve in unhealthy tropical areas such as sub-Saharan Africa and Indochina, except in carefully-defined national emergencies, only volunteers were allowed to serve in the colonial regiments of the marine infantry, which did most of the fighting in such places. These colonial marines constituted, in effect, a professional army on the Bugeaud model. Their status was made permanent by a law in 1900 which created an all-volunteer *Armée coloniale*, drawn largely from the troops of the old marine infantry.[30]

The razzia

The Algerian war of the 1840s offers us the legend, already fully-formed, of how the European armies won their colonial wars in Africa: mobile columns

on the march, driving the enemy before them; devastating firepower pouring from the security of the square to smash foolhardy attackers; officers
leading from the front and winning the undying loyalty of their men. As is
usually the case with legends, there is a kernel of truth in this one. But, as
Bugeaud and his emulators knew, there was a harsher and darker side to
colonial warfare which the legend played down or left out. Having once
experienced the effects of the fire discipline of European infantry, the enemy
often wisely refused to give battle. This meant that, since classic European
methods of securing victory, such as triumph on the battlefield and/or
conquest of the enemy's capital, did not apply in places like Algeria, other
ways to force submission had to be found. General Pierre le Comte de
Castellane, a veteran of the fighting in Algeria, put the French dilemma this
way:

> In Europe, once [you are] master of two or three large cities, the entire
> country is yours. But in Africa, how do you act against a population
> whose only link with the land is the pegs of their tents? . . . The only
> way is to take the grain which feeds them, the flocks which clothe
> them. For this reason, we make war on silos, war on cattle, [we make]
> the *razzia*.[31]

What de Castellane was referring to was Bugeaud's adaptation of the time-
honoured Arab practice of the *razzia*, or raid, to French use. For whereas
traditional *razzias* had been a means of obtaining booty or demonstrating an
enemy's vulnerability, the French variant of the practice bordered on total
war. Bugeaud's flying columns seized Arab flocks and herds, destroyed crops
and orchards, looted granaries and burned villages. Arab peoples who did
not succumb to this kind of persuasion and accept French rule could expect
a war of extermination. This was not a theoretical proposition. On two
separate occasions in 1845, French troops asphyxiated an estimated 500 Arab
men, women and children by setting fires at the mouths of caves where
fleeing tribes had taken shelter.[32]

Reports of these and other atrocities aroused a storm of criticism back in
France. Bugeaud, however, not only approved of such tactics but promised
their continuation. Civilian "softheads" at home did not understand the kind
of war his army was forced to wage in Africa, he said.

> Far from being ineffective or dangerous, such liquidations [as the cave
> massacres] would finally convince the natives that they had no choice
> but to "accept the yoke of conquest" and to devote themselves to
> that "agriculture and commerce which rapidly heal the ravages of
> combat."[33]

Besides, said Bugeaud, in words that would be paraphrased endlessly during the years of imperial conquest by generals in all the European armies:

> We have never got anything from these people except through force. We often tried to bring them around by means of persuasion, but it didn't work. Either they never responded or they told us that we would first have to shoot it out and that if we won, then they would submit.[34]

War without end

In his way, Bugeaud was correct about the efficacy of force. From 1845 to 1847, as the numbers of French troops in Algeria soared, the country was laid waste from end to end, in some areas repeatedly. By 1847, with over 100,000 French soldiers in the field, Abd el-Kader concluded that further resistance was hopeless. In December 1847, he surrendered, not to Bugeaud, who had been recalled by Paris, but to one of the men the marshal despised the most, the *polytechnicien* La Moricière, a dashing commander of *zouaves*.

The amir's surrender was, of course, no more than a truce in what would be a long war of national liberation. The Algerians did not, as Bugeaud had hoped, "accept the yoke of conquest". In 1871, while France was preoccupied with the Franco-Prussian War and the Paris Commune, Algeria rose in revolt. The repression, whose calculated ferocity was intended to cow the Algerian population permanently, took nearly a year to complete and cost the lives of many thousands of resisters.[35] The sequel to these nineteenth-century wars, culminating in Algerian national independence in 1962, is well known, and does not require rehearsing here. Nonetheless, at least one school of thought contends that it was rendered inevitable, not simply by the French presence in Algeria, as some might argue, but by the, to Algerians at least, unnatural violence of the total war waged against the indigenous population by the *Armée d'Afrique*. This reasoning is perhaps best captured in the thought of the French West Indian psychiatrist-turned-revolutionary Frantz Fanon, whose book *The wretched of the earth* made such a profound impact on the post-colonial Third World. Fanon, who had worked as a psychiatrist in a French government hospital in Algeria during the early 1950s before going over to the side of the Algerian rebels, argued that, since the colonial world had been created through violence, it could only be effectively "decolonized" through what he called "counterviolence".

> At the level of individuals, violence is a cleansing force. It frees the native from his inferiority complex and from his despair and inaction; it makes him fearless and restores his self-respect.[36]

Senegal

Introduction

Some two hundred years before the descent on Algiers, France had established its first foothold on the African continent, a trading post called St. Louis at the mouth of the Senegal River in West Africa. French traders had seen the Senegal as a highway into the interior of West Africa, to exotic places like Timbuktu, which they believed to be the source of a rich trade in ivory, gems and gold. This romantic vision of the Western Sudan continued to have an impact on French policy toward the region well into the nineteenth century.[37] But disease and powerful African opponents made expansion into the interior an extremely difficult process, and for a long time French commerce in West Africa was largely confined to the trade in human beings. In the seventeenth and eighteenth centuries, St. Louis and the island of Gorée off Cape Verde served as the main embarkation points for the hundreds of thousands of African slaves dispatched to the French sugar islands in the West Indies. By the 1820s, however, the slave trade had been outlawed and efforts were underway to find some other lucrative item of trade that could justify a continued French presence on the Senegal coast. At this point the only local product that commanded a good price back in Europe was gum arabic, derived from the sap of the acacia tree and widely used in the textile industry to fix dyes. Although the product was marketed in Europe by French merchants in St. Louis, who represented firms in Bordeaux and Marseille, its price in-country was dictated by Berber tribes – the so-called Trarza Moors – from Mauritania, north of the Senegal River, where much of the gum arabic was harvested.[38]

Compared to Algeria, for much of the nineteenth century Senegal was of only secondary interest to the government in Paris. Administered by the Ministry of Marine, which until the 1890s had responsibility for the administration of all French colonies outside North Africa, Senegal was in effect a ward of the French navy, which operated a naval base at Gorée, supplied most of the colony's governors, and stationed marine infantry there as garrison troops. But Senegal was so low on the navy's list of priorities that until the 1850s the St. Louis garrison seldom boasted more than one battalion of marines. Even later, when the government in Paris had adopted a more aggressive policy in Senegal, the governor in St. Louis found he could count on no more than "three battalions of infantry, two of them African; a mixed squadron of *spahis* [part African, part European]; and two batteries of artillery."[39] If France continued to hang on to Senegal, therefore, it was not because of French power, but because the Moors and the African peoples of the interior, such as the Tukolors, whose empire in the 1850s stretched from the Senegal River to the bend of the Niger, tolerated its presence for trading purposes.

The Moors and Tukolors, in fact, tended to regard the French coast dwellers as *dhimmi*, "people of the Book", who would be allowed to retain their seaboard enclaves and riverine trading posts only as long as they paid tribute to their overlords of the True Faith. In return, they were willing to grant these Europeans the status of "masters of the water", rulers over both the African seas and the rivers that emptied into them.[40] They, the Moors and Tukolors were, of course, the more important "lords of the land", a role the Europeans could never aspire to. "The whites are afraid to leave their stone houses for fear of dying in the African heat", Tukolor holy men assured the faithful.[41]

The failure of attempts to develop a plantation economy in Senegal in the 1820s and 1830s had convinced some observers that the colony had no future and ought to be abandoned. In 1850, a parliamentary committee on foreign trade conducted hearings on the fate of the colony. Effectively lobbied by "municipal imperialist" interests, particularly trading companies from Bordeaux and Marseille, the committee decided that the colony was worth retaining, but warned that its "commercial prosperity was dependent on political security, and that [this] security would require the establishment of French political supremacy over the whole course of the Lower Senegal."[42] In 1852 credits were allocated by Paris to finance the building of new forts along the Senegal River and the launching of a military campaign against the Moors. The initiative for this more aggressive policy emanated from two sources: first, from local French merchants and their Bordeaux and Marseille parent firms, who wanted to eliminate the Berber and African middlemen who controlled trade with the interior; secondly, from the new government which seized power in France in 1851, the imperial regime of Louis Napoleon, nephew of Napoleon Bonaparte. Louis, or Napoleon III as he styled himself, was keen to restore France to the status she had enjoyed in the days of his more illustrious uncle. Imperial expansion was thus high on his agenda. It was during the Second Empire of Napoleon III that France first gained a foothold in Indochina and managed to impose French rule briefly on Mexico in the 1860s.

The Faidherbe era, 1854–65

In Africa, expansion into the interior of Senegal led to the first real colonial war south of the Sahara. The drive up the Senegal River was commanded by General Louis Faidherbe (1818–89), who had become governor of Senegal in 1854, following tours of duty in Guadeloupe and Algeria and a term as head of the army engineers in St. Louis. Faidherbe would turn out to be one of the great French colonial proconsuls, the predecessor of and in some ways more of a model than Bugeaud was for Joseph-Simon Galliéni and Hubert Lyautey. His tenure as governor (1854–61, 1863–5) witnessed the transformation of Senegal from a beleaguered trading post into the hub of a budding French West African empire. He founded the port of Dakar, soon to replace St. Louis as the colony's capital, linked the two towns by telegraph, and stimulated the growing of groundnuts, which remain the staple cash crop of the region. During Faidherbe's years as governor, the Moors were defeated and forced to allow St. Louis merchants to set the terms of the gum trade, additional forts were built along the Senegal and up and down the coast, and lands adjacent to St. Louis were either annexed or brought into the French sphere of influence. Finally, Faidherbe's blueprint for the gradual expansion of French influence from the Senegal basin to the bend of the Niger laid the groundwork for French conquest of the Western Sudan later in the century.

There is still considerable controversy over the extent to which Faidherbe's programme in Senegal reflected policies followed in Algeria. Roger Pasquier, an expert on colonial Senegal, for example, sees Faidherbe as a disciple of Bugeaud and a continuator of the ideas of the "*Algériens*" in the West African setting. "In times of uncertainty and despair," he reasons, "what could have been more natural for those concerned with the future of Senegal than to turn for lessons to the prestigious accomplishments of Bugeaud in Algeria?". Pasquier believes that, although the governor diverged from the Algerian model in cases where Senegalese specifics demanded it, "the influence of Algeria . . . was determinant" in the development of the colony in Faidherbe's time. Faidherbe said as much himself: "Having served in Algeria, I had to be in favor of a more serious occupation of Senegal."[43] What this appears to mean was a more aggressive stance toward the Moors, who dominated the vital gum arabic trade, and the Tukolors, whose homeland lay in the path of French expansion and who had just commenced a tumultuous jihad against pagans and wayward Muslims in the Senegal basin to the east.

Faidherbe's masters at the Ministry of Marine in Paris seem to have been reasonably sanguine about his campaign against the Moors, which he prosecuted with success in 1855–8, but were much less happy with the looming confrontation with the Tukolors. In the opinion of Kanya-Forstner, it was Faidherbe's habit of ignoring the wishes of Paris in this regard and presenting the government with the occasional *fait accompli* that stamps him as a disciple of Bugeaud.[44]

But there were also important differences between Faidherbe and Bugeaud, or, more properly, the Bugeaud "type." To begin with, Faidherbe was no country squire. His petty bourgeois parents ran a dry goods shop in the northern city of Lille. And, while Bugeaud has all the earmarks of a throwback to the *Ancien Régime*, Faidherbe is clearly a product of the French Revolution, with its stress on careers open to talent. A talent for maths and drawing won him a scholarship to the elite *École Polytechnique* (although he seems to have profited little from the experience, preferring drinking and gambling to studying, and passing out only 98th in a class of 124).[45] The future governor of Senegal also qualifies as a flaming political radical in comparison with Bugeaud. Faidherbe may not have studied much at the *École Polytechnique*, but he seems to have found time to discuss politics. He emerged from the school a utopian socialist of the Saint-Simonian stripe, a republican, and an ardent abolitionist.[46]

Faidherbe differed most markedly from the Bugeaud model in his intellectual outlook. The *"Algériens"* as a rule despised anything that smacked of learning, including military science. Bugeaud's only real interest aside from war was scientific estate management, which he practiced with some success on his domains in the Dordogne. Faidherbe, on the other hand, was a recognized scholar in his own day, a student of African culture and one of the founders of the discipline of ethnography in France. He was also an accomplished linguist, being fluent in Arabic and Wolof, the language of most of the indigenous population of the French settlements, and possessing "notions" of a number of other West African languages. And unlike many French officers, especially those who had served in Algeria, Faidherbe held Islam in high esteem. In fact, he believed that Islam was destined to become the religion of most Africans and viewed this as a largely positive development. He considered Islam a considerable advance over the African animist faiths and believed that its spread would make the African population more susceptible to European influences and modern ideas.[47] It was the threat of their radical brand of Islam to political order in the French enclaves and in neighbouring states, not the spread of Islam as such, that persuaded Faidherbe to take the field against the Tukolor jihadists.

In terms of military strategy and tactics, Faidherbe "belonged to both the past and the future." He came to Senegal believing like Bugeaud and so many other European commanders in Africa during the nineteenth century that there could never be peace with indigenous peoples until they had been shown who was stronger and forced to submit. And so there were *razzias* against Moorish and Tukolor villages: sudden descents by *spahis*, homes burned, crops destroyed, herds driven off. But, Faidherbe "gradually came to perceive the disadvantages of military violence unaccompanied by supplementary strategies. In time he became convinced that the threat of force might reap even greater fruits than its employment."[48]

Faidherbe's great objective was the spread of French influence and commercial power across the Western Sudan to the bend of the Niger and down the coast into the rain forests of Guinea. But he was not unalterably convinced that this expansion need be in the form of military conquest. No doubt he believed that some day these regions would be part of a French West African empire, but he also believed that this could be achieved by the gradual submission of the population to market forces and the superior qualities of French civilization. In the shorter term, Faidherbe was even prepared to envisage French interests marching hand in hand with African states of the region, not excluding the Tukolor empire of al-Hajj Umar.[49]

Jihad empire of al-Hajj Umar

The dominant ethnic group in this vast empire, the Tukolors, were related to the wandering pastoral people known as Fulbe or Fulani in the Western and Central Sudan. They fascinated Faidherbe, the amateur ethnographer and student of African languages, since while "[t]hey were physically distinct from the bulk of negroid Sudanese, being of paler skin and more like Berbers in appearance . . . unlike the Berbers they spoke a language belonging to the Niger-Congo group."[50] The Tukolors, unlike their Fulani herdsmen cousins who had emigrated to the kingdoms of Bornu and Sokoto in the central Sudan, tended to be settled farmers and traders. Based on the region of Futa Toro, about 150 km east of St. Louis, they controlled some 600 km of the south bank of the Senegal River. The Tukolor lands could not have been more squarely in the path of the eastward thrust of the French. A second reason for the outbreak of conflict between the two peoples in the 1850s, and perhaps an even more important one, was that the Tukolors were in the grip of a particularly militant brand of Islam. Theirs was the stridency of the recent convert: Muslims had only succeeded in overcoming animist rule in Futa Toro in the 1770s. Religious fervour had in turn opened up the region to the influence of the most messianic of the Sufi brotherhoods in the Western Sudan, the *Tijaniyya*.[51]

In 1853, the year before Faidherbe's accession to the governorship of Senegal, the Tukolors launched a great jihad under the leadership of al-Hajj Umar Tal (1794–1864), one of the foremost religious and political leaders of pre-colonial West Africa. His career illustrates once again the powerful integrative impact of religion upon resistance movements in Africa, but, and this point needs to be emphasized, it also bears witness to religion's equally strong potential for disruption. Like Abd el-Kader, Umar was born into a family of prominent Muslim clerics. Like his Algerian near-contemporary, he had made a pilgrimage to Mecca from which he returned an acknowledged holy man with a large following. While on his pilgrimage, Umar, who had joined the *Tijaniyya* order as a young man, was named *khalifa* of the order (literally, deputy to its founder) in the Western Sudan. He appears to have returned from Mecca determined to carry out a crusade for religious reform, dismayed by the gap between the Islamic ideal he had observed in Mecca and "the disenchanting reality of mixed [impure] Islam in the Western Sudan."[52]

In the 1840s he began to gather around him a band of disciples, or *talaba* in Arabic (*talibés* in French), at Dinguiray, a fortified town which also served as a religious hostel, on the borders of Futa Jallon to the south of his native Futa Toro. It was here, among his *talaba*, that Umar began to build an army whose major purpose would be to carry out a jihad against the animist Bambara peoples to the east, rulers of the kingdoms of Kaarta and Segu. Modern writers who have portrayed the Umarian jihad primarily as a movement of resistance to the French would appear to be mistaken. It was one of the unfortunate aspects of Umar's career that his wars against the Bambara coincided with the decision by the French to project their influence into the interior of Senegal. This created an unwelcome diversion which Umar first sought to resist and then to negotiate away, with only partial success.

Tukolor army

Umar's jihad army had as its elite corps his close disciples, the *talaba*, who, in the great tradition of warfare in the Western and Central Sudan, served as mounted shock troops. These cavalrymen were frequently full members of the *Tijani* brotherhood and, as students of Umar, could boast some education, even if it was of a doctrinaire religious kind. The Tukolor infantry, meanwhile, was composed of volunteers from Futa Toro and converted animists, known as *sofas*, and conscripted levies, called *tuburru*. Many of the latter had been forced to serve, and were liable to desert at the first opportunity. The *sofas*, in addition to bearing arms, functioned as servants to the *talaba*, setting up camp, cooking, and caring for the horses. Their loyalty was reinforced by the right to plunder the enemy alongside their *talaba* masters. The *tuburru*, on the other hand, were forbidden to take booty. Most of Umar's soldiers were Tukolors from the Futa Toro, but there were also contingents drawn from other peoples in Senegal and from Guinea to the south, from Bornu and Sokoto in the Central Sudan and even from among the Arabs and Berbers of Mauritania.

The Tukolor army was reasonably well equipped with modern weapons. Generous monetary donations by the faithful, together with the early capture of the gold mines of the Bambuk region, made possible large purchases of muskets, powder and ball and some rifles and ammunition from English and French traders. The army also possessed four artillery pieces taken from the French. These were used to great effect in the capture of Segu and other cities in the Bambara kingdoms to the east. And, again like Abd el-Kader in Algeria, the khalifa employed his own gunsmiths to manufacture and repair weapons. Just how much of a help this was to his army remains open to conjecture. Says one writer:

> No doubt this corps [of gunsmiths] could service flintlock muskets and supply locally made ball and powder. One wonders, however, how well they were able to cope with the miscellany of European rifles which the army also possessed. It is difficult to believe that al-Hajj Umar's gunsmiths, without access to the proper workshop facilities required to repair precision weapons and to manufacture cartridge ammunition, can really have kept such weapons in service for any length of time.[53]

During the era of al-Hajj Umar, in the 1850s and 1860s, the Tukolor army enjoyed a reputation as a formidable fighting force. No doubt some of this was due to the ability of the khalifa's *sofas* and cavalry to manoeuvre in formation – the Tukolor army was one of very few West African indigenous fighting forces with this capacity as early as this in the century – but the real source of the army's strength lay in the zeal of its soldiers. For the more devout in the ranks, war under Umar was an opportunity to spread the faith by crushing pagans and infidels. Others served loyally because they identified with the army's Tijani leadership.

Common soldiers, for example, would have appreciated the more egalitarian outlook of the *Tijaniyya* order. Unlike other Sufi brotherhoods, such as the rival *Qadiriyya*, the *Tijaniyya* accepted all the faithful into membership, even women and slaves. Other soldiers might have welcomed the brotherhood's anti-authoritarian tendencies. One of Umar's favorite Sufi aphorisms concerned the inherent wickedness of kings. "The best of princes are those who repair to the learned," he wrote early in his career, "but the worst of the learned are those who frequent princes . . . Men of learning are trusted by God's Prophets so long as they do not mix with sultans; if they do so, they have betrayed them."[54]

Like Abd el-Kader in Algeria a decade earlier, al-Hajj Umar was a powerful charismatic figure, and it may well have been the fanatical devotion of his soldiers to his person that made the Tukolor army of his day such a potent fighting force. He had returned from his pilgrimage endowed by the master Sufis of his order with *baraka*, the blessing of God, and the gift of *istikhara*, "a formula of prayers [going back to the Prophet] which would always indicate to him the right line of action and lead him out of all difficulties". His troops knew of these powers and believed that they would be invoked if necessary to save them from defeat in battle.[55] Umar promised his followers that their deaths on the battlefield would ensure their entry into heaven. His description of paradise was a compelling one.

> Its palaces are high, its light radiant, its rivers flowing, its bunches of fruit close at hand, its towers unbroken . . . Its buildings are of silver and gold. There is no clamor there, no illness. Even the pebbles are pearls and jewels. The rivers are of milk and honey . . . The palaces are of hollow pearl, towering seventy miles into the air, of green chrysolith of dazzling brilliance, of red ruby rising high.[56]

No wonder Faidherbe could write of Umar's warriors: "They charge our lines as if they are seeking martyrdom; it is clear they want to die."[57]

Nevertheless, despite the religious fervour which inspired it, there was considerable potential for disorder and indiscipline within the Tukolor army which only the charisma and prestige of its commander, al-Hajj Umar, seemed capable of holding in check. The *tuburru* as well as some *sofas* resented the preference shown to the *talaba* in matters of booty and positions of influence. The issue of booty was of critical importance, since loot was the only payment for service most of the soldiers ever received. In addition, "[m]any of the sofas were men of great personal courage and while some were brought into [Umar's] counsel, others never received the distinction for which they had angled so hard".[58]

The army's grumbling may simply have reflected social tensions within the evolving Tukolor state. As the later example of the Mahdist state in the Sudan will bear out, it is difficult to sustain the fervour and commitment of religious crusades for very long, especially when they triumph. Once the struggle ends, the movement finds itself confronted with the often more difficult challenges of governing. Koranic wisdom does not always provide adequate answers to these. Like Sudanese Mahdism once again, the Tukolor empire toward the end of Umar's lifetime, but especially during that of his son and successor, Ahmadu Seku, evolved into a traditional hierarchical state. The old ruling class in the conquered lands gave way to a new one composed largely of al-Hajj Umar's faithful *talaba*. Indeed, B.O. Oloruntimehin sees the whole Tukolor empire-building process as a gigantic exercise in social mobility, with the new clerical elite, the *talaba*, generally emerging as the winners.[59]

This crisis of the maturing jihad state was complicated by the fact that the majority population, the defeated Bambara, by and large never reconciled themselves to their new masters or their religion. But even among Muslim subjects there was frequent tension. Many of these were followers of the *Qadiriyya* brotherhood, and resented the scorn directed their way by their new Tijani overlords. These divisions, which only grew sharper with time, naturally played into the hands of the French. Their ability to find allies among disgruntled subjects of the Tukolors was eventually instrumental in giving the French military control of the Senegalese interior and the Western Sudan.

Whatever tensions may have seethed in its ranks, the Tukolor army held together well enough to overrun the Bambara states of Kaarta and Segu between 1854 and 1858 and to go on to conquer the neighbouring Muslim kingdom of Masina. By 1864, Umar's army stood on the banks of the Niger far to the north-east, engaged in battle for control of the great city of Timbuktu. Until Samori's empire was forged later in the century, the Tukolor empire

was the largest and most powerful state in the Western Sudan. At its greatest, it spread along the river Senegal and included the Niger river basin north-eastwards to Timbuktu. It covered the present area of the Republic of Mali (excepting the largely desert areas north of Timbuktu), the Moorish emirates which now form the southern part of the Islamic Republic of Mauritania, the Dinguiray province in the northern part of the Republic of Guinea and parts of modern Senegal.[60]

The siege of Médine

Meanwhile, the jihad army had fared less well against its French opponents. Although the Tukolors won the odd skirmish against Faidherbe's troops, most of the battles ended in French victories. "By all accounts al-Hajj Umar's troops fought valiantly" against the French, a recent scholar has written,

> But in the pitched battles their formations quickly broke up into formless frontal assaults, carried out with great impetus, but helter-skelter, and, more often than not, across open ground. They offered rewarding targets to the French-officered African regulars, in their tight squares and with their measured fire control. The drenching volleys usually saturated the attack before the jihadists with their inadequate weapons could get within killing range.[61]

Firepower and fire control, however, were not the ultimate reasons for the French triumph over the Tukolors. What really determined the outcome of the Franco-Tukolor wars was the greater mobility of the French, the factor which had won Algeria for Bugeaud and the *Armée d'Afrique*. This was dramatically illustrated in the famous siege of the French fortress of Médine related below.

The object of Franco-Tukolor conflict during the Médine campaign was access to the strategic Futa Toro region, Umar's native turf and the source of much of his support. Although the *khalifa* was prepared to concede *physical* control of the region to the French, it remained crucial to him as a source of soldiers for his jihad, and he continued to visit it on recruiting drives. The French, in turn, saw Umar's jihadist agitation in the area as a threat to order and security in the whole western Senegal region, and naturally took steps to restrict his access. In 1855 Faidherbe personally oversaw the construction of a fort at Médine, on a bluff above the farthest navigable point of the Senegal River and astride Umar's easiest line of communication with Futa Toro. The fortress also served as a rallying point for the Khassonké, the people of the surrounding kingdom of Khasso, part of whom were in revolt against the Tukolors, their nominal overlords. In 1857, urged on by his *talaba* and apparently against his better judgment,

Umar ordered an assault on Médine. The ensuing siege has enjoyed a reputation as one of the epic battles in French colonial *and* Tukolor history.

From mid-April to mid-July 1857 some 15,000 Tukolors besieged the fort and its outlying walled village. Although the defenders numbered some 10,000, only about 1,000 of them were able-bodied men, of whom just 64 – including six French marine infantrymen and 40 African soldiers and sailors – had any military training. The rest were Khassonké women, children and old men. Nevertheless, strong in its bluff-top location and the cannon posted at each of its four corners, the fort withstood several massed assaults. The Tukolors, who, strangely, never brought their siege artillery into play, were unable to get close enough to the fort to place scaling ladders against the walls. By early July, however, the defenders were running low on food and ammunition. Fearing the worst, the fort's commander, a mulatto merchant and militia captain from St. Louis named Paul Holle, had a huge banner hung over the fortress gate inscribed with the words, "Long live Jesus! Long live the Emperor! Conquer or die for God and our Emperor!"

But help was on the way, in the person of no less a figure than Louis Faidherbe, the governor himself. With 500 men crammed into two armed steamboats, he left St. Louis on 5 July and ten days later was approaching Médine, when his flotilla touched bottom in the river. The resourceful Faidherbe disembarked his troops in order to refloat the steamboats, then marched overland in time to join the boats in attacking the Tukolor host outside Médine. A cannonade from the steamboats and a bayonet charge by Faidherbe's men scattered the enemy. And not a moment too soon. When rescue came, Paul Holle and his defending force were down to their last artillery round and were contemplating blowing themselves up in the powder magazine.[62]

The relief of Médine makes clear that the story of the French conquest of Senegal and ultimately of the Western Sudan is in large part the story of the effective use of naval power.[63] This has not been sufficiently recognized. Nor has sufficient credit been given to the sailors, French but especially African, who manned the vessels on the Senegal and Niger rivers and, in so doing, made a contribution to the French military effort in West Africa as important as that of the much-touted African light infantry, the *Tirailleurs Sénégalais*. It was the armed steamers of the French navy's river fleet that brought Faidherbe's troops inland for lightning raids on enemy villages. And as was seen in the siege of Médine, without the river fleet and its ability to bring forward troops and supplies, the whole French strategy of projecting power into the interior through the onward march of forts would have been impossible.

Hijra and truce

Umar's army lost 2,000 of its best troops in the failed siege. "I told you that you could not defeat the cannon", the khalifa is said to have reminded his *talaba*. Worse, the failure to take Médine was a major blow to Umar's prestige throughout the Senegal region. A new strategy was urgently needed.

> Umar could not afford another confrontation like Médine . . . nor [could he] force the French back into the old dhimmi mould. He could, however, preach the corruption of association and dependence on European power by adding the weapon of *hijra* to the arsenal of jihad. *Hijra* was the holy act of removal from opposition and pollution which Muhammad had inaugurated in AD 622 as he went from Mecca to Medina.[64]

Umar began appealing to Muslims in Futa Toro and other parts of western Senegal to leave their "polluted" homelands and join him in building a new, more godly state in the east. Observers at the time, including Faidherbe, saw this appeal as a threat to the future of the French colony. The French authorities were keenly aware of their dependence upon the largely Muslim population of Senegal. Already, significant numbers of peasants, artisans, and workers had gone east to fight for Umar. It is estimated that about 20 per cent of the population of Futa Toro decamped permanently for the east during the decade of the jihad.[65]

Fearful of the impact of the call to *hijra* on his Muslim subjects and eager to get down to the business of consolidating his hold over western Senegal, Faidherbe proved receptive to Tukolor feelers for peace talks in 1860. For his part, Umar was weary of the seemingly endless warfare on two fronts, against the French in the west and the restless subjects of his jihad empire, the Bambara peoples of the newly-conquered states of Kaarta and Segu, in the east. On 10 September 1860 a treaty of peace was signed between Umar and Faidherbe at Médine. The settlement drew a boundary line between the French and Tukolor empires along the course of the Upper Senegal and Bafing rivers, and thus put an end to hostilities between the two sides for the next two decades.

In 1863 Faidherbe dispatched a delegation headed by a young naval officer, Abdon-Eugène Mage, to negotiate a new treaty with al-Hajj Umar that would permit French commercial penetration of the region between the Senegal and Niger rivers. Although the *khalifa* died before Mage could reach him, the French envoy, after being held a virtual prisoner for nearly two years, was finally able to negotiate a pact with Umar's son and successor, Ahmadu Seku. The treaty of 1866 demonstrates the limitations which still faced French expansionist designs in the Western Sudan at mid-century. It is true that the French came away with the right to trade in the area between the Senegal and Niger rivers, but this was only at the price of agreeing to pay ten per cent of their earnings to the Tukolor government. Wiping out the stigma of paying tribute to indigenous rulers had been at the heart of Faidherbe's more agressive policy toward the Moors and Tukolors in the 1850s. Now, it appeared that all of this had been for nothing and, while the Tukolors won back access to the Futa Toro region in the treaty, thus reversing for a time at least the verdict of Médine, the French were denied the right to build trading posts on Tukolor territory. Finally, Ahmadu Seku managed to wrest a promise from his negotiators that he would be supplied with artillery from the French arsenal at St. Louis. By the time Mage returned from the Tukolor capital with his treaty, however, Faidherbe was gone, his dreams of expansion in the Sudan placed in abeyance, if not rejected outright by an imperial government more interested in its Mexican and Indochinese adventures.[66]

Legacy of Faidherbe

Despite the ambiguous conclusion of his career as empire-builder in the Western Sudan, Louis Faidherbe nonetheless bequeathed to his successors both a vision of the way ahead and the instrument to make it a reality. The vision was of a French West Africa, perhaps a protectorate rather than a colony, stretching from the Atlantic to the bend of the Niger River, from the deserts of Mauritania to the rain forests of Guinea.

The instrument to achieve the goal set by Faidherbe was the famous Senegalese light infantry, the *Tirailleurs Sénégalais*, whose first four companies were formed in 1857 at Faidherbe's urging. A chronic shortage of troops had led him to call for the recruitment of African troops in Senegal along the lines of the French experience in Algeria. An imperial decree of July 1857 stipulated that the *tirailleurs* were to serve as regular infantry, not labor battalions as had been the practice with earlier African formations, and would enjoy the same rights and privileges as troops in French marine infantry regiments.[67] There was one important difference, however. They were not to be paid in the same way or at the same rate as French regulars.

The pay of Tirailleur soldiers was to be excluded from normal navy stipends and, instead, was to be determined locally by the governor of

Senegal and his officials. Faidherbe had shrewdly and accurately calculated that this economy would appeal to planners and politicians in Paris.[68]

This provision did find favour with the government in Paris which, like all European imperial governments of the era, sought expansion on the cheap. But it also meant that, since local government was now responsible for footing the bill, the pay of *tirailleurs* would be kept as low as possible. Consequently, the taking of booty came to assume as great an importance to *tirailleurs* as it did to al-Hajj Umar's *sofas*. Faidherbe was opposed to using the right to take booty as an inducement to enlist, and sought other ways to make the troop attractive to volunteers.

He personally designed their dashing uniform: black cloak and hood, short blue cloth jacket and waistcoat, red sash, blue cotton Turkish trousers, boots and white gaiters, and a red zouave cap [tarboosh or fez].[69]

During the Scramble in the 1880s and 1890s, when efforts were made to increase sharply the number of *tirailleur* companies, the promise of booty once again emerged as a prime incentive to African recruitment. It was not this alone, however, which enabled the French to triple the number of *Tirailleurs Sénégalais* between 1884 and 1900. Higher enlistment and re-enlistment bonuses and better pay had some impact. But what really swelled the ranks was the aggressive recruiting of former enemy soldiers, as the Tukolor empire disintegrated, and recourse to an older method of recruitment: the *rachat* or purchase of domestic slaves for military service. The French practice of *rachat*, also followed to some extent by the British in Nigeria, was reminiscent of the system employed by the Egyptian Mamelukes and Ottoman Turks to obtain recruits for their elite units. In any case, the *rachat* system was well known in both France and West Africa and gave the *tirailleurs* a "slave-soldier" profile that would fade only with the First World War, when African soldiers fought in large numbers for France on the Western Front, at Gallipoli and in the Balkans.[70]

In 1865, Louis Faidherbe left Senegal, never to return. After five years in an Algerian command, he returned to France in 1870 to take part in the Franco-Prussian War. His resourceful leadership of the Army of the North during the war casts doubt on the claim that colonial service rendered officers unfit for European command. His great rival, al-Hajj Umar, meanwhile, had been killed in the course of a revolt against his rule in 1864. Besieged in his new capital of Hamdallahi by Muslim rebels from Masina, Umar broke through the enemy lines and, when pursued, took refuge in a cave. When enemy soldiers found him, the *khalifa* either committed suicide by blowing himself up or was blown up in a fire started by his pursuers. Or, as some sources would have it, "Al-Hajj Umar has no known grave, since his followers deny the fact of his death and believe [instead] in his disappearance . . . some say to Mecca."[71] Before his death the *khalifa* had named his eldest son, Ahmadu Seku, as his successor. The legacy would be an unhappy one. Except perhaps for Galliéni, the Frenchman who followed in Faidherbe's footsteps in the 1870s, while adopting his expansionist vision, had little patience with his notion that expansion could be commercial and cultural in nature, and might be achieved through coexistence with the Tukolor empire. Their chosen solution to the power struggle being waged in Senegal and the Sudan was French military conquest.

The Ashanti war (1873–4)

Prelude

As French military activity in West Africa eased with Faidherbe's departure and ground to a halt altogether in the aftermath of France's catastrophic defeat at the hands of newly-united Germany in 1870, Britain found herself locked in a dispute on the Gold Coast of West Africa with the kingdom of Ashanti, one of the great empires of pre-colonial Africa. The subsequent Anglo-Ashanti war was Britain's first major conflict in the rain forests of tropical Africa.

Her adversary was one of nineteenth-century Africa's largest and most powerful states. The product of some two centuries of expansion outward from its capital, Kumasi, the kingdom of Ashanti in 1870 claimed sovereignty over a territory of some 140,000 sq. miles, larger than England, on the site of present-day Ghana.[72] Ashanti wealth, based on trade in slaves and gold, was legendary, as was Ashanti power, rooted in a remarkable talent for diplomacy and bureaucratic organization and in the exploits of the Ashanti army, in the 1870s probably the largest, best organized and most feared in tropical Africa. And, as the Ghanaian historian J.K. Fynn has noted, "Of all the states of West Africa involved in resistance against European occupation, Asante had by far the longest experience".[73] Ashanti's rise to power in the interior was roughly commensurate with the setting up of European trading posts, including British, on the shores of the Gold Coast. From time to time,

84

disputes over trade and the British rejection of Ashanti claims of sovereignty over the coastal area led to war.

In 1823, following a breakdown in relations with British officials at Cape Coast Castle, the largest British post in the region, an Ashanti army had descended toward the coast to enforce its claims. An army comprised of warriors of the Fante people, who were local British allies, and a small detachment of British troops under the command of the Governor of Sierra Leone, General Sir Charles McCarthy, had sallied forth to meet them in January 1824. The allied force, outnumbered and outflanked, had fled in disarray, leaving the governor to be killed and beheaded by the victorious Ashantis.[74] McCarthy's skull, whose fate would become something of an obsession with two generations of British statesmen and soldiers, was carried off to the Ashanti capital, where it became a highlight of the annual Yam Festival.[75] Forty years later, by which time the British government had declared a protectorate over the land in the proximity of its trading posts on the Gold Coast, another British-led army had advanced against the Ashantis, only to be caught in the rainy season and forced to withdraw when disease put half of its troops out of action.

According to an early Western historian of the region, this 1864 fiasco was "the greatest failure in the history of the British occupation of the Gold Coast."[76] These British defeats at the hands of the Ashantis clearly rankled, and can be seen as major contributing factors to the conflict between Britain and the Ashantis in 1873–4.

Origins of the Anglo-Ashanti War

The creation of the Ashanti state had coincided with a shift in the regional economy toward the slave trade. Up to that time external trade had been largely in gold – hence the name "Gold Coast" given to the area by Europeans. By the 1680s, however, slaves accounted for some 75 per cent of regional exports. Ashanti military activity during this period was geared closely to seizing slaves for sale to the Europeans, who had begun setting up trading posts like Cape Coast Castle or Accra along the Gold Coast.

The end of the slave trade in the early nineteenth century was a blow to the Ashanti economy, but one from which it was able to recover, unlike the once powerful state of Oyo in western Nigeria, for example. Unlike Oyo, Ashanti survived because it was prepared to switch to other commodities –

gold and kola nuts – and to find other customers than the European traders. Following the abolition of the slave trade, Ashanti greatly expanded its trade with the Muslim states in the central Sudan to the north. Kola nuts, which it had in abundance, were the only stimulant Muslims of the Sudan were allowed to use.

Although not a fatal blow economically, the end of the slave trade undermined the political consensus on which the Ashanti empire had been built. The army, always a powerful prop of the state, now found its existence threatened, since it was no longer needed for slave raiding. By the 1820s two rival factions dominated political discourse in Ashanti: a middle-class "peace party" that wanted to play down the importance of the military and to enrich its members by promoting free enterprise; and an imperial party, centred on the nobility, which wanted to preserve the state monopoly on trade and maintain a strong army in order to hold the empire together and overawe its neighbours. The battle lines in this dispute resembled those of nineteenth-century Europe, where a bourgeoisie with the wind in its sails was also contesting power with an entrenched aristocracy.

The "peace party" held the upper hand during much of the first half of the nineteenth century, in the course of which something like a capitalist revolution began to take shape in Ashanti. The growth of alternative trade in kola nuts, gold and palm oil had favoured this process and had enhanced the position of the merchants who made up the peace party. The king was obliged to make concessions to these people, allowing individual traders to enter the market alongside the state trading company. These developments, however, fell short of satisfying the well-to-do merchants of the peace party, who now began to agitate for, among other things, the full dismantling of state trade monopolies and the abrogation of the right of the king to inherit any property held in gold dust, one of the main sources of wealth in Ashanti. The merchants took on as political allies the Ashanti lower classes, who objected to conscription and, by extension, to the military faction in the imperial party itself.

But the political winds shifted abruptly in Ashanti in the 1870s, as the imperial party staged a comeback. The issue was the continuing bad relations with Britain, which had earlier declared a protectorate over an area of the Gold Coast claimed by Ashanti, and which was now in the process of closing off Ashanti access to the sea, the source of the state's arms and ammunition. In 1873 the Ashanti army mobilized for a descent on the coast, setting the stage for war with Britain. Despite what were widely seen as British provocations, Ashanti was to enter the war with serious political divisions and would pay the price in defeat.

The ostensible cause of the war with the British in 1873–4 was Ashanti opposition to an 1871 pact by which the Netherlands had agreed to sell its forts on the littoral of the Gold Coast to Britain. The *Asantahene*, or king, of Ashanti, Kofi Kakari, had protested against the agreement, but to no avail. The Ashanti claimed the coastal region as part of their empire, and saw the forts as mere trading posts operated at their sufferance, a position which the Dutch had accepted. The Dutch enclave of Elmina, whose African inhabitants were loyal subjects of Kumasi, was a vital Ashanti outlet to the sea, where Ashanti merchants could trade directly with foreign suppliers of guns, gunpowder and iron rods (which were cut up to make bullets). In order to preserve the *status quo* in the former Dutch ports, King Kofi had demanded British recognition of Ashanti sovereignty over the coastal enclaves and payment of an annual rent.

What Ashanti opposition to the pact with the Dutch signified to the British was continued proof of the hostility of the kingdom's ruling class to free trade. What had more than anything else bedevilled Anglo-Ashanti relations over the previous half-century, above and beyond disputes over ground rent and sovereignty or even the British desire for revenge for the defeats of 1824 and 1864, had been the Ashanti state's refusal to accept the creation of a free-market economy on the Gold Coast. Despite the rise of a free-enterprise bourgeoisie in its midst, the Ashanti government had turned a resolutely mercantilist face toward European traders throughout the period. Trade with the coastal enclaves continued to be controlled by a Company of State Traders dominated by the king. The state trading firm was able to dictate prices of gold and other commodities on offer, and to choose its trading partners among the European merchants. The Ashanti kingdom's "mercantilist outlook was anathema to British traders, although they profited greatly from it", according to Ivor Wilks. British traders were also discomfited because the Ashanti state, after the cessation of the slave trade, had not readjusted its economy by increasing its trade with the coast in more conventional goods, especially gold, but instead had redirected much of it to the Muslim states of the Central Sudan to the north.[77] Blunt Henry Stanley probably offered the best short explanation of the origins of the Anglo-Ashanti war. "King Coffee", he said, "is too rich a neighbour to be left alone with his riches".[78]

In 1872, when the Anglo-Dutch treaty was officially consummated, a large Ashanti army was mobilized and began moving toward the coast. By 1873, the few British troops on the Gold Coast were under siege in Cape Coast Castle and the people who lived in the former Dutch enclaves had risen up in support of the Ashantis.

Immediate background to war

It was not a war either government was particularly eager to fight. On the British side, the Liberal government of William Ewart Gladstone, in addition to the prime minister's usual reservations about imperial wars, feared the expense both in blood and money of a serious campaign in the tropics. These fears were shared by the Duke of Cambridge, Queen Victoria's cousin and commander-in-chief of the British army, who believed that the West African climate was too inhospitable for white troops.[79] On the Ashanti side, the kingdom's powerful peace party, although momentarily outnumbered in the royal council by proponents of war, was ably led by the Queen Mother and the leading Ashanti general, Asamoa Nkwanta. The advocates of peace argued that, with the end of the slave trade in the region, war was no longer a profitable undertaking and that, therefore, Ashanti interests might best be served by a negotiated settlement with the British. Kumasi's neighbours were of the same opinion. When Ashanti envoys approached their old enemies, Dahomey, about a possible alliance against the British, they were told that the king had consulted his "great fetish" and had been advised to decline, as the Ashantis were certain to be beaten by the white man.[80]

General Nkwanta, head of the Ashanti army's general staff, had similar forebodings. In 1872–3 he had had an opportunity to assess "the potentialities of the new breech-loading Snider [rifle] with which the British had equipped their troops". He had not been reassured by what he had seen.[81] The Ashanti muzzle-loaders, as General Nkwanta knew, lacked both the range and rate of fire of the British rifle. Indeed, one has the impression that muskets were used by the Ashantis as much for pyrotechnic effect as for killing enemies. Musketeers did not use wadding to compact the powder they put down the musket barrel, but simply poured in large amounts and then dumped an assortment of lead slugs, nails and even stones on top. When the musket was fired, the explosion was such that it might frighten an enemy into running away, but it was unlikely to hurt him unless he was within extremely close range. This was partly because the projectiles spewed out by the muskets tended to fan out over a wide area and lose their force after about fifty yards, but also because Ashanti musketeers seldom aimed their weapons. The explosion caused by the huge powder charge in the musket barrel produced such a kick that musketeers chose to fire from the hip rather than the shoulder. This meant that they usually fired high.[82]

If the British government as a whole and a good part of the British military establishment were not enthusiastic about a war with the Ashantis, there were two members of Gladstone's cabinet who were. Lord Kimberley, the Colonial Secretary, and Edward Cardwell, the Secretary of State for War, both appear to have believed that it was time to break the Ashanti power once and for all. In fact, the two men appear to have begun planning for a confrontation with the Ashantis as soon as news of their descent on the coast reached England in May 1873. Their "co-conspirator" in the planning process was the man who would eventually lead the British expedition to the Gold Coast, Cardwell's protégé and one of the foremost military heroes of the hour, Sir Garnet Wolseley (1833–1913).[83] Wolseley, who seems to have believed that the goal of the Ashanti invasion was the seizure of coastal towns that could be used to revive the slave trade, was adamant that victory on the battlefield offered the only permanent solution to Britain's long-standing differences with "this nation of warriors". Hope of "making any definite and lasting peace with the Ashanti king until his army had been utterly defeated," he wrote, "was merely the wild dream of timid men . . ."[84] This was, of course, precisely the viewpoint articulated by "Père" Bugeaud three decades before, as we have seen, and one that would echo down through the years of the European conquest of Africa.

Cardwell's part in the coming of the Anglo-Ashanti war requires more careful scrutiny. Oddly enough, earlier in his career Cardwell had acquired a reputation as an advocate of British retrenchment in Africa. As Undersecretary of State for Colonies in 1865 his name had been linked to the recommendation of a Select Committee of Parliament that Britain withdraw altogether from the Gold Coast.[85] Since then, however, Cardwell had changed jobs and also, presumably, his mind about British policy with respect to Ashanti.

In 1868 Cardwell had been appointed Secretary of State for War in the Liberal cabinet of William Ewart Gladstone. Three years later, he engineered, with the aid of Wolseley, a series of major reforms of the British army, including the abolition of "purchase", the ancient system under which the command of regiments could be bought by gentlemen, and a reduction in the length of enlistments from twenty to six years. The latter reform had been proposed to solve the volunteer army's perpetual problem of shortfalls in enlistment. The reforms had been strongly opposed in the more conservative circles both inside and outside the army, and Cardwell and Wolseley had emerged from the successful struggle to impose them with a formidable host of enemies in "Society". For Cardwell a "splendid little war" in West Africa would serve two purposes. First, a victory over the powerful Ashanti would reassure the country of the prowess of its reformed army. Secondly, it has been suggested that "Cardwell arranged for Wolseley to command the military expedition" to West Africa as "a reward for his services in resuscitating the army from the suffocating effects of prejudice and tradition".[86]

One suspects that Cardwell and his friends may also have had more than an inkling that a war with the Ashantis would be popular with the British public. For the kingdom was not an unknown quantity in the Britain of the 1870s, as Alan Lloyd demonstrates.

> 1874 welcomed Ashanti avidly, if belatedly, to the booming Never-Never Land of barrack-room fable which served much of Victorian Britain for a knowledge of "abroad". If there was some doubt in British minds about the geographical location of Ashanti, there was no doubt that in spiritual terms it lay pretty close to Inferno and Gehenna. Stories of the unremitting ferocity of the Ashanti people, of a gigantic cauldron at Kumasi filled to the brim with human blood, and so on, were used to cruel effect by the soldiery on susceptible kitchen-maids; while Kofi [Kakari] himself, the terrible "King Coffee", reigned supreme for many a long month among the shadowy ogres lurking around night-lit nurseries, the ultimate deterrent to juvenile delinquency. Fervent, indeed, were the prayers offered up in the mansions and hovels of their home-towns for husbands, sons or brothers in the expedition to Ashanti.[87]

But, before the plans of Kimberley, Cardwell and Wolseley could be translated into action, two hurdles needed to be cleared. First, concern over the susceptibility of British troops to the heat and fevers of the "white man's grave" had to be dealt with. Here the trio appear to have engaged in a subterfuge, making plans for what they believed to be the necessary introduction of British troops into the campaign, while telling government colleagues that every effort would be made to repulse the Ashantis with local African levies.[88] The second problem to be overcome was Royal Navy opposition to the expedition. The Gold Coast, like the rest of West Africa, had been the navy's "patch" since at least the beginning of the anti-slave trade patrols in the early part of the century; when "natives" proved truculent, gunboats had been sent to shell their villages and landing parties put ashore to burn down what remained. Now the army was intending to poach on the navy's territory. Admiralty opposition was strenuous. It took a table-thumping threat to resign by the Colonial Secretary before the navy would agree to support the decision to form an army under the command of General Wolseley to invade Ashanti. The proponents of Wolseley's expeditionary force had also to agree to give the navy a piece of the action. A second invasion force was authorized, to proceed up the Volta River in the direction of Kumasi under the command of the swashbuckling naval officer and governor of the Lagos Protectorate in Nigeria, Sir John Glover. In all, four columns, including Wolseley's main force, were eventually launched against the Ashantis. Two of these, which were to have been recruited among local tribes by officers from Wolseley's staff, never really got underway, and Glover's undermanned, fever-ridden column arrived at the Ashanti capital only after Wolseley's army had departed. None of this would upset Wolseley, who had actually conceived of the other columns as mere diversions and not part of a concerted attack on Ashanti. In this, Glover's force and the other two largely mythical columns seem to have enjoyed some success.

On 13 August 1873 Wolseley was given command of the expedition against the Ashantis, and at the same time made administrator of the Gold Coast protectorate. He was promoted to the rank of major-general for the occasion, becoming the youngest general officer in the British army. He was just forty.[89]

"Wolseley. It is strange how quickly that name has passed into oblivion", remarks Joseph Lehmann, who has dedicated his recent biography of the general to restoring "that great soldier to his rightful place in history".[90] This may still be something of an uphill battle, if the entry on Wolseley in the most recent edition of John Keegan's *Who's who in military history* is any indication. Here Wolseley is presented as a Dublin shopkeeper's son, with the added editorial comment that "a more unpromising start in life for a Victorian soldier with a career to make could not have been wished on him by the harshest of fairies".[91] This leaves one to wonder how it came to pass that in 1852 Wolseley was awarded a commission without purchase, a favour "rarely granted in those pre-Cardwell days", by none other than the Duke of Wellington. The answer seems to be that Wolseley was descended from a long line of army officers, which included a general who served in Ireland in the seventeenth century under William III, and his own father, who had retired from the army a major after 29 years of service.[92]

It was his family's military reputation – and Anglo-Irish background, one suspects – that recommended Wolseley to the attention of the "Iron Duke". Wellington's confidence was not misplaced. By the age of twenty-seven, just eight years after receiving his commission, Wolseley was a lieutenant-colonel, having served with distinction in the Second Burma War, the Crimean War, the Indian Mutiny and the Second China War. A nine-year tour of staff duty in Canada followed, during which he led an expedition halfway across North America to crush the Red River rebellion in Manitoba, and paid a respectful visit to Robert E. Lee and Stonewall Jackson in Northern Virginia during the American Civil War. Wolseley's Red River campaign in 1870, a triumph of logistical planning and audacity, established him "as one of the most efficient and forward-looking officers in the army".[93]

For General Wolseley, the looming war with the Ashantis fell into the category of "small wars" Callwell would later label "punitive".

> As might be expected from a very warlike, proud and barbarous people, our having left them [the Ashantis] unpunished for the invasion of our territory was attributed to cowardice . . . Such a condition of things always means war sooner or later.[94]

There is, however, a sense that the Ashantis were to be punished for "crimes" that ranged far beyond their current invasion of the Gold Coast protectorate. There were old wounds that required healing – McCarthy's defeat and decapitation in 1823, the 1864 debacle – if what Wolseley termed "national dignity" was to be preserved.

But "punishment" of the Ashantis could also serve useful future purposes, Wolseley believed. The Ashantis, he wrote, were "the only dangerously strong native power in Western Africa", and "until we had utterly defeated their army and taken Koomassee, we should never have any assured peace in our West African settlements". Wolseley sensed that the eyes of all black Africa were fixed on the impending conflict with the Ashantis, that there were many Africans who thought, given what had happened in the past, that the Ashantis would win. The British, then, had something to prove, and, like Antonio Enes and the Portuguese Generation of 1895 in Mozambique, Wolseley saw threatened national honour in racial terms: it would not do to wage war against the Ashantis with "native" troops; the defeat had to be administered by *white* troops or "the natives of all tribes and races would continue to believe that if we dared to push forward beyond the River Prah [into the Ashanti heartland] we should be exterminated."[95] The general was right to assume that this belief existed, as Alan Lloyd has pointed out. Remarkable as it might have seemed to the next generation of Britons,

> neither the Ashantis nor the the Fantes at that time had any real evidence that Britain was a great military power in her own right. To the tribes of West Africa all white men were aristocrats riding in hammocks and living like kings. The idea of an army of such people, marching through the jungle and going into battle like ordinary warriors seemed ludicrous to the majority of people on the Gold Coast. "Do white men know how to travel to fight?" Kofi Kakari asked incredulously of one visitor to Kumasi.[96]

So there was never any question about the composition of the invasion army: there would be African auxiliaries, of course, but the majority of the force would be white soldiers, elite troops of the British army who would master both the rigours of the bush and the fearsome Ashantis and thus bring home "to the minds of all the negro rulers on the coast the greatness of the White Sovereign beyond the seas . . ."[97]

Wolseley had already begun drawing up his expeditionary plans in May, at Cardwell's urging, not long after the news of the Ashanti invasion of the Gold Coast protectorate had reached England. In his autobiography, *The story of a soldier's life*, he sketched out what had been the general thrust of his strategy for the Ashanti war.

> My plan was to concentrate [the British troops at my disposal] and all my native fighting forces at Prahsu [on the edge of the Ashanti homeland], and push thence with all possible haste for Koomassee. I hoped to defeat the Ashanti army on the way, and having taken the capital and its far-famed [royal] palace, to make peace there. Should the king refuse my terms, I intended to burn both city and palace, and then to get the white troops back on board ship with the least possible delay. The deadliness of the climate forbade me to calculate upon any greater military results.[98]

It is clear from the above that Wolseley's overriding concern in working out the details of his strategy was to reduce as far as possible the health risks to which his British forces would be exposed in this "white man's grave". Before his white troops embarked from England, Wolseley had prepared and distributed to them in pamphlet form what amounted to "the first comprehensive instructions ever issued to a British army on what would now be termed jungle warfare".

Soldiers were reassured about their exposure to malaria. Quinine would be dispensed every morning, along with tea or chocolate and a bit of biscuit. There was advice about the two great enemies of European troops in the tropics: heat and damp. Soldiers were urged to keep their heads covered at all times and to avoid contact with the damp earth: "sleeping off the ground [even a few inches] is a great preservative of health."

Attention was also paid to the crucial problem of supplies. The men were "strongly urged" to treat African carriers with kindness, since if they were ill-treated, "the troops run the risk of being left without food and ammunition".

But much of Wolseley's pamphlet was given over to morale-raising. Soldiers were told that, as white men, God had given them an edge over Africans on the battlefield.

> It must never be forgotten by our soldiers that Providence has implanted in the heart of every native of Africa a superstitious awe and

dread of the white man that prevents the negro from daring to meet us face to face in combat. A steady advance or charge, no matter how partial, if made with determination always means the retreat of the enemy.

In case "superstitious awe and dread" did not suffice to drive the Ashantis from the field, however, soldiers were assured that, armed with their breech-loaders, they were "equal to at least 20 Ashantis, wretchedly armed as they are with old flint-muskets", and that "Our enemies have neither guns [artillery] nor rockets, and have a superstitious dread of those used by us".[99] Like his near-contemporary, the French general Faidherbe, Wolseley took a hand in the design of his soldiers' campaign uniforms. Although critics contended that the traditional scarlet uniform terrified and confounded the enemies of the Queen and was, therefore, indispensable garb, Wolseley simply found it impractical for bush fighting and had it replaced by an outfit of gray homespun.

The general began making detailed plans for the Ashanti campaign on the long voyage out from Liverpool. He had gathered around him for the trip a large picked staff of volunteer officers, some veterans of his Red River campaign in Canada, others chosen for their reputations for daring or their intellectual abilities. Dubbed the "Wolseley Ring" or "Ashanti Ring" by critics, this clutch of young officers would produce in the decades to come some of the British Empire's foremost soldiers. The "Ring" included General Sir Henry Brackenbury, who served as a captain and Wolseley's military secretary in the Ashanti war before becoming head of the Army's Intelligence Division in the 1880s and Director-General of Ordnance during the Second Boer War; General Sir John Frederick Maurice, a lieutenant and Wolseley's private secretary in the Ashanti war who went on to become Professor of Military Art and History at Camberley in the 1880s, owner and editor of the influential *United Services Magazine*, and one of the editors of the official history of the Second Boer War; and General Sir Redvers Buller, who served as a captain and Wolseley's intelligence chief in the Ashanti war and would succeed to commands in the Zulu War and the Sudan before suffering ignominy as the commander of British forces in South Africa during the disastrous opening weeks of the Second Boer War.[100]

It might usefully be added that the era of imperial conquest seems to be unusually replete with cliques like Wolseley's "Ring". In other European armies, there were, of course, the Portuguese Generation of 1895 in Mozambique and the guild of *officiers soudanais* among the French marines in West Africa. But perhaps the most famous counterpart to Wolseley's "Ring" was the "Circle" centered around his deadly enemy and rival, General Sir Frederick Roberts, the much-loved "Bobs" of the Imperial Army in India. Together with the members of his "Ring", Wolseley pored over documents about the Gold Coast he had brought with him – government reports, travellers' accounts, histories of the region – in an effort to get a picture of the sort of enemy they would be facing and of the terrain in which they would be facing him. It was as well they did their homework on the tedious voyage out; they would gain precious little other intelligence about the enemy once they had arrived on the Gold Coast. [Wrote Wolseley]

> In no campaign where I have served was it so difficult to obtain trustworthy information of the enemy's whereabouts, doings and intentions as it was upon the Gold Coast... The amount of our information regarding the Ashanti army, or upon the topography and climate of the country lying between the River Prah and Koomassee was provokingly meagre.[101]

Wolseley began implementing his plans for the campaign as soon as he landed at Cape Coast Castle in October 1873. He knew he would be operating within a very tight timescale: the only dry months on the Gold Coast are from December to February, when warm winds blow from the Sahara. The troops would, therefore, have to be brought forward very quickly once they landed, if the mission Wolseley had set for them was to be accomplished before the rains set in again. This posed a number of formidable engineering problems. The company of sappers sent out from England began by widening and improving the traders' road north from Cape Coast Castle to permit the passage of the troops and their even larger army of carriers. In addition, 237 bridges were built over the endless streams that cut through the 70-mile stretch of savannah and forest from the coast to the army's forward base at Prahsu, 60 miles from the Ashanti capital. Every ten miles along the road to Prahsu, way stations were set up to feed and shelter the white troops. Huts featured bamboo bedsteads to keep the men off the ground at night and large filters processed a constant supply of pure water. Carriers with hammocks waited at each way station to transport the sick and wounded back to the coast, where three hospital ships were standing by to receive them.[102]

But all of these careful plans and feats of engineering would go for nothing if no reliable system of transport could be arranged to bring up supplies. Animal transport could not be used because of sleeping sickness. Wolseley toyed for a while with the idea of building a railroad to Prahsu, and track and some construction equipment were actually brought out. But the terrain proved unpropitious and the project was abandoned.[103] Thus, the

British campaign in Ashanti, like so many others in tropical areas during the wars of imperial conquest, came to depend very heavily on human transport, on carriers. There was a lot to carry: over a million rounds of Snider ammunition; 30 days' rations for 6,500 men – a total of some 400 tons of food. Nor was that all. To avoid collapse in the heat, the white troops had been ordered to carry a strict minimum of gear on their persons; the rest – everything from extra ammunition and clean underwear to groundsheets and tents – moved forward on the heads of carriers, one to every three British soldiers.[104]

That logistics was the weak spot in Wolseley's careful preparations became evident even before his three British battalions – drawn from the Royal Welch Fusiliers, the Rifle Brigade and the 42nd Highlanders (Black Watch) – came ashore on New Year's Day 1874. In December the carriers had begun deserting *en masse*, partly out of fear of the Ashantis, and partly because of dissatisfaction at the conditions of their employment. Matters were not put right, or so we are given to understand, until the arrival on the scene of Colonel George Colley, Professor of Military Administration at the Staff College at Camberley and a leading member of the Wolseley Ring. The carrier system was removed from civilian control and placed in Colley's hands. The solution to the labour shortage, however, owed much less to Colley's principles of scientific management than to the old-fashioned practices of eighteenth-century press gangs.

> Desperate for carriers, Wolseley cast [aside] all forms of legality. Kidnapping began on a large scale . . . The commandant of Accra, with a man-of-war at his disposal, went up and down the coast collecting carriers. If the chiefs were unco-operative, a party of sailors would land at night, surround his village and carry off the entire adult population, leaving only a few old women to care for the infants.[105]

His carrier problem eased, at least for the moment, Wolseley could now bring his troops forward to the Prah. His army comprised some 1,500 white troops and 700 blacks, among which elements of the West Indian Regiment from Barbados. The African contingent included a force of Hausas from Northern Nigeria, described by a young Royal Marine officer as "first-rate fighting men, that is, for Africans, very morose but in the heat of battle very wild and excited".[106] The Hausas, one of Africa's widely-touted "martial races", would become a mainstay of British forces in the region, forming the nucleus later in the century of the West African Frontier Force. They were also recruited by the French marine infantry for duty in Dahomey and the Western Sudan, and by the *Force Publique* in the Congo Free State.[107]

Meanwhile, the Ashanti army which had invaded the protectorate had fallen back across the Prah. It was not in retreat but suffering, as most African armies long in the field did, from the weaknesses of its logistical system. The army was riddled with smallpox and dysentery and short of food. Nevertheless, a strategy was worked out for its employment, once it was heavily reinforced, against the British invader. The strategy called for the forward units of the Ashanti army to carry out a fighting withdrawal and thus coax Wolseley's force deep into Ashanti territory. A strong defensive position would be created at the village of Amoafo, about twenty miles from Kumasi. Here the British would be pinned in place, while a wing of the Ashanti army outflanked them and passed across their rear, destroying the bridge over the Prah and cutting them off from the sea.[108]

This was a traditional Ashanti battle strategy, and one which was common to a number of other African armies as well.[109] It usually worked for Ashanti armies against African rivals and it had prevailed against the unfortunate Governor McCarthy.

Successful against enemy armies that failed to protect their flank and rear areas, this strategy did not work against Wolseley because he had anticipated it and had firmed up his flanks and assigned one of his best units, the Rifle Brigade battalion, to cover the rear of the British army, as, formed up in a loose square, it slowly cut its way through the thick rain forest toward Kumasi.

As the Ashantis had planned, the two armies collided for the first time on the outskirts of the village of Amoafu. The British army had advanced in what Wolseley described as a "parallelogram", with its two seven-pounder artillery pieces and service troops bunched in the centre and rocket troughs at the front angles.

Each face of the square had its own commander, who had been briefed carefully on the position to be occupied by his men. Given the difficult terrain, Wolseley had believed from the beginning that maintaining a functioning command structure in battle would be his greatest challenge. He had brought along a disproportionately large number of officers, on the grounds that "Owing to the dense cover, an officer can only exercise control over the men closest to him, and for this kind of work there should be at least one officer to every 20 men". Any less and the soldiers were likely to "get entirely out of hand" and to "fire indiscriminately and recklessly into the bush".[110]

Wolseley was clearly worried about the chances of panic among his troops as the British square became enveloped in the dense rain forest by a numerous enemy.

97

In the semi-darkness of those jungle recesses, the nerves are tried by the feeling that you are more or less cut off from any immediate support, and by hearing the triumphant shouts of a barbarous, inhuman enemy on all sides.[111]

The battle of Amoafo was like no other British soldiers had fought in Africa up to that time. It was a battle in which Wolseley's troops ended up fighting "not as battalions, or even as companies in the accepted sense, collected to the will of a single mind, but . . . in which, sooner or later, almost every soldier was alone, dependent on his own resources." There was "no maneuvering, no brilliant charges, no general concentration of troops" and "scarcely a man saw an enemy from the commencement to the end of the fight". For the British infantry, the battle consisted for the most part of "creeping through the bush, of gaining ground foot by foot, and of pouring a ceaseless fire into every bush which might conceal an invisible foe."[112]

At the front of the square, the Black Watch pushed ahead, gaining twenty yards or so, regrouping, repeating the pattern, over and over again, in the dense undergrowth. Slowly, the Ashantis gave ground. On the flanks, meanwhile, where soldiers were expected to hew their way through the underbrush and fight at the same time, the square began to come unstuck, as columns moving at different speeds lost touch with each other. A gap opened between the Black Watch, surging forward at the front of the square, and the left flank column, into which the Ashantis attempted to insert themselves. In the confusion, soldiers fired wildly, and there were some casualties from friendly fire.[113]

For the Ashantis also, however, this was a battle like no other they had ever fought. At such close quarters the enemy artillery and breechloaders left "Heaps of dead and wounded." And, for all their ability to keep up an astounding rate of fire with their "Long Danes", the Ashantis knew that they were seriously outgunned.

Troops returning to the capital . . . were clearly appalled by the extent of the casualties and had confirmed their fears about the inadequacy of their weaponry . . . "The white men have guns that hit five Ashantis at once", they said. "Many great men and princes have fallen".[114]

The Ashanti troops in front of the British square fell back beyond Amoafo. But the battle was not over. An Ashanti counterattack fought to within 100 yards of British headquarters and, in the rear, sustained attacks by Ashanti raiders succeeded in shutting down the supply line from Prahsu. "Thus, sixteen miles short of Kumasi, with an ever increasing number of soldiers reported sick, the general was faced with a protracted halt."[115] And with the rains just days away.

Meanwhile, in Kumasi, the losses sustained at Amoafo had brought the peace party to power in the king's council. Attempts were made to negotiate with Wolseley, but when his terms proved too severe, the Ashanti government was forced to take the unpopular step of remobilizing. "That the government was in fact able to put forces back into the field was a result in no small measure of its political wisdom in entrusting" the command of the frontline troops to Asamoa Nkwanta. Nkwanta, the army chief of staff and a key member of the peace party, "was immensely respected and liked by the Asante troops, and was popularly known as *Srafokra* [or] 'the soldiers' guardian spirit'". Under his command, the hastily remobilized Ashanti army put up a fierce resistance at the battle of Odahsu just a few miles from the capital.[116]

But the Black Watch, ordered to break through to Kumasi at all costs, succeeded in its mission and on the evening of 4 February 1874 Sir Garnet Wolseley's expeditionary force entered the capital of Ashanti. It had been Wolseley's hope, as it had been Napoleon's in Moscow, that the enemy would now come forth to negotiate. But as in the case of the Emperor of the French, no one came forth and two days after entering Kumasi, the conqueror was obliged to leave. On 6 February, after having sacked, then destroyed, the royal palace and burned down the rest of the city, Wolseley's troops left for the coast. "It was out of the question", wrote Wolseley's military secretary, Sir Henry Brackenbury, "to undertake any operations which might involve another battle; because any increment to our list of sick and wounded would have placed it beyond his power to remove them back" to the coast.[117]

On the way back across the Prah, the Ashanti king's emissaries caught up with the retreating British and a peace treaty was signed which both sides desperately sought – the British because it gave them a fig leaf with which to cover what had been in the end an inconclusive campaign despite their victories in the field, the Ashanti government because it wished to cut its losses in order to face a political crisis as conquered provinces began to bid for independence. It should be noted that a key clause in Wolseley's draft peace treaty, eventually accepted by Kumasi, called for a guarantee of free trade between Ashanti and the British protectorate.

The number of Ashanti casualties will never be known, but British estimates of as many as 3–4,000 dead and perhaps twice as many wounded and missing do not seem wide of the mark. Beyond this and the destruction of the capital city, the military defeat threatened to destroy the Ashanti empire, as provinces and tributary states began to declare their independence of Kumasi. As it was, an independent Ashanti would survive for only another 12 years, at which point another British army would invade the heartland of the empire, this time bent on occupation and the absorption of Ashanti into the Gold Coast Protectorate. It is instructive that this time the Ashanti people chose not to resist, but stood by passively as British troops, disease–resistant African soldiers from Nigeria for the most part, seized Kumasi and carried off their king into exile.

The return to the coast of Wolseley's army in February 1874 was a more sombre affair than might have been expected. The casualty rate among officers was "disproportionately heavy". Wolseley was accompanied by only one member of his "Ring", Captain Brackenbury: the other thirty-five were dead, wounded or had gone down with fever. Of the some 2,500 white soldiers who had set out for Kumasi, 68 had died, 394 were wounded, and a total of 1,018 were invalided for one reason or another. "Proportionately, no less than forty-three per cent of the combined strength of the white regiments was invalided home and there was seventy-one per cent sickness in two months".[118] This, despite the most careful preparations yet made for a tropical campaign by a European general. "So ended", concluded Wolseley, "the most horrible war I ever took part in".[119]

Despite their considerable inferiority in weaponry and having been at the receiving end of one of the best-planned and executed European campaigns in the annals of jungle warfare, what really cost the Ashantis the war of 1873–4 was a lack of political will. The kingdom's leadership had entered the war badly divided, and only achieved unity of purpose when the enemy's army was already at the gates of the capital. Although it is not likely that the Ashantis could ever have beaten the British on the field of battle, given their inferiority in armament, they might still have staved off defeat through a more vigorous defence.

One recent observer of the war has charged the Ashanti leadership with being inflexible in its choice of strategy; they might have done better, he says, if they had taken advantage of their numerical superiority and massed their troops at the front of the British square rather than dispersing a large part of their force in flanking manoeuvres.[120] Another critic has suggested that the Ashantis committed "a great strategic error" in not resorting to guerrilla warfare once they realized that they were outgunned by the British.[121]

Had they succeeded in holding off the British force until the rains began, Wolseley would have had no choice but to retreat. Had this happened, the resultant political embarrassment in Britain would very likely have precluded a repeat engagement, at least for some time into the future. It certainly would have called into serious question the army reforms carried out by the Liberals and with which General Wolseley had been so closely associated.

As it was, however, the Ashanti campaign transformed Wolseley into a national hero. Tory leader Benjamin Disraeli lauded him on his return as "our only general", while Gilbert & Sullivan added even greater lustre to his name by making him "the very model of a modern major-general" in their popular operetta, "The Pirates of Penzance".

After Ashanti Wolseley became a kind of imperial fireman, picking up the pieces after Lord Chelmsford in Zululand in 1879, putting down the revolt of Arabi Pasha in Egypt in 1882, leading an unsuccessful attempt to rescue "Chinese" Gordon in Khartoum in 1884. Finally, in 1895, he capped his career by being named commander-in-chief of the British army. The post was to bring Wolseley little joy, however. It would be his misfortune to be at the head of the British army when the Second Boer War broke out in 1899. The string of defeats suffered during "Black Week" at the outset of the war took place while his one-time disciple, Sir Redvers Buller, was in command in South Africa, and so was laid at his door. Never short of enemies, he was pilloried in Parliament for having failed to prepare the British army for war. Although the charges were unfair, they nonetheless stuck, and Wolseley retired from government service under a cloud. The remaining decade of his life would be a sad anti-climax. Britain's greatest imperial soldier died on 26 March 1913, a recluse in self-imposed exile in the south of France.[122]

As for the Ashanti, the fragmentation that shook the empire in the aftermath of the 1873-4 war was never entirely repaired. This continuing weakness opened the way for the Gold Coast government to meddle actively in Ashanti politics. Political exiles from Ashanti who took refuge in Cape Coast Castle were treated like a virtual government-in-exile. By the early 1890s the Ashanti kingdom was for all practical purposes a British dependency. Alarmed that they might be beaten to the punch by the Germans in Togo to the east or by the French in the Ivory Coast to the west, Britain made haste to occupy Ashanti in 1896. This was not the last act, however.

In 1900 the Ashantis rose up against British rule and waged the kind of guerrilla war they had refused to fight in 1873-4. Invaded by an army composed largely of African troops from Nigeria and Central Africa, with a sprinkling of Sikhs, the Ashantis gave the British "their last as well as the hardest battle the latter had ever fought in their longstanding attempts to control and finally subjugate Ashanti". The Ashanti Queen Mother, who had captained the insurgents, was deported to the Seychelles and the kingdom was formally annexed to the Crown.[123]

The Zulu war (1879)

Introduction

In his recent book about the fate of the Ashanti empire in West Africa, Robert Edgerton complains that "for most people in Europe and America, recognition of the valor of African fighting men begins and ends with the Zulus".[124] While one could quibble about whether he really means "Europe" or simply its British component, Edgerton is probably right. Thanks to films like "Zulu" and books like Donald Morris's The *washing of the spears*, the Zulu warrior very likely has replaced "Fuzzy Wuzzy" of the Sudan as colonial Africa's "first-class fighting man" in the popular mind, in the Anglo-Saxon world at least.

Popular appeal aside, the Anglo-Zulu War that commenced in January 1879 merits the close attention of students of the African wars of imperial conquest because it furnishes the quintessential example of a clash between an unmodified traditional African military system and that of an industrialized European state. In most other such confrontations, including the celebrated squaring-off between the British and the Mahdists in the Sudan, the African armies involved had made more or less serious efforts to adopt European weapons and European methods of fighting as a way of resisting European penetration. Not so the Zulus. In the years before war with the British broke out, large quantities of shoulder arms were imported into Zululand – from 10,000 to 20,000 such weapons a year between 1875 and 1877, according to official sources. Yet, for the most part, these firearms were never used in any serious way in the fighting against the British. As they had for decades, the Zulu armies relied instead on their short stabbing spears or *assegais*, and on the tactics of frontal assault intended to bring them close enough to their foes to use them. An intelligence report circulated on the eve of the war in 1879 informed British officers that the Zulu "methods of marching, attack formation, etc., remain the same as before the introduction of firearms among them".[125]

"Blood River"

The first clash between whites and Zulus in South Africa came in the 1830s as a result of the "Great Trek" of the Boers away from the British-dominated Cape Province with its laws promoting equality between black man and white. The Trekboers had come down through the Drakensberg passes from the Orange Free State into Natal, on the western edge of Zululand. Zulu resistance to Boer settlement in Natal led to a major battle in December 1838, in the time of Shaka's successor (and murderer), Dingaan. It was a rude shock for the Zulus, who fell by the thousands to Boer elephant guns on the banks of the Ncome River in Natal. In a sense, however, this battle of "Blood River" gives a misleading impression of the fighting abilities of the Zulus. It was a battle a cleverer leader than Dingaan would not have fought. The Boer position was close to unassailable. The Zulus were forced to attack a *laager* or circle of wagons on a narrow front between two high banks. "[T]he mass of the charging [Zulus] was hemmed between the banks, and the press grew intolerable as the regiments strove to reach the wagons. . . . It was only necessary to fire and reload and fire again at the black mass that seethed out of the smoke." More than 3,000 Zulus died on the banks of the Ncome without killing a single Boer.[126]

Toward war with the British

Having driven off the Zulus, the Boers took possession of fertile Natal and declared it a Boer republic, independent of Cape Province and the British. In 1846, however, the Boer dream of a Natal homeland faded as the British, fearing alien domination of the port of Durban and the strategic waters off the Natal coast, annexed the republic and brought it under rule from Cape Town. The Boers left the area in large numbers for the still-independent Boer republics in the Orange Free State and the Transvaal. The Zulus now had a new white neighbour, the British, to contend with.

Conflict between the two peoples remained latent until the 1870s, when, in British eyes, the Zulus suddenly replaced the Boers as the greatest obstacle to the peace and stability of South Africa. In analyzing the sources of this fateful development, a distinction has to be made between longer-term and immediate factors. Imperial soldiers like Sir Garnet Wolseley believed that coexistence between Britain and the Zulus was impossible. In 1875 Wolseley, then the governor of Natal, wrote to the British Secretary of State for the Colonies, Lord Carnarvon, that

> [I do] not believe it is possible for the two races to live together on perfect terms; one or the other must be the predominant power in the State; and if the very small minority of white men is to be that power, the great native majority must be taught not only to confide in its justice, but to realize and acknowledge its superiority.[127]

Thus, for Wolseley, the Zulus, like the Ashantis he had just fought (and like Bugeaud's Algerians), would have to be shown who was the master and who the servant before there could be peace.

What turned lingering incompatibility into confrontation in the 1870s, however, was the way the Zulus impinged upon what the British government saw as the supreme task of the moment in South Africa: the effort to forge a confederation which would bring together Boer and Briton in a largely self-governing dominion like the one created to reconcile Québecois and Briton in Canada in 1867. The confederation scheme for South Africa was the brainchild of Wolseley's correspondent, Lord Carnarvon. The great sense of urgency that surrounded it in the 1870s derived from the discovery, a decade earlier, of diamonds at Kimberley on the frontier between Cape Province and the Orange Free State. As well as assuring British control of the Kimberley diamond fields, Carnarvon looked to the proposed confederation to assume the administrative and military costs of empire in South Africa, thus relieving the exchequer in London of a growing burden. The Zulus were seen as figuring in this scenario in two ways.

First, the new British governor of Cape Province and commander-in-chief for South Africa, Sir Bartle Frere, appears to have been convinced by the "old Zulu hands" in his entourage, principally Theophilus Shepstone, that the Zulu king, Cetshwayo, had built up a huge army in imitation of his hero, Shaka, and was preparing to put it at the head of a massive pan-African onslaught against white power. Frere probably did not need much convincing. The governor also saw a struggle looming, a great contest between the forces of progress, represented by Britain, and the great mass of Africans, who seemed to believe "that the time was come for them all to join to resist the flood of new ideas and ways which threatened to sweep away the idle, sensuous elysium of Kaffirdom . . ."[128] What appeared to give credence to the conspiracy theories of Shepstone and Frere was the recently ended Ninth Frontier War between the Xhosa and the British on the eastern border of Cape Province, resistance to British efforts to disarm the peoples of Basutoland to the west of Natal, and continuing warfare between the Pedi people and the Boers in the eastern Transvaal. Frere chose to believe that Cetshwayo was the puppet master behind this widespread agitation.

Secondly, Frere and his advisors, again on the counsel of Shepstone, had concluded that the surest way to reconcile the Boers to British rule was to take a hard line against the Zulus. At issue was a contested Boer claim to land along the border between Zululand and the Transvaal. Shepstone, who after thirty years as Native Affairs Commissioner in Natal had left his post in 1887 to engineer the annexation of the Transvaal, reversed an earlier stand in favour of the Zulus in the land case and espoused the Boer claim. In a letter to the colonial secretary in London, he seemed to justify this about-face by portraying Zulu society "as a vicious military despotism" and concluding, ominously, that "Had Cetewayo's 30,000 warriors been in time changed to labourers working for wages, Zululand would have been a prosperous, peaceful country instead of what it now is, a source of perpetual danger to itself and its neighbours".[129]

When the boundary commission set up to adjudicate the land dispute found in favour of the Zulus, Frere attached conditions to the award that he knew the Zulus could not accept, prominent among them being the demand that Cetshwayo disband his army within thirty days. Given the centrality of the army to Zulu society, this requirement was tantamount to demanding that the Zulus abandon their way of life. When Frere's ultimatum expired on 11 January 1879, an 18,000-man British army marched on Zululand under the command of Lieutenant-General Frederick A. Thesiger, shortly to become the second Baron Chelmsford.

These machinations, worthy of a Bugeaud or Faidherbe, were carried out against the wishes of the government in London and largely without its knowledge. In October 1878, Sir Michael Hicks Beach, who had replaced Lord Carnarvon as colonial secretary, had advised Frere that "by the exercise of prudence, and by meeting the Zulus in a spirit of forebearance and reasonable compromise, it will be possible to avert the very serious evil of a war with [Cetshwayo]".[130] A month later, he told the governor that, with problems mounting for Britain in Afghanistan and the Balkans, "we cannot now have a Zulu war".[131] But Frere ignored London's wider concerns and Hicks Beach's instructions. He "believed he could crush the Zulu before the British Government had an opportunity to question either the efficacy, or the morality, of the methods he used".[132]

Unfortunately for Frere, the Zulus refused to play their part in his plans. Their resounding victory over British troops at Isandlwana on 23 January 1879 ruined his chances of a *fait accompli* and brought his career as proconsul to an abrupt close.

Isandlwana

The force which invaded Zululand under the command of Lord Chelmsford consisted of just under 18,000 men. Of these only 5,746 were British regulars, including two battalions of the veteran 24th (or 2nd Warwickshire) Regiment. Irregular colonial horse, white frontiersmen whose main function was scouting, accounted for another 1,193 men. The major part of this

"British" army, however, was African: the 9,350 troops of the Natal Native Contingent.[133] In addition, some 300 Zulus, rivals or enemies of Cetshwayo, marched with the invasion army. Their numbers would increase as the campaign wore on.

Chelmsford had also led British troops in the recently ended Ninth Frontier War in eastern Cape province. His soldiers had had a difficult time trying to corner the mobile Xhosa fighters, and Chelmsford was eager to avoid a repetition of this in Zululand. Like Sir Garnet Wolseley in Ashanti, he divided his invading force into separate columns, whose mission would be to drive the enemy before them and eventually to join together to fight a final battle on the outskirts of the enemy capital, in this case Ulundi, the principal kraal of King Cetshwayo. The southern column, under the command of Colonel Charles Pearson, wended its weary way through the hot stifling coastal zone of Zululand, while a second column commanded by Sir Evelyn Wood, a member of the "Wolseley Ring", closed in from the north. Both of these columns came under assault by Zulus on 22 January, but were able to fight off their attackers. The central column, under the command of Lord Chelmsford himself, which found itself being shadowed by a Zulu scouting party on 21 January, was not so lucky.

The next day, Chelmsford set off with half of his troops in pursuit of the Zulu reconnaissance force, and sent the remaining 1,700 men of his command to occupy high ground on his flank, from which they presumably would be able to alert the main column to the approach of a large Zulu *impi* known to be in the area. The detachment made camp at the foot of a Sphinx-shaped hill called Isandlwana. It was there that most of them died on 23 January 1879, at the hands of a Zulu force of some 20,000 men.

The Zulu army, which had passed unseen around Chelmsford's flank, was discovered by scouts from the camp on the morning of the 23rd, resting in concealment in a ravine about five miles from Isandlwana. Having been spotted, the Zulus quickly emerged from their hiding place and began trotting in their famous "cow horns" formation toward the camp. Lieutenant Horace Smith-Dorrien, a future general and one of the few British officers to survive the battle of Isandlwana, described the Zulu advance. It "was a marvellous sight", he wrote, "line upon line of men in slightly extended order, one behind the other, . . . bearing all before them".[134]

The British garrison, surprised, was strung out in a straggling line. Colonel Anthony Durnford's colonial troops found themselves isolated from the main body of British troops and tried to fight their way back to the camp. It was around this vulnerable right wing of the British force that the left wing of the Zulu crescent would pass into the British rear. The British commander, Colonel Henry B. Pulleine, tried to make a stand in front of

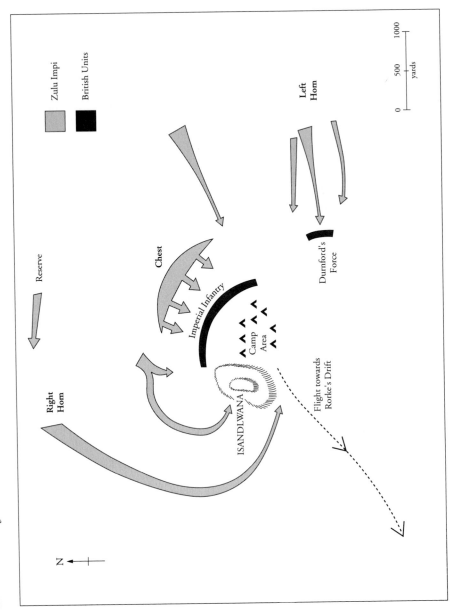

2. *The Battle of Isandlwana*

the camp, forming up his men in "an angled line, placing three companies on a north-facing side, three companies on an east-facing side, and two companies of the Natal Native Contingent at the angle". The positioning of the African troops, bracketed by British regulars, gives an idea of the low esteem in which they were held. Another indication is that they had only thirty rifles among them and few rounds to fire in them; when the shooting started, quartermasters refused to replenish their supply. Not surprisingly, many of these unfortunates broke and ran for their lives when the Zulus bore down on them, fragmenting the British line. Out-flanked, their angled defence line broken, Pulleine's men tried to regroup. It was too late. The Zulu right and left wings burst into the camp, nearly cutting off all retreat; the Zulu centre, which had taken horrible punishment from British riflemen as it held its place in front of the camp, now resumed its advance. In the ensuing massacre, over 1,300 African and British soldiers of Chelmsford's army were killed, most of them in desperate hand-to-hand combat.[135]

Isandlwana was the greatest triumph of the classic Zulu battle strategy. Despite terrible punishment from British rifle fire, the "chest" of the *impi* had stood its ground while the wings of the formation passed to the rear of the British line and came close to joining hands in an African Cannae.

Donald Morris provides the butcher's bill for the British side of the battle line.

There had been almost 1,800 men in the camp at Isandhlwana at noon – 950 Europeans and 850 Natal Kaffirs. By late evening 55 of the Europeans were still alive, scattered [all over the surrounding area]. Perhaps 300 Natal Kaffirs still survived; 470 of their bodies were found in the camp and along the fugitive's trail. The rest had vanished, but scores must have been hunted out in the kraals and crannies and killed far from the field. Six full companies of the 2nd Warwickshire had died without a single survivor – the 24th Regiment had lost 21 officers and 581 men.[136]

Back home in Britain the news of the massacre was greeted with disbelief, then shock. The Zulus had killed more British officers at Isandlwana than had gone down before Boney's grenadiers at Waterloo.[137]

But the Zulus had paid a high price for their victory. They

had given battle with a high-hearted courage that bullets had not been able to quench, and their losses had been fearful. 'An assegai has been thrust into the belly of the nation,' Cetshwayo said when the news reached him. 'There are not enough tears to mourn for the dead.' ... There was never a count, but over 2,000 Zulus were dead, and scores of them dragged themselves away to die for miles around the camp. Those who could, walked home, to recover or die, and in later years men who visited the kraals were shocked by the fearful wounds warriors had sustained and survived without medical attention.[138]

Chelmsford had learned of the battle only when it was over. By the time his force returned from its fruitless chase to Isandlwana, the Zulus were long gone. Although Chelmsford could not know it, the victorious *impi* had in fact disbanded and would not be reassembled for another month.

As soon as the slaughter at Isandlwana was concluded, the 4,000-man Zulu reserve, which had not been involved in the battle, jogged twelve miles across country in hopes of surprising a small British garrison at a Natal border crossing known as Rorke's Drift. The garrison comprised less than 150 men, soldiers of the South Wales Borderers, part of the 24th Regiment whose 1st Battalion had just been wiped out at Isandlwana. But, the Rorke's Drift post proved to be a reasonably strong defensive position, as the men were able to use a stockpile of supplies intended for Chelmsford's column to build barricades. Warned by survivors of the fate of their comrades at nearby Isandlwana, the garrison, under the command of Lieutenants John Chard of the Royal Engineers and Gonville Bromhead of the 24th Regiment, nonetheless chose to put up a fight. The first Zulu assault came at about 4.30pm, and attacks continued almost without pause throughout the night. Although one of the post buildings was set on fire, the Zulus failed to penetrate the barricades, and gave up the fight just before dawn. They left some 500 of their number behind on the battlefield. The British garrison, meanwhile, had lost just seventeen men, only six more than the number of defenders who were later awarded the Victoria Cross.[139]

To uncertain victory

Chelmsford's invasion plan fell to pieces in the aftermath of the defeat at Isandlwana. Pearson's coastal column came under renewed attack and was forced to take refuge in a former mission station at Eshowe. Here they remained under siege for three months, sick, short on rations, and continually sniped at by Zulus. Wood's northern column also lost momentum and entrenched at a place called Kambula hill.

Fearful of the loss of British prestige, the government in London now moved quickly to provide Chelmsford with reinforcements. At the end of March, the British returned to the offensive: Pearson's besieged column at Eshowe was relieved, and the march on Ulundi was resumed. In order to mask the real thrust of his offensive from the Zulus, Chelmsford called upon Wood to create a diversion on the northern flank. Wood took advantage of the opportunity to launch an attack on Zulus who had been harassing his position from a nearby mountaintop called Hlobane. It was also from here that on 12 March the Zulus had delivered an attack which had badly pummelled a British convoy at Ntombe River. On 28 March Wood sent columns of horsemen to attack the mountain position at either end, in the hope of trapping the Zulus in a pincer movement. When the cavalry reached the mountain top, however, they discovered that they were the ones who were trapped – by the sudden arrival of a 20,000-man Zulu army, as large as the one which had fought at Isandlwana, on the way to attack Wood's position at Kambula. The stage was set for the worst disaster of the war after Isandlwana, as British and colonial horsemen streamed down from the mountain in a disorderly rout.[140]

The débâcle at Hlobane did, however, serve the purpose of warning Wood of the approach of the main Zulu force, giving him ample time to prepare for its attack the next day. The battle of Kambula of 29 March 1879 was a major disaster for the Zulu *impi*, and served to cancel out the victory gained the previous day at Hlobane, as Ian Knight relates.

> For several hours the Zulus made determined assaults on [Wood's] position, a chain of wagon-laagers and earthwork redoubts on the top of Kambula ridge, until they were routed by a particularly ruthless mounted pursuit.[141]

Fortified by the Kambula triumph and a victory of his own on 2 April at Gingindlovu, Chelmsford could now begin the final descent on Cetshwayo's kraal. Toward the end of May, however, as his columns moved slowly in the direction of Ulundi, he learned that he was being relieved, and that the great imperial fireman, Sir Garnet Wolseley, was on his way out from England to replace him. Lord Chelmsford did not, however, now pause in the field to await the arrival of his successor, as some in government back home might naively have hoped. The not entirely unexpected news of his replacement made him all the more determined to strike a blow at Ulundi, in the hope of bringing the war to a successful conclusion and banishing the spectre of Isandlwana before Wolseley arrived. He did not, however, sprint. Lumbering onward in a giant square formation, proof against further Isandlwanas, he would only reach Ulundi at the beginning of July.

On the 4th of July, 1879 Chelmsford's army finally delivered its long-awaited attack on the capital of the Zulu king. Advancing methodically in a great hollow square bristling with Gatling guns, breechloaders, and artillery, the 5,000-man British army fought off repeated attacks by a Zulu army of some 20,000 men. Ulundi was burned to the ground. The Zulu soldiers who remained in the field dispersed to their home kraals. Following his victory, Chelmsford resigned his command, leaving to his successor Wolseley the final mopping-up of Zulu resistance. Not long afterward, Cetshwayo was hunted down and sent to Robben Island, already a place of detention for black enemies of South Africa's white rulers.

The Zulus lost the war because their traditional military strategy of head-on engagement in the long run could not prevail against the breechloading rifle. The Zulu victories at Isandlwana and Hlobane were anomalies. Although there was little the Zulus could have done about it, it is clear that the terrain on which so much of the fighting took place, the open veldt, favoured the British style of warfare. Their volley-firing infantry usually had an open field of fire and profited from it accordingly. The British mounted arm could also be used to advantage in Zululand. With no cavalry of their own and either lacking or eschewing cover, the Zulus were particularly vulnerable to pursuit by horsemen.

It was not, however, defeat on the battlefields of Kambula and Ulundi that ultimately cost the Zulus their kingdom. The British government were unwilling to risk the resumption of warfare that seemed likely to accompany an attempt to occupy Zululand in the aftermath of Ulundi. The strategy employed by Wolseley, to divide authority in the kingdom among a number of chiefs, would accomplish the same end without conflict. The final defeat of the Zulu people and the absorption of Zululand into the British South African empire, stemmed from the British ability to intensify, in the post-conflict period, divisions within the Zulu hierarchy that had surfaced before and during the war. It was the ensuing, bloody civil war between Zulu factions in the 1880s, not the war with the British, that finally destroyed the Zulu kingdom.[142]

Aftermath

The British defeat at Isandlwana was the central event in a decade in which more than one observer must have wondered if European arms were after all destined to prevail over the lesser breeds. Three years before the Zulus decimated the 2nd Warwickshire Regiment at Isandlwana, George

Armstrong Custer's US Seventh Cavalry had paid the price of overconfidence and indifferent scouting at the Little Big Horn. Within two years after Isandlwana, the British would suffer two equally devastating defeats – at Maiwand in Afghanistan and, back in Africa, against the Boers at Majuba Hill. Only time and the onset of new, more potent military technology would reassure shocked Western governments and publics that these defeats were no more than temporary setbacks. Over the next two decades, the shoe would be firmly on the other foot, as European armies seemed to move almost effortlessly from victory to victory in North America, Africa, Asia and wherever else they were on the march. But, even then, as the European Century was reaching its apogee, there would be surprises, rare perhaps but filled with portents of the future.

Chapter Four

Flood tide, 1880–98

Introduction

The period 1880–98 encompasses the years of the European "Scramble" to divide up Africa. At its conclusion, Liberia, Ethiopia, Northern Nigeria, Mauritania, Morocco and Libya were the only parts of the continent still free of European domination, and the last four areas would also fall into European hands in the course of the succeeding decade. The gap between European military capabilities and those of indigenous armies, in Africa and elsewhere, would never be greater than it was during this era.

Technological disparity

African peoples who took the path of armed resistance to European invasion in the years 1880–98 faced daunting technological disadvantages. The disparity in armaments that had begun to appear in the 1870s was now a yawning gulf. European troops and, to a limited extent, their African levies, now carried magazine rifles accurate beyond 1,000 yards, while, with a couple of prominent exceptions, their African foes were still armed with muskets or at best single-shot breechloaders. Europeans were now also able to field a much-improved machine gun, the Maxim gun, replacing the unwieldy, crank-operated Gatling and Gardner guns and the Nordenfelt. There were also notable innovations in artillery. The French, who were frequently obliged to besiege cities in their West African campaigns, found their 75 mm cannon incapable of breaching the thick mud or stone walls around them, and in the early 1890s brought in 95 mm siege guns with new high-explosive shells. On water, a new class of low-draught armoured gunboat was turned out, vessels capable of navigating the African rivers to transport supplies and troops, and to supplement the fire power of the European armies.

The presence of gunboats illustrates the heightened capacity of European armies for combined operations during this period. Close co-ordination between gunboats and land columns had contributed greatly to earlier French successes in Senegal and the Western Sudan, and naval control of the upper Niger would be instrumental in completing the conquest of the Western Sudan in the 1890s. British penetration of the Niger delta region of southern Nigeria also profited from the use of naval vessels to shell villages and ferry troops and supplies.

Kitchener's armoured steamboats on the Nile were credited by his Sudanese foes with providing the winning margin at the battle of Omdurman. Less well known perhaps is the contribution of gunboats on the Incomati and Zambesi rivers to the gradual "pacification" of Mozambique by the Portuguese army in the 1890s. Ships were an important means of communication available to European armies in the late nineteenth century, but they were not the only one. Few modern-day generals have ever "enjoyed" such close communications with their political leaders as Italian general Oreste Baratieri in Ethiopia, bombarded almost daily by telegraphic advice (most of it bad) from his prime minister in Rome in the run-up to the battle of Adowa. Field telegraph was also beginning to come into its own, but semaphore and couriers continued to account for most communication on the battlefield. Neglecting to bring forward their field semaphore gear did not improve Italian chances at Adowa.

The most crushing disadvantage faced by resistance forces in Africa was, however, in logistics. This is perhaps best borne out by the stately progression of Kitchener's army toward Omdurman in the Sudan in 1896–8. While their Mahdist opponents starved, the Anglo-Egyptian-Sudanese forces received regular supplies by Nile steamer or by the railroad which Kitchener's conscripted Egyptian navvies had built south across the desert. And, while desertion undermined the Mahdist army with little prospect of replacement, Kitchener could call up additional troops at will by sea or train.

But these technological advances are only the most obvious signs of a burgeoning European hegemony in the African wars. What is less obvious but more important is the heightened *will* of European governments to use military force to seize and occupy territory during this period. By the 1890s European armies are everywhere on the march. The motivations behind these military operations will differ from one imperial power to

114

another, even from one set of circumstances to another, but almost every-where the effect will be the same: not simply to punish African "trouble-makers" and render them more biddable, but to conquer and colonize African territory.

Yet, in spite of all this, it should not be forgotten that this same period opens with a startling series of British defeats in Africa and elsewhere, is punctuated by a mysterious mid-1880s hiatus that John Hargreaves has aptly dubbed "the loaded pause", and features the greatest victory of the African resistance over European troops during the whole of the wars of imperial conquest, the Ethiopian defeat of the Italian army at Adowa in 1896.

Long march to Timbuktu (1880–98)

Introduction

The fall of the Second Empire and the trauma of defeat in 1870 brought a temporary halt to French expansion in West Africa, but by the end of the decade it had resumed again at an accelerated pace. Much of the new impetus was due to the appointment of Colonel Louis-Alexandre Brière de l'Isle of the marine infantry as governor of Senegal in 1876. The colonel, as Galliéni would write later, was an admirer of "le go-ahead des Américains".[1] His goal was much the same as Faidherbe's had been in the 1850s and 1860s: to establish a French empire in West Africa. There were a couple of new twists, however. Faidherbe had pursued a policy of gradualism, mixing diplomacy with the use of military force, whereas Brière had a preference for the sword. He also wanted to speed up penetration of the Western Sudan by convincing the French government to finance a railroad that would link up the military's forward base at Kayes with the Niger. This was not, of course, the way the railroad scheme was presented to a sceptical parliament. Its real purpose, the deputies were told, was to open up the Western Sudan to French commerce. For a time, the governor's project was tied to a scheme for a railway across the Sahara, linking Algeria and the Sudan. The Trans-Sahara plan was abandoned in 1881, however, when a surveying party was massacred in the desert by Tuareg tribesmen. This left the field to the Senegal railroad project, but, for some time, little more than start-up money could be wheedled out of the Chamber of Deputies.

Nevertheless, the plan to advance into the Sudan went forward. It gained momentum from the arrival in office in Paris in 1879 of a new cabinet, headed by Charles de Freycinet as prime minister and with his friend and fellow imperial enthusiast, Admiral Jean Jauréguiberry, as minister of marine and colonies. Freycinet, an engineer who had studied at the École Polytechnique and was something of a railroad fanatic, eagerly embraced Brière de l'Isle's Senegal railway scheme. The Sudan was no desert, he told the French president, but the homeland of 100 million people who were eager to receive the blessings of French civilization and the fruits of French industry. (There were, at most, about eight million people living in the Western Sudan at this time.) What was at stake, the railway enthusiasts claimed, was the creation of a "French India" in the Sudan, representing at one and the same time revenge for the imperial defeats of the eighteenth century and a future rival for Britain's "jewel in the crown".

The arrival in office of Freycinet and Jauréguiberry meant that for the first time the schemes and unofficial initiatives of the men on the spot in West Africa became official policy in Paris. Where Faidherbe had been obliged to dissemble to get his way, Brière de l'Isle could count now not only on the support of cabinet ministers for his expansionist plans, but could also expect them to go before parliament to demand the funds to pay for their realization. This was a turn of events of some magnitude, not only for French imperialism, but for Western expansionist ventures as a whole.

> The unusual, or at least the new, feature was the acceptance by the French government that colonial expansion could no longer be left to the free play of social forces, but demanded intervention by the authorities. This new conception of the role of the state in colonial affairs was the crux of the new imperialism. It reflected a transition from "informal," that is, private, to "formal," that is, state, imperialism. This transition would make itself felt later among other [western] colonial powers, but France was its pioneer.[2]

It did not take the new government in Paris long to move from the planning stage to action. Their measures had, however, the ironic result of giving a green light to the forces of expansion in West Africa, while at the same time effectively denying the government any control over them. In September 1880 Jauréguiberry took the fateful step of placing the western Sudan under military control. Major Gustave Borgnis-Desbordes, an aggressive marine artillery officer and yet another graduate of the École Polytechnique, was named Commandant-Supérieur of the upper Senegal region and given full authority over all operations in the territory between the Senegal and Niger rivers. The powers granted to Borgnis-Desbordes had the effect of shifting the centre of power in Senegal from the governor in St. Louis to the military commander in the field. And, as the governor's control over the soldiers diminished, so did that of the authorities in Paris. This marks the real beginning of the phase of French expansionism in Africa christened "military imperialism" by Kanya-Forstner. For the next twenty years marine commanders, not government ministers, would determine the pace and extent of French expansion along the road to Timbuktu.

The basic French field unit in the wars which now commenced, first against the Tukolors and later against Samori, was the self-contained column. The size of these columns varied according to the mission. Some were veritable armies, comprising several thousand infantry, with supply trains, artillery and cavalry; others were raiding parties no larger than a company of riflemen (about 100 men). As we have seen, after the mid-1880s the bulk of the forces under French command in the Western Sudan were African *tirailleurs*. Because of their tendency to sicken or to fall out from the effects of the heat and humidity, white troops, to the extent that they were used, were increasingly put on horseback. By the 1890s the great majority of white troops in the Western Sudan were mounted infantry, marines on horseback.[3]

As was so often the case with European armies operating in Africa, logistics was the Achilles' heel for French troops in the Western Sudan. Supplies had to come over 900 km by river from St. Louis to the main base at Kayes before they could be transferred to supply columns or, after 1887, to railway cars, for distribution to the growing number of French forts or to troops in the field. The river could not be used beyond Kayes because of a succession of rapids and falls. The navigable end of the river was, however, not without its problems. Vessels could only come upstream at the end of the rainy season when the river was in flood. In 1880, because of an unusually low water level in the river, most of the supply fleet failed to reach Kayes and had to be towed several kilometres by gangs of soldiers and sailors on the riverbank. Beyond the base at Kayes supply columns and trains had to be heavily guarded, since they were prime targets for enemy attack.

Logistical problems in the Western Sudan were eased somewhat by the introduction in 1883 of a deceptively simple innovation in transport. This was the *voiture Lefebvre*, a two-wheeled cart that could be pulled by a single mule. The wagon box mounted on the cart could accomodate 250–300 kg of supplies, while a mule could carry only 80–100 kg on its back. The Lefebvre carts served a variety of uses. They could carry up to four wounded soldiers and could be drawn up in a *laager* to protect against marauding cavalry. Perhaps their most novel use was as "portable truck gardens", growing radishes and lettuces so that the troops could have fresh salads in the field.[4]

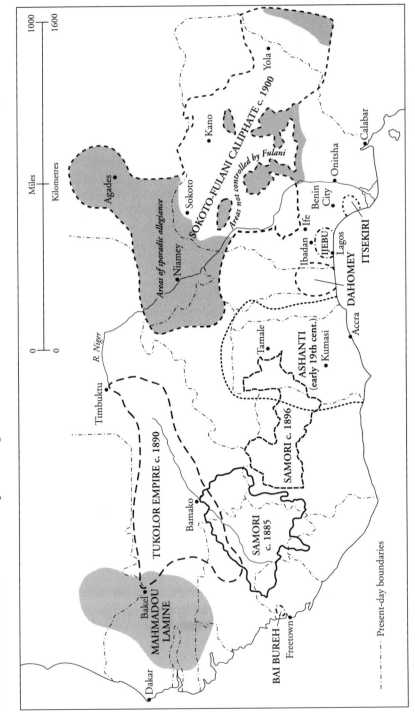

3. West Africa on the eve of European conquest

At about the same time, communications also improved considerably for French troops in the Sudan. In December 1885 it became possible to communicate by telegraph between Bamako on the Niger and Paris. The hook-up proceeded by telegraph wire to St. Louis and then to the Bay of Yof north of Dakar, whence submarine cable made the connection through Tenerife in the Canary Islands to Cadiz in Spain, which had a land link to Paris. Thanks to this improvement, the time required to get reinforcements from France out to Senegal, for example, was cut from two months to a couple of weeks.

Destruction of the Tukolor empire

Troubled succession

The Tukolor empire, now in the hands of Ahmadu Seku, the eldest son and chosen successor of al-Hajj Umar, was the first major obstacle in the way of Borgnis-Desbordes and his marines. It was, however, not nearly as formidable a barrier to French expansion as the empire of Ahmadu's father had been.

Although al-Hajj Umar is said to have passed on his *baraka* to his son, Ahmadu's lack of charisma and his recurrent difficulties with family members who resented his rise to power boded ill for the future of the Tukolor empire. Despite his assumption in 1868 of the title of Commander of the Faithful, Ahmadu never succeeded in winning the loyalty of the *talaba* or in reviving the crusading spirit of the jihad era. The bad feeling between the *talaba* and *sofa* regiments, which had festered below the surface in Umar's time, now came out into the open. Many *talaba* quit the army to return to Futa Toro. Family opposition to Ahmadu's assumption of his father's mantle stemmed from the fact that his mother was a commoner. His blue-blood half-brothers never accepted him as their equal and in 1872 conspired, albeit unsuccessfully, to overthrow him. One of them, Aguibu, eventually rallied to the French. Ahmadu's personal problems undermined the cohesion of the empire he had inherited. Masina, lost by Umar in 1864, was never regained. The empire's Bambara subjects were in a state of almost permanent rebellion. Kanya-Forstner has neatly summarized the situation of the Tukolor empire by the 1880s, when the French were preparing to resume their eastward march into the Sudan.

Rent by dissensions from within and sapped by rebellions from below, Umar's once dynamic and self-confident community was gradually transformed into a rickety, alien and essentially secular empire of conquest.[5]

Defence through diplomacy

With his army weakened by the departure of many *talaba*, and given the generally demoralized state of the troops who remained, Ahmadu was in no position to mount effective opposition to the French advance on the field of battle. Indeed, Ahmadu offers perhaps the best example of an African resistance leader who sought to compensate for military weakness by relying upon diplomacy. Most resistance movements in Africa had recourse to diplomacy from time to time. We have seen how Abd el-Kader negotiated with his French enemies in order to take pressure off his army at crucial junctures, and how he tried to play off the British and French against each other. Few resistance leaders, however, were obliged to rely as heavily on the diplomatic option as Ahmadu.

Ahmadu appears to have believed almost until the collapse of his empire that the French needed him to guarantee order and security for their commercial interests in the Western Sudan as much as he needed them to supply him with weapons and ammunition. This wishful thinking survived increasingly brazen French intrigues with his enemies, particularly his rebellious Bambara subjects, as well as unprovoked attacks on his fortresses. The seizure of the major Tukolor bastion of Murgula by French troops in 1883 opened the way to Bamako, the first French lodgement on the Niger. Now what Umar had tried to so hard to forestall on the Senegal River would come to pass on the Niger as well. A gunboat was brought overland in pieces, reassembled at Bamako and launched on the Niger. Soon it was cruising up and down the river to Timbuktu. This was profoundly disturbing to Ahmadu, who had been told by his father that "when French gunboats sailed above Segu, the collapse of the Tukolor Empire would be at hand".[6]

Although it would not be obvious at the time, the capture of Bamako would be the high water mark for the French in their war with the Tukolors over the next few years. The French faced formidable logistical problems in the Western Sudan. Railroad construction was absorbing more and more money and manpower and making very slow progress. By 1884 it had become painfully apparent to the French commanders that their rapid advance to Bamako had placed them at the end of a long and vulnerable line of supply and communications. Protecting this lifeline and garrisoning and supplying the chain of forts now being erected from the Senegal to the Niger absorbed so much manpower that offensive operations virtually ceased. The Chamber of Deputies back in Paris, already in the throes of the Third Republic's most pronounced anti-imperialist spasm, was incensed by the spiralling costs of the military campaigns and railway project, and threatened to terminate the whole Western Sudan adventure. Thus, at the very moment that the Berlin West Africa Conference was presumably opening the way to a European "scramble" for African territory, the French advance into the Western Sudan ground to a halt. It may have been a "loaded pause", in John Hargreaves's phrase, but it was a pause nonetheless.

To make matters worse, in 1884 Borgnis-Desbordes had foolishly launched an unprovoked attack south into the territories of an even more formidable regional power, the Mandingo empire of Samori Touré, about whom we will shortly be hearing a great deal. Although no full scale conflict with Samori resulted from this provocation, the *Tirailleurs Sénégalais* and their marine officers now had a new danger to worry about in their war with the Tukolors: the threat of an alliance between Ahmadu Seku and the Mandingo leader.

Fortunately for the French, relations between Ahmadu and Samori never prospered. Distrust between the two camps in the end proved insuperable, fed as it was by Samori's justified suspicion that Ahmadu was tacitly supporting the French against him, in the hope of receiving the guns and cannon he needed to firm up control over his crumbling jihad empire. Samori also had before him the example of the Tukolors' open alliance with the French in the 1885–7 suppression of a revolt by the Sarrakolé people in central Senegal. This upheaval, led by Mahmadou Lamine, a holy man from a rival Muslim brotherhood, the Sanusis, took place on territory partly controlled by the Tukolor empire.[7] Again, it is necessary to return to the point made above: against mounting evidence to the contrary, Ahmadu continued to believe, almost down to the day of his demise, that a deal could be struck with the French which would allow him to retain his empire. In the long term, this belief outweighed any consideration of alliance with other African states against the French. The failure of West African statesmen to join together to fight the French, a failure for which Ahmadu was largely responsible, has been severely censured by African historians. Writes the Ghanaian scholar, Adu A. Boahen:

> Had Samori, Ahmadu, Lat Dior,[8] and Mahmadou Lamine, or even the first two alone, allied against the French, the course of events in the Senegambia region could well have been different.[9]

121

The Galliéni interlude (1886–8)

The only time the kind of rapprochement Ahmadu sought might have been effected were the years of the "loaded pause" between 1884 and 1888. During this period support for expansion in Africa was at its lowest ebb in France; there was talk of pulling out of the Western Sudan altogether. Inclinations toward retrenchment were reinforced by the emergence of Samori Touré as a major element in the politics of the area. No one in France – neither soldier nor politician – was eager to fight a two-front war in Africa. In addition, there were the logistical problems alluded to earlier: the railroad that wasn't getting built and the dribbling out of combat troops as garrison soldiers along the string of forts on the road to the Niger.

Finally, these were the years when Joseph-Simon Galliéni served as French commander in the Western Sudan. Of the second generation of French soldiers in West Africa, Galliéni comes closest to being a disciple of the cautious expansionist, Louis Faidherbe. According to Galliéni's biographer, Marc Michel, although the young marine officer shared his fellow soldiers' belief that "an extension of French sovereignty in Africa was a matter of great urgency" (to fend off the British), he would have preferred to achieve this by "finding common ground with the great African leaders" (Ahmadu, Samori). These were entirely pragmatic considerations.

We know also from his reports to his superiors and his own writings that Galliéni had little liking for the Tukolors. They were exploiters and parasites, he informed the French governor in St. Louis. Their Bambara subjects did all the work, while the Tukolors "produce nothing; far from it, they are destroyers". Nor did the colonel bother to hide his disgust for what he saw as the "religious fanaticism" of the Tukolors. The Bambara animists and the less than fanatical Mandingo Muslims over whom they ruled "express the deepest distrust and hatred for the shaved heads who are always praying with their foreheads to the ground and their rear ends sticking up in the air", he wrote contemptuously.[10] While Michel ascribes Galliéni's dismissive views to "Eurocentrism", they may also have derived something from the colonel's rather pronounced anti-clericalism. Galliéni would become one of the leading "republican generals" in a military better known for conservative, even monarchist, officers such as Ferdinand Foch and Hubert Lyautey. Like other French republicans of his day, Galliéni favoured the curbing of church influence in politics and education. He would have had little sympathy for the Muslim theocracy the Tukolors sought to impose in the Western Sudan.

Yet, Galliéni believed that war was not the most efficient way of dealing with these "fanatical" enemies. He thought that the Tukolor empire had become such a ramshackle affair that it would soon collapse under its own weight. In the meantime, it could be manipulated for French advantage. So long as French commercial interests enjoyed unimpeded access to the markets of the region, there would be no need for invasion and conquest.

It was in the Western Sudan that Galliéni first employed his famous "oil stain" policy of expansion. The idea was to establish markets in the shadow of the new forts which the French were building; the markets would draw the local population into their orbit; French goods, ideas and influence would spread through the countryside like an oil stain. In time, Tukolor hegemony would become a hollow shell and, with its collapse, France would achieve the empire she sought without recourse to the sword.

As it turned out, however, time was working against such peaceful solutions to the Franco-Tukolor rivalry. Galliéni had done his job too well. During his short tenure as commander, the obstacles that had held up French expansion earlier in the decade were largely overcome. To begin with, the Tukolor empire's best protection, the failure of the French to create an effective supply system in the Niger-Senegal valley, was largely removed. Roads were repaired and the railway had at last reached the key post at Bafoulabé. Now the chain of forts from the Senegal to the Niger could be provisioned with relative ease.

The time for a *modus vivendi* with the French was over. In 1888 Galliéni was replaced as commander in the Western Sudan by Major Louis Archinard, a partisan of *la manière forte* in the tradition of Brière de l'Isle and Borgnis-Desbordes.

Enter Archinard

In the course of his five years as commander in the Western Sudan, Archinard would destroy the Tukolor empire and force Samori to evacuate his first empire. For this he became a hero to the first generation of French colonial historians – Jacques Méniaud, for example. Of late, however, Archinard's star has waned. He has come to symbolize "military imperialism" in its most reckless and violent form. Recent historians tend to see him as a vulgar careerist who scheduled offensives to coincide with the drawing up of promotion lists back in Paris and who rivalled "Père" Bugeaud in insubordination and contempt for civilian superiors.

The "military imperialism" that Archinard practiced so assiduously rested on two foundations. He and his cohorts had early come to realize that the way to secure an authorization to advance was to tell their civilian superiors that French prestige was at stake, that to fail to advance would make France appear weak, both to the Africans and to other imperial powers. The other sure-fire method for winning support for expansion during these years was to suggest to one's superiors in Paris that, if France failed to occupy a certain area, the British were prepared to do so. Such cynical appeals to prestige and nationalism were key weapons in Archinard's arsenal, to be deployed each year when he returned home to spend the rainy season. Much of his holiday was spent politicking in Paris, explaining away the excesses of the previous campaign and winning authorization for the next one. He had powerful friends who could be mobilized to promote his cause and, increasingly, to rescue him from the wrath of his civilian superiors – Brière de l'Isle and Borgnis-Desbordes, for example, who had risen high in the hierarchy of the marines. He also had powerful enemies – men of the stature of Eugène Étienne, leader of the Colonial Lobby and Under-Secretary of State for Colonies, and Théophile Delcassé, Minister of Colonies and future Foreign Minister. In the end, his enemies proved to be more powerful than his protectors, and in 1893 Archinard was forced to resign his post as commander in the Sudan.

For the moment, however, all was well. In 1889, a year after he replaced Galliéni, Archinard received the go-ahead from Paris for a resumption of hostilities against the Tukolors. Ahmadu's capital at Segu was swiftly taken, then Kaarta fell and, after a futile last stand in the eastern part of his collapsing empire, Ahmadu fled across the border with what remained of his army and took refuge at the court of his father-in-law, the sultan of the Sokoto Caliphate in northern Nigeria. Ahmadu's troops would take a second bow on the historical stage, in 1902, as the only veteran soldiers in the army of the Sokoto Caliphate, as it faced an invading British force under the command of a bumptious and remarkably Archinard-like Colonel Frederick Dealtry Lugard.

The Franco-Tukolor war was an uneven struggle in the end. So many Bambara auxiliaries accompanied Archinard into battle in Kaarta that, on some occasions, his force outnumbered that of the enemy. The Tukolor obsession with fortresses, besieging or being besieged in them, proved to be their ultimate undoing. The 95 mm siege guns Archinard brought with him for the 1891 campaign, whose shells contained a new high explosive called melinite, wrought such devastation in Tukolor-occupied cities that, eventually, the resisting forces either abandoned them without a fight or drew up to do battle outside the walls.

Kanya-Forstner writes that in the end Ahmadu faced two choices: to surrender unconditionally or resist.

[H]e chose to fight and save his honour if not his empire. Like his brother Aguibu [who collaborated with the French], he might have tried to settle for a comfortable old age. That he did not merits him some consideration as a leader of African resistance to European imperialism.[11]

But the defeat of Ahmadu was for Archinard and his fellow *officiers soudanais* only the overture to a long awaited and much rehearsed final act: the conquest of fabled Timbuktu. At this distance, it may be a bit difficult to appreciate the fervour which gripped these French officers as they turned their attention to the final objective in the Western Sudan. For we are aware that they had reason to know that the Timbuktu of 1893 was but a pale shadow of the great commercial and cultural centre of the African Middle Ages. European travellers and military men had visited the city in recent years and had brought back what should have been disillusioning reports. What we miss from our latter-day perspective, however, is the overpowering *will to believe* of the French officers who now began jostling for the honour of being the first to enter the ancient city. For what was at stake was not just booty, although booty would not have gone amiss, or even fame, but something more important to these French officers, a commodity that had been in short supply in French military circles in recent years: *la gloire*.

This makes it all the more ironic that the first Frenchmen to enter Timbuktu, arms in hand, were not marines at all, but sailors!

On 16 December 1893, the tricolor was raised over this desert city, some 800 miles from the sea, by a detachment of 19 sailors (of whom 11 were Senegalese) from the French gunboats *Mage* and *Niger*. The two craft, under the command of the impetuous Lieutenant H.G.M. Boiteux, had ascended the Niger River from their anchorage at Mopti, near Segu, in violation of orders to the contrary from their erstwhile commander, Marine Colonel Étienne Bonnier. (Bonnier had replaced Archinard, who, as we know, had been forced to resign his position as commandant and governor of the Western Sudan.) The colonel was headed toward Timbuktu himself with two columns under his command and had no desire to share any of the glory of taking the city with a mob of sailors.

On their arrival, Boiteux and his *matelots* had found themselves more or less invited into Timbuktu by the local authorities, who were desperately searching for someone to liberate the city from those inveterate desert warriors, the Tuaregs, who had been holding it to ransom for a number of years. Although the sailors were few in number, they were well armed, with repeating rifles and a French version of the Gatling gun. Nonetheless, a small detachment managed to get themselves ambushed just outside the city walls by the Tuaregs, and a call was sent out for reinforcements. This was balm to the ears of Bonnier, whose columns had been ordered to turn back by the Colonial Office. Paris wanted an end to the fighting in the Western Sudan, which had been going on for the better part of two decades. Now Bonnier had the excuse he needed to continue his march; he was going to the rescue of fellow Frenchmen. Even better, he could now also claim that the sailors he was obliged to save from their folly had never really been in control of Timbuktu, so that he, not they, was the real conqueror of the city. So, Bonnier, having rushed his column up the Niger in a huge fleet of canoes, marched into the desert city, ordered off Boiteux and his sailors in disgrace, and declared himself the conqueror of Timbuktu. Then the colonel rushed off in pursuit of the Tuaregs and fell into a night ambush, losing his life and that of 81 of his men – the largest single day's loss of life in France's Western Sudan adventure.

The remains of Bonnier and his slain soldiers were later found by a relief column led by Major Joseph Joffre, future Marshal of France and commander of French armies during the first two years of the First World War. The tragic irony of Bonnier's demise brought to an end one of the most bizarre episodes in the history of European imperial warfare in Africa: the quest for the fabled city of Timbuktu.[12]

The eclipse of Ahmadu and the Tukolor empire and the fall of Timbuktu meant that only one obstacle remained to French conquest of the lion's share of West Africa. But that would prove to be the biggest obstacle of all: Samori.

The Bonaparte of the Sudan

Introduction

Samori Touré (1830–1900) is one of the greatest figures in the recent history of West Africa. His French biographer, Yves Person, explains why he has achieved such stature among his fellow Africans.

> Samori arouses the highest passions because more than any other leader in pre-colonial Africa he symbolizes heroic and determined resistance to the European conqueror. Over seventeen years separate his first

contact with the French and his arrest in 1898. Fighting was by no means constant during this period, but no other confrontation between colonised and coloniser had ever lasted so long without the former surrendering his liberty.[13]

French soldiers have also paid homage to Samori's greatness. One of his adversaries, Captain [later General] Albert Baratier, wrote of him, in the paternalistic tone typical of the time:

> It is not an exaggeration to say that he showed himself superior to all the Negro chiefs who were our adversaries on the African continent. He was the only one who gave proof of those qualities characteristic of a chief of a people, a strategist and even a politician . . . an outstanding leader of men, possessing audacity, energy, the ability to follow up an advantage and plan in advance, and above all an irrepressible tenacity which could not be destroyed.[14]

There is, however, another Samori of legend: *Samory le Sanglant*, "Bloody Samori". To begin with, there was the matter of his involvement in the slave trade. His army's purchases of guns and horses were financed to a large extent by the sale into slavery of war captives. This provided fertile material for a French propaganda campaign against him, a campaign which grew in intensity as his war with the French widened. Under the pens of his enemies, the "Bonaparte of the Sudan" was transformed into the "Attila of the Sudan".

While it is clear that the French command deliberately set out to cast Samori in the worst possible light in order to arouse public and parliamentary support for their war against him, there is also no doubt that the he could be utterly ruthless when the situation seemed to warrant it. He sometimes ordered captured *Tirailleurs Sénégalais* to be decapitated and their heads sent back to their comrades, in order to sow terror in the ranks of France's African soldiers.[15] Officers in his army suspected of truckling to the enemy or neglecting their duties risked summary execution. The extent of Samori's ruthlessness is shown most dramatically in his treatment of Karamoko, at one time his favourite son. In 1886–7 the young man had been invited to visit France, where he had been lavishly entertained and exposed to equally lavish displays of French martial prowess and technological mastery. When he returned home, Karamoko had advocated a more conciliatory policy toward the French, to the great displeasure of his father. He fell out of favour, was rehabilitated, but, finally, when evidence of treason was brought against him, he was walled up alive on his father's orders.[16]

Apprenticeship

The future "Bonaparte of the Sudan" was born around 1830 in the Guinea Highlands, not far from the commercial centre of Kankan. Both of his parents were members of the Mandingo tribe. His father was a merchant or *dyula*, and Samori is often described as the chief protagonist of the Dyula Revolution, West Africa's equivalent of the European bourgeois revolution. The *dyulas* were long-distance traders, often in imported European or North African goods. Like their European counterparts under the *Ancien Régime*, they possessed wealth and often superior education but lacked political influence, which remained in the hands of the chiefly caste. The *dyulas* had another cause for complaint: most of them were Muslims and the establishment leaders they had to contend with were often unsympathetic animists. In the beginning, at least, this sort of religious discrimination was not a problem for Samori's family. They seem to have converted from Islam back to animism in order to further their business interests among their non-Muslim neighbours. But around 1850 Samori experienced a dramatic conversion to Islam, and later in his career became not only a great general and statesman but also a religious leader.

In 1884, he took the title of *almamy* or "spiritual leader". By now this will be recognized as a familiar pattern. All the North and West African resistance leaders whom we have discussed up to this point – Abd el-Kader, al-Hajj Umar, Ahmadu Seku and now Samori Touré – exercised both spiritual and secular authority. It should be noted, however, that in Samori's case, the spiritual aspect never weighed as heavily in the balance, largely because he lacked the credentials of his great Algerian and Tukolor predecessors: he had not made the pilgrimage to Mecca; he was not a holy man; he was unable to read and write in Arabic; and he had converted to Islam relatively late in life, a fact which undermined his credibility in some circles. Samori, wrote Jacques Méniaud, "was a self-made man".[17] But he proved to be enough of a statesman and military genius to compensate for these shortcomings.

He began adult life as a long-distance trader, a *dyula* like his father. Legend has it that he returned home after one of his long journeys in 1853 to find that his village had been raided by a local warlord and his mother carried off. Samori is supposed to have agreed to serve as a soldier in the warlord's army in order to win his mother's freedom. This story may not be true, but it is clear that it was during this time that Samori began a long and formative career as a soldier. Over the next two decades he fought his way as a mercenary through the ranks of a number of regional war bands to become one of the great soldiers of the Guinea Highlands. By the early

1880s, he had either outfought or outlasted all of his competitors, and had pieced together an empire embracing the eastern portion of modern-day Guinea, southern Mali, and chunks of northern Sierra Leone and Liberia. It is remarkable, but nonetheless true, that Samori Touré is the only major African resistance leader who had a professional military career behind him when he came to power.

Samori as statesman

What most clearly sets off Samori from the other African resistance leaders presented in these pages is his possession in approximately equal parts of military genius and political acumen. He emerges not only as a great war leader, but also as a statesman. The only other African resistance figure who approaches him closely in this respect is the Ethiopian king, Menelik. But, although he seems to have been an effective strategist, Menelik hardly ever found it necessary to occupy himself with military affairs at the operational level. He had at his side great generals like Ras Mekonnen (the father of Haile Selassie) to devise and execute his battle plans for him. Samori, on the other hand, although he had many competent subordinates, was his own general in every sense of the word, operational as well as strategic.

Whereas Menelik took his army to war to preserve – and expand – an empire whose origins go back to the pre-Christian era, Samori used the army he had created to fashion an entirely new polity, a centralized state in an area where the previous operative basis of authority had been the local clan, and a multi-ethnic and religiously-mixed empire in a region fractured for centuries along tribal and religious lines. Samori's awareness that there was "a political end" that transcended the purely military side of his activity was a key aspect of his greatness, according to Yves Person.[18]

This intuitively Clausewitzian understanding of the purposes of war was married in Samori to a political pragmatism that failed him only once, but then almost fatally. In 1886, largely as a result of the search for an effective unifying principle for his sprawling multi-ethnic state, Samori allowed himself to be persuaded by the more fanatical clerics in his entourage to proclaim Islam as the exclusive faith of his empire. This, it is generally agreed, was the biggest mistake of his career. It led in 1888 to a major revolt in the empire that required much bloodshed to stamp out. Galliéni, the French military commander in the region at the time, was of the opinion that this upheaval, which coincided with a failed 18-month siege of the rival city of Sikasso, in which a number of key officers and many soldiers were lost, spelled the end of the Samorian empire. That it nevertheless remained standing owed something no doubt to Samori's decision to quietly drop Islamicization, but probably even more to the fact that, in the throes of the profound crisis of 1888, the *almamy* continued to enjoy mass support. The middle class *dyulas* and commoners of artisan and peasant background, animists and Muslims alike stayed loyal to him because the Dyula Revolution he was promoting had brought domestic peace and greater prosperity. And among his fellow Mandingos, who constituted a majority of the inhabitants of his empire, Samori was regarded as a nationalist who had created a Mandingo state. These factors enabled him to recover relatively quickly from the divisive effects of his mistaken policy and to develop his first empire to its broadest extent by 1891.

This original empire, centred on the Guinea Highlands, was about two-thirds of the size of France. Its capital was at Bissandugu, where the *almamy* ruled from "a palace protected by a double wall of earthworks".[19] The empire was divided into ten districts. The two in the centre, surrounding the capital, came under Samori's direct control. These were home to the army's elite, a force of around 500 *sofas* personally selected by Samori, which served as the source of most of the officers for the rest of the army. Also present in the capital were the *almamy's* personal bodyguards, who were issued with repeating rifles as early as 1887. Each of the eight outlying districts was administered by a civilian governor, whose authority was enhanced by the presence of an army corps of some 5,000 men under the command of a general officer. Each army corps had a nucleus of around 300 highly-trained, veteran *sofas*. Conscripts made up the rest of the force. While in peacetime only about 10 per cent of able-bodied males were conscripted, in wartime up to 50 per cent could be called up. The army corps had an economic as well as a military function. Like the Zulu regiments, in peacetime Samori's troops devoted half their time to training and half to labouring in the fields. French Marine Lieutenant Marie-Étienne Péroz, who was sent to Bissandugu to renegotiate a treaty with Samori in 1887, later wrote of "the superb and well laid out agriculture of an area of some 200 square kilometers on which thousands of workers were engaged".[20]

Not surprisingly, the imperial economy was devoted to meeting the needs of the military. Taxes, most often paid in kind, along with the sale of gold from the mines of Buré and foreign trade receipts helped pay the army's bills. The empire's external trade included an active commerce in slaves. Income from the sale of slaves, most often to buyers in the neigh-bouring Futa Jallon, was used to buy horses for the cavalry in the Sudan to the north and, especially, rifles and ammunition from European traders on the coast.

Samori as soldier

Samori's empire was a product of war, and the army held a central place in it. It was the army that kept the empire together in the general crisis of 1888, and in the equally traumatic years when Samori was forced to abandon his first empire and build a new one in the east. Without the army, the eastern empire, constructed among alien and hostile peoples far from the *almamy's* natural base, could never have taken shape.

Although it existed long enough to sink roots as an institution in its own right, the Samorian army remained to the end very much the instrument of its founder, as Yves Person has noted.

> Samori . . . knew exactly what his men wanted and what their difficulties were and it was because he took care to satisfy them that their loyalty never faltered. Where the wounded were concerned, every possible effort was made to save them; the dead were buried decently and the maimed were given jobs to help them live in reasonable comfort. His warriors' love for him was also founded on a proper basis of confidence: they were convinced that he would lead them to victory.[21]

What strikes the observer about Samori's army is that, of all the armies of the Sudan, it was the only one since the days of Usuman dan Fodio that relied upon infantry rather than cavalry. This is significant in more than a strictly military sense. Although the armies of al-Hajj Umar and Ahmadu Seku did have infantry components, they were still dominated by men on horseback, the *talaba* elite nurtured by the ruler and waited upon by the *sofas*. Samori's army thus not only represents a rational adaptation to the methods of warfare of his enemies, but also reflects the social revolution which was underway in his empire. Samori's army is the army of the Dyula Revolution.

Like Abd el-Kader, Samori learned early to avoid set-piece battles against the French, where the superiority of their weapons and fire discipline would be decisive factors. After receiving a few bloody noses in engagements of this sort in the 1880s, Samori, again like the great Algerian resistance leader, went over to guerrilla warfare. His troops became proficient at cutting the long, vulnerable French supply lines and laying ambushes for French columns. They were aided in this by their remarkable mobility. Samori's *sofas* travelled light, living off the land and carrying little more than their arms and ammunition. Each soldier was equipped with a musket or rifle, a sabre and a dagger in a red-leather scabbard. On campaign, the *sofas* wore great conical straw hats, not unlike those worn by the peasants of East Asia; rust-colored trousers and tunics, the latter covered with good-luck charms; and leather sandals. Squad leaders were distinguishable by the red scarves they wore, while company commanders wore a red turban, a robe with wide sleeves, and doeskin boots. Officers were usually mounted.

This was also an army that knew how to fire and manoeuvre.

> After a particularly bloody engagement in the marshes of Diamanko, [Lieutenant-Colonel Gustave] Humbert was forced to admit that they were by far the strongest military force the French had so far encountered in the Sudan. "Samori's troops fight exactly like Europeans," wrote the embattled colonel, "with less discipline perhaps, but with much greater determination".[22]

Of all the African resistance armies, with the exception of the Ethiopians, Samori's was probably the best equipped with modern weapons. Until nearly the end of his struggle, the *almamy* was able to buy repeating rifles and ammunition from suppliers in Sierra Leone, including French merchants based there. Jacques Méniaud claimed that the British would have sold him artillery as well, if French authorities had not intervened to dissuade them.[23] As was traditional in African armies, the most advanced weapons went to Samori's bodyguard first and were only later distributed to the rest of the troops. However, the process of diffusion seems to have moved more swiftly in the Samorian army than in most others. By the 1890s most of Samori's troops had been issued with breechloaders, while the elite of the army were equipped with magazine rifles, French Kropatscheks for preference. Some of the breechloaders carried by Samori's *sofas* were of domestic manufacture.

The arsenals that supported Samori's armies were probably the most sophisticated south of the Sahara. Baratier estimated that they employed some 300–400 men. They were able to manufacture gunpowder; reload cartridges (200–300 a day); make spare parts for and repair a range of weapons, including magazine rifles; and, most important, build single-shot breechloading rifles from scratch (about a dozen per week). (One author suggests that the repertoire of Samori's gunsmiths also included the Kropatschek magazine rifle – which was, after all, basically a Gras single-shot breechloader with a tubular magazine fitted below the barrel – but this has not been verified.[24]) It was this ability to reproduce relatively complex European weapons that places Samori's gunsmiths in such a special category. Abd el-Kader's artisans could repair muzzle-loaders, but their attempts to manufacture muskets or build cannon ended in failure. The same is true of the gunsmiths employed by the armies of al-Hajj Umar, Ahmadu Seku, the Barue kingdom in Mozambique, and the Mahdi in the Sudan: they could repair weapons or cast spare parts for them, but they could not manufacture the weapons themselves. Only the Ethiopians had a greater capacity to repair and manufacture modern weapons of war than Samori's smiths. What is surprising is that Samori managed to achieve this level of sophistication without recourse to the European soldiers of fortune or prisoners of war who played such major roles in the arms programmes of the other resistance movements, including those of the Ethiopians. It would appear that the knowledge required to reproduce weapons in Samori's factories was brought back by Mandingo blacksmiths who had worked undercover in the French arsenal at St. Louis. That the copied breechloaders sometimes lacked the range of the originals, or even sometimes blew up in the faces of their users, defects that the *almamy's* nemesis, Colonel Archinard, was quick to point out, should not detract from the achievement of Samori's artisans.[25]

Early on Samori had acquired a reputation as a master of the strategic withdrawal. In 1893, his skill in this aspect of war was put to a stern test. When his first empire in his Guinea homeland was no longer sustainable, he withdrew to the east with the intention of forging a second one. Michael Crowder describes how this was done. As Samori moved east,

> One part of his army fought the French [while] another part conquered new lands to the East into which he could withdraw when the French could no longer be held. Then the lands which the French were about to occupy were "scorched". This involved a fantastic administrative ability, for not only was an army on the move, but a whole empire. Yet during all this time Samori managed to keep his constantly shifting empire under firm control. Samori's flight to the east involved the painful uprooting of whole communities and sometimes the destruction of those who refused to leave, so as to deny their resources to the French.

Dénouement

In 1896 the noose began to tighten. In January, the British deployed an almost all-African army to do what Wolseley had been unable to do in 1874 – to occupy Ashanti, with whom Samori was in the process of negotiating an alliance. At first, the *almamy* chose to see the establishment of a British protectorate over Ashanti as a positive development, believing he would be able to play the British off against the French and, in the process, replenish his arms supplies from the new masters in Kumasi. This proved to be wishful thinking. In fact, the occupation of Ashanti had been undertaken at least in part to forestall what the British thought was an impending alliance between Kumasi and Samori to drive them off the Gold Coast.[26] Furthermore, British forces in the region actually saw Samori as an obstacle to their own planned expansion northward along the western border of the Gold Coast to outflank the French. This led to fighting in the area between British troops and Samori's *sofas* in March–April 1897. Although the British troops got the worst of it, Samori elected to pull back in order to further his chances of acquiring arms from the British. But the *almamy* quickly learned that the new rulers of Ashanti had no intention of selling him arms; his requests were met with references to the Brussels Act of 1890 forbidding the sale of breechloaders to Africans.[27] The news was bad elsewhere as well. In Sierra Leone, where the British had also declared a protectorate in 1896, no further weapons were to be had. And now the French could harass him from the south, from the Ivory Coast, which their armies were in the process of conquering. The final blow was the French defeat of Samori's ally, Ba Bemba of Sikasso, and the occupation of that city in 1898. This closed off any chance of escape to the north. It was almost over.

His room for manoeuvre now dangerously reduced, Samori fled with a picked band of followers into the mountains of the western Ivory Coast. As he moved, the *almamy* attempted to negotiate at arm's length with the French, seeking honourable terms on which to surrender. By late September 1898, he believed he had secured agreement to his offer to surrender in return for being allowed to retire to his homeland as a private citizen. As Jean Suret-Canale has argued,

> It is these negotiations which explain the circumstances of his capture at Guélému on 29 September 1898. That same morning he had sent negotiators to the French post at Tuba, and when [French Captain Henri-Eugène] Gouraud's small party of riflemen crossed his camp, they were not resisted since everyone supposed that they, too, were negotiators.[28]

But Gouraud's men were not negotiators, and Samori was taken prisoner and transported to the French base at Kayes.

There is a temptation to believe that Samori's defeat was basically the result of a combination of bad luck and the closing of European ranks against him. This would be a mistake. One does not have to agree with Yves Person's chauvinist claim that Samori fell because "his field of action happened to coincide with that of the French Marine Corps, . . . possibly one of the best instruments of conquest ever used by any country", to recognize that the tenacity of the French marines and *Tirailleurs Sénégalais* had a great deal to do with his downfall. Many of the campaigns described in this book were affairs of a season, or of a year at most. The war against Samori, it should be recalled, went on for over a decade and a half, from one dry season to the next. In the end, to bring the *almamy* to heel, the French troops were obliged to fight in the rainy season as well.

On 22 December 1898, while still in custody in Kayes, Samori was told that he would be exiled to Gabon. "The old man, believing that his earlier negotiations were still valid, felt that he had been tricked and attempted to commit suicide before embarking from Saint-Louis".[29] On 2 June 1900 Samori died of bronchial pneumonia on the small island of Ndjole in the middle of the Ogooué River in Gabon. Captain Baratier drew the obvious conclusion, observing in his usual patronizing fashion that

> this conqueror whom the blacks, if they had known history, would have compared to Napoleon, found his St. Helena in the island of Ogowé [sic] where he had been confined.[30]

Legacy of Samori

Michael Crowder believes that the capture of Samori closed the most clearly-marked, autonomous African path to modernization. The *almamy*, he wrote, was

> the most interesting of all the resisters of colonial penetration for in him we can see the sort of leader who might well have achieved modernization of his own state, independent of European control. That he had the ability and the instinct is clear from his military tactics, his organization of trade and his spectacular administration of his constantly moving empire. Certainly if Samori had not had to fight the French, there is every indication that he had the organizing genius and sufficient control of his people to have created a state responsive to the needs of the approaching twentieth century.[31]

Yves Person did not agree. Although Samori was endlessly resilient and adaptable in the strategy, tactics and technology of war, in Person's view his political and, especially, social outlook was deeply traditional.

> His conservatism . . . surprises us, for example, his scrupulous respect for the established local chiefs and other notables. It is clear that the action of Samori, in spite of its revolutionary aspect, belonged to the

traditions of his society. It is, therefore, quite difficult to see him as the forerunner of modern nationalism.[32]

That Samori was a great military innovator, there can be no doubt, Person contended.

In the space of a mere twenty-five years he made the most profound changes in the art of war as fought in his country, turning from the old Konya warrior bands to the new dyula army, and from this to companies specially trained to fight the white men. These changes were possible only through the mobilisation of all the resources of the empire and no other African ruler would ever have dared to attempt this.

But, concluded Person, Samori's "military undertakings have all the sadness of wasted efforts".

His great work was condemned from the start, for neither his energy nor his farsightedness, nor even the fierce love he inspired in his men could make up for the technical insufficiency which doomed Africa to colonisation.[33]

Leopold's Congo Free State

Introduction

The outlines of what was to become the Congo Free State were sketched in for Leopold II by Henry Stanley, following a series of expeditions into the region at the king's behest in 1880–4. In the course of these journeys Stanley had actually begun to lay rough claim to the territory through a series of outposts, most of them on the lower Congo toward the Atlantic. Stanley's vision of the future was more important than anything he did on the ground in this early period. Having explored much of the region, he knew that the key to the military conquest – efficient administration and commercial exploitation of the Congo – was the development of an efficient transportation system.

Eventually, this would have to include the construction of a railway from the Atlantic Coast to Stanley Pool (site of Léopoldville, present-day Kinshasa), to circumvent the rapids and falls that disrupted navigation on the lower Congo River. For the moment, however, the main priority was to achieve domination of the region's waterways by the use of a fleet of steamboats. Already in 1881 Stanley had supervised the launching of the first steamboat on the Congo River. It had been brought in pieces for some 250 miles, from the Atlantic coast to Stanley Pool, on the heads of African carriers. From there, steamers could cruise for 900 miles, to Stanley Falls (today's Kisangani), beyond which point the Congo River became the Lualaba, navigable for another 500 miles, deep into the rain forests and savannah of the southern Congo.

It was the development of a river fleet, at enormous cost in Belgian francs and in the lives of African porters, that would enable Leopold and his administrators to claim "effective occupation" of the vast Congo region. So important were these steamers to the development of the Congo, that it is estimated that they absorbed some 90 per cent of the capital invested in the Congo Free State from 1887 to 1896. Until completion of the railroad Stanley had envisioned in 1895, the steamboats continued to be brought to Stanley Pool in pieces. Between May and October 1887, some 60,000 African carriers transported 992 tons of freight, mostly steamer parts, over the long route from the Atlantic to Leopoldville.[34] Unknown numbers died, victims of exhaustion and the brutality of overseers.

It was, therefore, Stanley's vision – and the heavy expenditure in blood and resources he was prepared to make in order to realize it – that made it possible for the Belgian king to lay claim to Congo territories stretching far beyond Stanley's outposts when the European powers convened in Berlin in 1884 to set out the parameters for dividing up Africa. Even so, the Congo Free State, as finally set up in 1885, was a "territory monstrously disproportionate to the resources at its disposal".[35] A makeshift administration was established at Boma, near the mouth of the Congo, and an army, called the *Force Publique*, was created in 1886 to assist in the "effective occupation" of the king's vast domain. For much of the history of the Free State, army and state were largely synonymous, as the key posts in the administration at Boma were held by "officers of the Belgian army assigned to African service".[36]

For several years the government at Boma had only a very limited influence over huge areas of the region. What little power it was able to wield was thanks to the presence of the river fleet. "Take good care of our Marine", Leopold wrote to his Free State administrators in 1886, "it about sums up all our governmental authority at this moment".[37]

The so-called "Arab zone" of the eastern Congo remained a largely autonomous entity until the early 1890s. So weak were Free State forces in the eastern Congo that an attempt was made in 1887 to pacify the Arabs by making the region's major slave trader and territorial magnate, Tippu Tip, governor of the zone, with headquarters at Stanley Falls. Several expeditions were sent to Katanga in the far south, but a lack of personnel delayed effective occupation until 1903. The region of Kivu on the border with Rwanda was still largely unoccupied on the eve of the First World War. Outside the Arab zone, resistance to Free State authorities was probably strongest in areas where pre-colonial kingdoms had existed: the Zande kingdom of the north Congo, the Yaka along the Kwango River in the western Congo, and the Luba at the headwaters of the Lualaba River in the south-central Congo. But not only kingdoms resisted. Some of the so-called "stateless peoples", communities without chiefs, also fought back. And traders involved in pre-existing networks, particularly the Chokwe of the southwestern Congo with their ties to Angola, refused to be integrated into the new commercial networks being promoted by the Free State. When Leopold's domain was taken over by the Belgian government in 1908, some of these resisters were still holding out.

In the view of two distinguished Belgian historians, neither the Free State nor its Belgian government successors were ever destined to acquire anything like legitimacy in the eyes of their subjects, so deep was the misunderstanding and mistrust between conqueror and conquered.

> To the whites, the Africans were lazy, cruel children. To the blacks of the Lower Congo and as far as Kasai, the whites were persons returned from the dead, from the land across the water or under the sea, whence their wealth and power came. Everywhere European technical superiority and wealth were attributed to special, supernatural power; Europeans were sorcerers or magicians. Even the "good" white man derived his power from some unethical unknown. In practice the Congolese never accepted European superiority. After resistance was broken they still did not accept the new order.... The mass of the population finally submitted, but never forgot.[38]

Two interesting themes encountered earlier re-emerge here. The first concerns the African perception of whites as "creatures" from the sea, a notion which was common to the Tukolors and Zulus as well as the Congolese. The second theme concerns the ultimate meaning of European physical victory over the Africans, the feat considered by soldiers from Bugeaud's time onward to be so vital to European hegemony. To the Congolese, European battlefield "victories" were barren of result, indeed illegitimate, since they were believed to be the product, not of moral authority or superior technology, but of witchcraft or magic.

Since European "victory" was perceived by the peoples of the Congo to be the result of sorcery or magic, it was quite natural that resistance to the Europeans should be couched in religious terms. The early years of European penetration of the Congo saw the rise of the Lugbara "water cult", a widespread movement which claimed the power to turn bullets into water. In 1892, a similar cult emerged along the lower Lomami River in the eastern Congo in opposition to Arab slave raiders.[39] "Water cults" were not confined to the Congo, however. Claims of powers to turn bullets into water were a prominent feature of later resistance movements in Mozambique and, especially, Tanganyika.

The Force Publique

In the beginning the private army King Leopold had decreed into existence in 1886, the *Force Publique*, was composed largely of African mercenaries recruited outside the Congo. Of the original 2,000 other ranks of the force, only 111 were Congolese. Preference in early recruiting was given to that much sought after "martial race", the Hausas of the Central Sudan. In the end, however, these foreign mercenaries proved to be too expensive and local recruiting was intensified. In 1891, chiefs were ordered to produce a certain number of recruits per year, and a militia was founded from which men could be drafted to fill out the ranks in emergencies. In 1900 the term of enlistment in the *Force Publique* was raised from five to seven years. The Free State also used large numbers of irregulars in its campaigns. The Azande people of the north Congo and the Batetela people, who lived between the Sankuru and the Lomami rivers in the south central area of the Congo, were frequently employed in this capacity. The main attraction was the promise of booty.

Although officials always denied it, there were continual charges that, in order to terrorize its enemies, the *Force Publique* went out of its way to recruit cannibals. An English visitor to the Congo in the 1890s, E.S. Grogan, described *Force Publique* recruits as "degraded and vice-sodden cannibals" and charged that their officers expected them to supply themselves with food and clothing through "commandeering" or looting.[40] During the Arab wars of the 1890s, *Force Publique* officers admitted that there were outbreaks of cannibalism in their forces, but claimed that this was the work of irregulars. Since these mercenaries were not subject to army discipline, wrote the authors of the official history of the *Force Publique*, "it was impossible to stop them from eating a certain number of victims after each battle".[41]

The *Force Publique* increased its numbers tenfold in the first decade of its existence, largely because of the requirements of the Arab wars. By 1898 it boasted nearly 20,000 men (although numbers plummeted thereafter, with the collapse of Leopold's plans to occupy the southern Sudan). The army maintained a military camp in each of the Free State's districts. More important were the base camps, where regional headquarters were located and basic training carried out. The most important of these camps were at Eambu Luku, near Boma, and at Irebu and Lisala, in the north around the junction between the Ubangi and Congo rivers. Since the latter region was a major catchment area for recruits, it was no coincidence that the Lingala language spoken there in time became the *lingua franca* of the army.[42] The greatest challenge faced by the *Force Publique* in its early years came in the 1890s, in the so-called "Arab wars".

> The sharpest struggles were those that had to be undertaken not against the Africans, but against Swahili slave traders (often called "Arabs" but rarely of pure Arab descent) and their followers in the eastern Congo.[43]

The Arab wars

The Congo Arab war was one of the bloodiest conflicts of the whole era of imperial conquest.

> The fighting [was] massive, because both sides enlisted the aid of thousands of irregulars. An estimate of 70,000 dead on the Swahili– Arab side is probably exaggerated, while figures for Congo State losses are not available. At all events, tens of thousands died in this campaign.[44]

The Congo Arab war also was (and remains) one of the most obscure of the wars of imperial conquest in Africa. Fought over enormous distances far from the centres of European authority, it was difficult for even Free State officials to follow the action, and it excited relatively little attention abroad. Nor has the war been the subject of many recent studies, even in Belgium or Congo. There is, for example, no good biography of the commander of the Free State forces, Commandant Francis Dhanis, who was made a baronet for his services during the conflict.

What is clear, however, to even the most casual observer is that the crucial factor in the eventual success of the Free State forces was their control of the waterways of the eastern Congo, an advantage gained thanks to the foresight of Henry Stanley. A glance at the map, for example, shows that the main population centres of the Arabs, principally the areas around the towns of Nyangwe and Kasongo on the Lualaba River downstream from Stanley Falls, were easily accessible to the Free State's river fleet. In anticipation of war with the Arabs, the *Force Publique* had moved to strengthen this advantage by building heavily fortified riverine bases at the edge of the Arab zone, at Basoko down the river from Stanley Falls and at Lusambo directly to the south on the Sankuru river. The fort at Basoko, with a garrison of 300 men, was "surrounded by loopholed walls, topped by an observation tower . . . crammed with victuals and thousands of cartridges [and] equipped with two Krupp cannons, four bronze artillery pieces and a Maxim machine gun".[45] It would prove an important jumping off point for the invasion of the Arab heartland during the war.

In 1890 the Free State authorities took another measure to improve their chances of triumph over the Arabs in the event of war by standing out "for the exact observance" of the Brussels General Declaration of 2 July 1890, which, among other things, forbade the sale of breechloading rifles and ammunition in the tropical zones of Africa. Before this time the same officials had been conspicuously liberal in their sales of firearms to the Arab zone.[46]

Not surprisingly the official version of the outbreak of hostilities puts the blame on the Arabs, first of all for refusing to terminate slave trading within the boundaries of the Free State. They had promised to do this in the Treaty of Zanzibar, signed in February 1887 between Henry Stanley and Tippu Tip. The Free State administration appears to have begun planning for a showdown with the Arabs as early as 1889, believing that this was the only reliable way for slave trading to be ended and the authority of the Free State firmly implanted in the eastern regions.[47]

The second element in the official version of the causes of the war was the dubious charge that Tippu Tip and his Arab cohorts were planning an alliance with their fellow Muslims, the Mahdists in the Sudan. This alleged conspiracy was used to justify the invasion of the southern Sudan by the *Force Publique* during the 1890s.[48] Less partisan writers have suggested that, while the Free State was indeed eager to put an end to slave trading on its territory, this was as much because it wished to be seen to be living up to the terms of its mandate from the Berlin Conference as for any humanitarian reasons of its own. These same writers have also pointed to the emerging competition between the Free State and the Arabs over the ivory trade as a factor in bringing on hostilities.[49]

At the outset of the fighting the *Force Publique* was too small to carry the battle to the enemy. The Arabs had the capacity to field 100,000 men, and only their seeming inability to co-operate among themselves stopped them from doing so. Thus, some 4,200 mercenaries had to be recruited by the *Force Publique*, and militia were incorporated into the regular army at an accelerated rate. These additions boosted the size of the army from 6,000 men in 1892 to 10,000 by 1894. During the course of the war, the *Force Publique* also absorbed some of the irregular troops of their defeated foes, principally members of the Batetela and Baluba tribes. The Free State forces had another interesting ally in their war against the Arabs – an armed force paid for by the Anti-Slavery Society and under the command of one Captain Jean Jacques. The Society's troops operated farther east than the *Force Publique*, in the vicinity of Lake Tanganyika, where they began attacking Arab strongholds in 1891–2.[50]

After desultory sparring in 1891–2, the *Force Publique's* "river war" against the Arabs moved into a higher gear in the spring of 1893 with assaults against the main Arab strongholds of Nyangwe and Kasongo on the Lualaba River. Troops under the command of Commandant Dhanis used artillery to bombard Nyangwe, provoking an Arab counter attack which was repulsed with great slaughter. Nyangwe fell on 4 March and Dhanis quickly moved downstream to attack Kasongo, supported by swarms of African irregulars. Kasongo was taken "after furious fighting. In wild flight the Arabs abandoned the field and many of them were drowned in the River Musokoi".

While Dhanis was subduing the Arabs south of the fortified base at Basoko, *Force Publique* troops commanded by Lieutenant L.-N. Chaltin used the fort as a base for operations against Arab forces to the north, in the vicinity of Stanley Falls. Moving swiftly by steamboat up the Congo River and into the Lomami, Chaltin's men occupied a number of Arab villages, only to realize that the light defence of these Arab strongholds meant that Arab troops were somewhere else – delivering, as it turned out, a furious assault against the Free State's base at Stanley Falls. Tobbak, the commandant at the Falls, "was holding out with difficulty against superior numbers, when on the 18th [of May 1893], at the moment of his greatest extremity, the [steamer] 'Ville de Bruxelles' drew near with the longed-for relief force under Chaltin". Shades of the siege of Médine!

The Arab war was brought to an end by a *Force Publique* victory on 20 October 1893 on the Luama River just west of Lake Tanganyika. The Free State forces, under the leadership of Commandants Dhanis and Ponthier (who died of wounds after the battle), succeeded in winning "a decisive victory . . . after heavy losses on both sides".[51]

While it seems obvious that the major factor in the success of the Free State forces in the Arab war was the mobility conferred upon them by control of the river system, there is surprisingly little reference to this in official accounts of the war. According to the authors of the official history of the *Force Publique*, the Arabs were beaten because they lacked the capacity or armament to wage offensive war. They "excelled" at defensive warfare and built strong field fortifications called *bomas*, but, presumably, the artillery and offensive *esprit* of the *Force Publique* proved too much for them. The arms available to the Arab army varied considerably: the chiefs presumably possessed modern repeating rifles, while the common soldiers carried everything from "Long Danes" to Winchester repeaters. The situation was made worse for the Arabs, the authors contend, because of their inability to work together. The final negative factor was logistical: the difficulty of supplying such a large army in the eastern Congo, which had been "depopulated and devastated" by the slave raiders.[52]

During and after the war, strenuous efforts were made by the Free State authorities to convince public opinion in Belgium and elsewhere that the bloody and costly conflict had been a struggle between the forces of enlightenment and progress (the Free State) and a vicious, exploitative regime (the Arabs) from which Africans were only too glad to be liberated. Until fairly recently this view won general acceptance, at least in the West. Modern scholars, however, have found reason to dissent. Using new sources (missionary records, Arab/Swahili accounts and oral histories) to supplement the sparse documentation made available in Belgian archives, historians like the missionary priest R.P.P. Ceulemans[53] have constructed a somewhat different picture of the Congo Arab zone on the eve of the 1890s war. Surprisingly, some of the most telling evidence comes from accounts of participants in the conflict on the Free State side. This description of the taking of the Arab town of Kasongo, written by Captain Sidney Hinde, a British medical officer with the *Force Publique* during the war, is particularly illuminating.

> We rushed into the town so suddenly that everything was left in its place. Our whole force found new outfits, and even the common soldiers slept on silk and satin mattresses, in carved beds with silk mosquito curtains. The room I took possession of was eighty feet long and fifteen feet wide, with a door leading into an orange garden, beyond which was a view extending over five miles. We found many European luxuries, the use of which we had almost forgotten; candles, sugar, matches, silver and glass goblets and decanters were in profusion. The granaries throughout the town were stocked with enormous

quantities of rice, coffee, maize and other food; the gardens were
luxurious and well-planted; and oranges, both sweet and bitter, guavas,
pomegranates, pineapples, mangoes and bananas abounded at every
turn. . . . I was constantly astonished by the splendid work which had
been done in the neigbourhood by the Arabs. Kasongo was built in the
corner of a virgin forest, and for miles around the brushwood and the
great majority of trees had been cleared away. In the forest-clearing
fine crops of sugar-cane, rice, maize and fruits grew. I have ridden
through a single rice-field for an hour and a half.[54]

Modern scholarship leaves the impression that by the 1880s the Arab/
Swahili raiders had put their slaving days behind them and had begun
to build permanent communities in the eastern Congo with viable agricultural and commercial infrastructures and efficient systems of administration.
This, it is suggested, was what made the Arabs so threatening to the
expansion-minded Free State authorities, not their penchant for slave raiding
or their religious fanaticism. Perhaps the best proof that there is something
to this argument is the quiet homage paid to it by Free State officials
themselves. Following conquest of the Arab zone, the government in
Boma kept the Arab administrative system in place and even retained most
of the middling Arab officials; the eastern Congo was ruled in this way until
the 1920s.[55]

The Nile expeditions

One would have thought that fighting the Arabs and keeping the peace
in the vast Congo region would have been more than enough of a task
for the modest-sized *Force Publique*. But Leopold had an even more grandiose mission in mind for his army: conquest of the headwaters of the Nile.
As early as the conclusion of the Arab wars, the king began laying plans
for annexing the southern Sudan to the Free State. In 1896 Leopold
dispatched Baron Dhanis to the Sudan with the largest army the *Force
Publique* had yet been able to muster, nearly 30,000 men, including a huge
element of irregulars. But the campaign came to an abrupt end in the
forests of the northeastern Congo, when Dhanis's army mutinied, killed
most of its officers, and began rampaging across the region. The mutineers
had complained of short rations, forced marches and mistreatment by their
officers.

The king had to be content with a slice of the province of Equatoria at the extreme southern end of the Sudan, called the Lado Enclave, captured for him in 1897 by another of his columns, led by Commandant Chaltin. This, however, was a consolation prize in the race for the control of the Nile headwaters. Both France and Britain had let the king know that they would look unfavourably on any more grandiose schemes for operations in the Sudan.

Subject of scandal

With the Arabs defeated and the Sudan project aborted, the *Force Publique* was able to focus its attention on its second important mission: the maintenance of order. In this capacity, it acted as a police force, charged with assuring tribal co-operation with the Free State government's schemes for developing the country.

The whole idea behind taking control of the Congo had been to exploit its wealth but, before the Congo could be made profitable, it had to be developed. The biggest problem faced by the companies and state officials involved in developing the Congo was the securing of labour. Since the Africans did not seem eager to volunteer their services, the king's administrators in Boma stepped in to help. They instituted a system of forced labour, under which Africans were rounded up by the *Force Publique* and turned over to special African overseers called *sentilles* who enforced work quotas with shotguns and rhinoceros-hide whips. Another way to get the Africans to produce more was to impose heavy taxes on them and, when they could not pay in cash, to order them to pay in kind – i.e. in natural rubber, or palm nuts, or ivory. If the Africans resisted, as some did, they received a visit from the *Force Publique*, which often burned the villages, killed the women and children, and took away the men as slaves. Africans who failed to meet their quotas – and the quotas were often set unrealistically high – were whipped or, in some highly-publicized cases, had their hands lopped off. Revelations about the mistreatment of Africans by the Free State regime and its army eventually provoked an international outcry, and in 1908 the king was forced to turn the territory over to the Belgian government. His *Force Publique* lived on, but as an arm of the Belgian state rather than the private army it had been for the first quarter of a century of its existence.

Portuguese campaigns, 1895–1902

Introduction

The Portuguese imperial renaissance of the 1890s, spurred on by national indignation at the country's humiliation at the hands of her imperial rivals, meant war for the peoples who inhabited the African lands over which Portugal claimed sovereignty. In Angola, beginning in the 1880s, Portuguese columns made increasingly vigorous efforts to break out of the coastal regions and on to the central plateau, to penetrate the northern rain forests, and to bring the arid lands of the far south under effective control.[56] In Guinea-Bissau, on the eve of the First World War, Portuguese military pressure on the interior increased, under the direction of Major João Texeira Pinto.[57] Mozambique, however, was the major arena of Portuguese colonial warfare. In northern Mozambique Portuguese troops faced a broad coalition of peoples, ranging from the Swahili-speaking Muslim sheikdoms of the coast, such as Angoche, to the fierce slave-raiding Yao in the interior, all well-armed and prepared to wage guerrilla warfare to forestall the spread of Portuguese sovereignty. Resistance in Mozambique's Zambesi valley at first devolved upon the great Afro-Portuguese estates or *prazos*, such as Massangano, seventeenth-century creations of the Portuguese crown whose ruling families had long since "gone native" and set themselves up as autonomous "secondary" states. From the 1880s onwards the Portuguese challenge in the central Mozambique region would be met by the kingdom of Barue on the south bank of the Zambesi. Under the leadership of its royal family, Barue mounted an opposition based on modern European weaponry, and, in a manner reminiscent of Samori's effort at roughly the same time on the other side of the continent, maintained armouries that could repair and copy European weapons.

It was, however, in the south of Mozambique, in the districts of Lourenço Marques and Inhambane, that the most widely heralded encounter between Portugal and its African foes would take place. In the 1890s the hinterland of these two coastal cities lay on the edge of the African kingdom of Gaza. Gaza was another of the realms carved out in the aftermath of the *Mfecane* by migrating Nguni peoples. Its ruling dynasty had been put in place in the 1830s by the warriors of King Soshangane, who had fled north to escape the wrath of Dingaan, the successor to Shaka Zulu. The Gaza Nguni or *Vatuás*, as the Portuguese called them, had over the years brought neighboring Chope and Tonga peoples under their sway and by way of warfare or intermarriage had made their power felt all the way to the banks of the Zambesi and across the western escarpment on to the high veldt of

146

present-day Zimbabwe. Although in the 1880s, under the rule of Soshangane's grandson, Gungunhana, the Gaza Ngunis were weaker than their forebears, they continued to evoke terror among their neighbours, including the small Portuguese population of the coastal cities. Gaza armies on the attack employed the same half-moon *impi* formation as their Zulu or Matabele cousins, and the battles they and their "Nguniized" Tonga subjects fought with Portuguese colonial troops in the 1890s evoked memories of the Anglo-Zulu wars two decades before.

The Generation of 1895

The humiliation imposed upon Portugal by Britain in 1890 aroused a fierce patriotic reaction among soldiers and civil servants as well as among the general public. This upsurge gave rise to a movement to regenerate Portuguese imperialism centred around a remarkable coterie of young colonial military officers known collectively as "the Generation of 1895". The group took its name from its involvement in the campaign of 1895–6 that subjugated the Gaza kingdom, thus launching the long process of bringing Mozambique under effective occupation. Its members and their deeds would have a profound impact upon the evolution of Portuguese colonialism in the next century.

Although the Generation of 1895 was overwhelmingly military in composition and cast of mind, the man who brought it to life and gave it purpose was a civilian, the Royal Commissioner for Mozambique (1895–6), António Enes, a former dramatist and journalist turned politician and civil servant. Despite his pivotal role, however, Enes was not the member of the Generation best known to the public. That distinction belonged to Captain Joaquim Augusto Mousinho de Albuquerque, the aristocratic cavalryman who would gain undying fame in Portugal for his capture of Gungunhana, the king of Gaza, and who would succeed Enes as Royal Commissioner for Mozambique in 1896. Another member, the equally aristocratic Aires de Ornelas, who acted as Mousinho de Albuquerque's chief of staff in 1896, went on to become colonial minister in 1906–7. The governor-general of Mozambique from 1906 to 1910, Alfredo Augusto Freire de Andrade, began his career as Enes's *chef de cabinet*. Enes's aide-de-camp over the same period, Henrique Mitchell de Paiva Couceiro, a veteran of colonial warfare in Angola, would return there to serve as governor general from 1907 to 1909. Eduardo Augusto Ferreira da Costa, who served as a provincial governor in Mozambique in 1896, was as close as the Portuguese came to having a colonial military strategist. Even better known for his theorizing on colonial administration, Ferreira da Costa went on to become governor of Angola a decade later.

The goal of this team was to assure the effective occupation of Mozambique and thus frustrate the acquisitive designs of foreign powers. But, equally importantly, effective occupation was seen as the vital prelude to the colony's economic development, which would, of course, eventually require the mounting of military campaigns over virtually the whole of Mozambique. Again, the aim was not simply to extend Portuguese influence or to establish a Portuguese presence inland as the previous generation might have been content to do. Rather, it was to use military force to crush the various, largely independent, peoples of the interior, and to transform them into obedient contributors of the head tax and productive labourers on the plantations of the chartered companies that were being created to help develop Mozambique.

There had never been any doubt in Portuguese minds that the Gaza kingdom held the key to the effective occupation and economic development of Mozambique.

> The task of bringing permanent order to the province [of Mozambique], had to begin in the south in order to vitiate the pretensions of the South Africa Company [of Cecil Rhodes] and to protect the swelling commercial movement through the port of Lourenço Marques, which was fast becoming the first city of the colony.[58]

This meant war against the Gaza Nguni kingdom of Gungunhana, which had been trying to shore up its independence of the Portuguese by negotiating for arms and moral support from both the British government and Cecil Rhodes's British South Africa Company.

Enes and his entourage believed that the challenge they faced was as much moral and psychological as material. To begin with, the Portuguese had to do battle with an enormous inferiority complex in undertaking to wage war against the Gaza Nguni. They had to struggle against the memories of the sacking of Lourenço Marques by the Zulu cousins of the Gaza Nguni in 1833 and the massacre of a large Portuguese army by the Gaza Nguni themselves in 1834.[59] They also knew that the Gaza Nguni and their subject peoples held them in great contempt. During his tenure as governor of Lourenço Marques province, Mousinho de Albuquerque expressed the Portuguese complex in its mildest form. "The blacks don't obey us, don't respect us, don't even know us over most of this province", he lamented.[60]

But Portuguese feelings ran deeper than this. They were painfully aware that a common Gaza Nguni epithet for them was *galinhas*, or pea fowl. It was for this reason as much as any other that Enes insisted that the bulk of the fighting against the Vatuás had to be done by Portuguese soldiers, the "white cocks", as he called them.[61] The Portuguese also knew that the Gaza Nguni compared them unfavourably to the British next door in South Africa. This had been manifest even before the British defeat of their Zulu cousins. In 1870 a delegation of Gaza Nguni had visited Theophilus Shepstone, the Natal Secretary for Native Affairs, "whose fame was well known to all the Nguni peoples", ostensibly to drum up trade. Shepstone had told his guests that, unhappily, he could do nothing for them because they were Portuguese subjects. The Gaza Nguni had indignantly replied that "they were not Portuguese subjects, for they never had and never would pay tribute to a people they despised".

Umzila [the current Gaza Nguni ruler] is a king [they said]; the Portuguese are women ... Umzila says 'I am like a girl wishing to become a bride, and to be married, like the Zulu and Amaswazi brides have been, to a strong and vigorous husband, who is able by his word [alone] to protect me.'

Shepstone, however, managed to resist this seductive offer. In yet another example of the remarkable solidarity of European powers in the face of African efforts to play them off against each other, he insisted that the Gaza Nguni were, in spite of their protestations, Portuguese subjects, and observed that "civilized white nations are always careful not to interfere with the rights of each other".[62]

War against the Gaza Nguni

The war which now broke out was sparked by an uprising of Tonga chieftaincies against high Portuguese taxes and Portuguese interference in a succession dispute. The rebels unsuccessfully attacked Lourenço Marques in October 1894 and their leaders, war chiefs Mahazul and Matibejana, fled to their nominal overlord, the Gaza Nguni king, Gungunhana, for sanctuary. When he refused to give them up to the Portuguese, Enes resolved to go on the offensive. Although the royal commissioner could now claim that he had been goaded into action, it seems clear that, if the provocation had not occurred, as far as the Portuguese were concerned it would have had to be invented. Before going out to Mozambique, Enes "had sworn to [Portugal's] Queen Amelia that he would bring Gungunhana as a prisoner to the king's feet or never return".[63]

Enes now called upon the king of the Gaza Nguni to surrender the Tonga chiefs who had carried out the attack on Lourenço Marques, and, when Gungunhana refused to do so, a Portuguese invasion force was formed. Its main components were one battalion of infantry from the Second Chasseurs, newly arrived from Portugal, and one from the Third Chasseurs, African troops from Angola under Portuguese officers, a company of militarized police and a large force of colonial cavalry. Fire support would be provided by four mountain guns and two Nordenfelt machine guns. A makeshift fleet of river steamers armed with machine guns would shadow the invasion force from the nearby Incomati River. Local African irregulars were recruited to act as a screen for the Portuguese column as it moved inland.

Enes's decision to take the offensive against the Gaza Nguni was widely viewed as a reckless gamble. Foreign observers believed that the expedition would end in disaster. Sir Hugh MacDonnell, the British minister in Lisbon, warned that defeating Gungunhana was beyond Portugal's powers. The US consul in Mozambique City, Hollis, "exaggerated the strength of Gungunhana as well as the weakness of Portugal, and even after the end of the 1895 campaign, he refused to believe that Gungunhana was beaten".[64] As he sent the 812-man punitive column off into the interior, Enes must have harboured doubts of his own. He had to face logistical problems that would have been incomprehensible to his European counterparts in Africa, such as Lord Cromer, the British proconsul in Egypt. Enes's own assessment of these obstacles, written in the aftermath of the fighting, merits quoting at length:

> Today colonial wars, even more than wars in Europe, are carried on with material well-chosen . . . even luxurious, satisfying all require-ments and minimizing inconveniences. The Portuguese of 1895, how-ever, encamped and fought . . . with scanty matériel almost as primitive as that which their rude ancestors employed in the conquest of the Indies and the exploration of Africa in the fifteenth and sixteenth centuries. . . . Transport, alike of food and munitions, of ambulances and wounded, was by means of wattle-and-mud carts drawn by slow-moving oxen; for tent or shelter there was the starry sky, or a hut in the bush − or, if the ground were damp, one found a bed of branches, a stretcher, or a hammock; for carrying rations, the iron pots used by the Kaffirs, and in place of sanitary and comfortable mobile infirmaries,

huts made of straw and banana leaves . . . while as for rations . . . their principal feature, for soldiers subjected to temperatures in excess of fifty degrees centigrade, were the classic macaroni and chick-peas, seasoned with paprika! . . . Nowadays, no one makes war in this way except ourselves and, perhaps, the Spaniards".[65]

But Enes and the Portuguese also had strengths that were not always apparent when placed alongside such glaring weaknesses. As António José Telo has reminded us, Portuguese infantrymen may not have had tents to crawl into at night or comfortable ambulances to carry off their wounded, but they were equipped with one of the best shoulder weapons available for use in Africa, the French-made Kropatschek magazine rifle.[66] Enemy soldiers would have nothing even remotely comparable to fight back with. The Portuguese troops also enjoyed a monopoly of machine guns and artillery. Even more important, the Portuguese army had friends next door who were willing to help with its most grievous problem area – logistics. The British in Natal sold Enes horses for the cavalry, mules, oxen and wagons and gave him the loan of ships.

The Portuguese possessed another advantage which only Enes seems to have fully appreciated. Portugal stood united behind his forward policy in Mozambique. The government in Lisbon was prepared to commit troops in unprecedented numbers and spend money it often didn't have in unprecedented amounts to attain the objective of a pacified Mozambique. For example, the expeditionary corps deployed to Mozambique in 1895, some 2,190 men, was the largest sent abroad by Lisbon in the nineteenth century. While small in comparison with the forces sent out by the French and, especially, the British, the units dispatched to Mozambique nonetheless amounted to about 14 per cent of Portugal's peacetime army.[67] This level of commitment was the upshot of the British ultimatum of 1890. Enes also seems to have understood that, by contrast, Gungunhana was presiding over an empire which was in the process of coming apart.

It is not possible to accept the late Walter Rodney's argument that the Gaza Nguni state in the 1890s, far from falling into decay, as others have suggested, was merely suffering from "manifestations of old tensions [ethnic and regionalist] that were being eliminated". Or that events demonstrate "the capacity of the [Gaza Nguni] state to survive, to take initiatives and to stabilize the society in the interest of the [Nguni] ruling class and of a broader 'nationality' covering the territory of the Gaza empire".[68] Far from "being eliminated", tensions within the empire appear to have grown in the 1890s. Subject peoples such as the Chope were in a state of near permanent rebellion. At the same time as he was attempting to cope with the Portuguese offensive, Gungunhana also had to send troops to put down a Chope rebellion. Enes was aware of this dissension, and made the encouragement of it one of the cornerstones of his policy. He appears to have succeeded in weaning away so many of the subject peoples of the Nguni that "at the end, Gungunhana's supporters were plainly outnumbered as well as outgunned".[69]

But the Gaza kingdom was suffering from other severe internal problems. Epidemics had decimated many of the cattle herds around which the Gaza Nguni society and economy revolved. Many of the young men who might have fought in Gungunhana's *impis* against the Portuguese were absent in Natal or the Transvaal, working for wages on the farms and in the mines; Mozambique's role as a reservoir of labour for South Africa was already a fact of regional life.

Gungunhana the negotiator

Like his contemporary on the other side of the continent, the Tukolor leader Ahmadu Seku, Gungunhana tried to compensate for his internal weaknesses by negotiating alliances with neighbouring European and African powers. However, although his persistence as a diplomat was remarkable, it was clear that his room for manoeuvre was narrowing. In October 1890 he had scored his greatest, albeit ephemeral, diplomatic triumph, in signing over mineral rights and the railroad right of way in Gaza to Rhodes's British South Africa Company in exchange for an annual subsidy and a thousand rifles. Gungunhana had then tried to gain international recognition of his kingdom's sovereignty by sending two representatives to London to lobby the British during the talks which followed Britain's ultimatum to Portugal in 1890. The British had not been moved. London and Lisbon had agreed that Gazaland was firmly in the grip of the Portuguese and Rhodes's company had subsequently been told by the British to discontinue its activities there. Gungunhana had also attempted to maintain close ties with the Ndebele in Rhodesia and the Swazi across the border in South Africa. One of his elder sisters was married to the Ndebele king, Lobengula. The value of these alliances, however, declined sharply on the eve of the showdown with the Portuguese. The Ndebele had been defeated and their lands occupied by Cecil Rhodes's Pioneer Column in 1893, and the next year the Transvaal Boers had taken over the administration of Swaziland.

But still the king persevered. As Enes's troops manoeuvred closer and closer to his kraal, he continued to parley with a Portuguese envoy, José d'Almeida. In September 1895, as the noose tightened, he dispatched emissaries to Pretoria, Natal and Cape Town, "hoping to gain some kind of protection or alliance". The envoys returned empty-handed. Even so, "to the last day of his reign, [Gungunhana] apparently believed that he could prevent the Portuguese conquest by bluffs, threats or by actually making an alliance with 'other whites'".[70]

Conquest of Gazaland

In the night of 1–2 February 1895 the Portuguese troops sent in pursuit of the "rebel" chiefs camped in square formation on the savannah not far from Lourenço Marques. Toward morning, as the camp was beginning to stir, the soldiers thought they recognized a patrol that had been sent out during the night returning to the square. Instead, the approaching men, some of whom spoke Portuguese and were wearing Portuguese soldiers' garb taken, as it turned out, from the bodies of the missing patrol, hurled themselves against the face of the square occupied by the Third Chasseurs from Angola. As the intruders pushed the surprised Angolans back, breaking the square, bands of men who had been hiding nearby charged forward. Some of the police who had accompanied the expedition now moved over to fill the gap in the square while the Angolans regrouped. Hand-to-hand fighting raged inside the square as the enemy fighters who had penetrated it were dispatched one by one.

> Now all sides of the square poured such a hot fire on the enemy that they dared not advance and began to melt away in the light of day. . . . It was 6a.m. The fighting had lasted an hour and a half. The column had won, as the enemy had conceded by leaving the field. All the same it was undeniable that the column had been on the edge of a terrible disaster.[71]

This mini-engagement at Marracuene, involving some 800 Portuguese and colonial troops and an estimated 3,000 African attackers, although it only involved the Tonga subjects of the Gaza Nguni and not the Gaza Nguni themselves, represented a great triumph for the Portuguese. For Enes, the victory had undermined the Gaza Nguni legend of invincibility and had tipped the all-important moral scales in his favour. Even Walter Rodney was forced to concede that the Portuguese

> won African allies after the demonstration of their effective firepower at Marracuene. . . . Nguni greatness was measured inversely to that of the Portuguese, and the myth of Gaza invincibility suffered as a counter-myth of Portuguese invincibility gained ground.[72]

The initial test successfully passed, Enes could now activate his strategy to subdue the Gaza Nguni. Two columns, one marching from Lourenço Marques in the south and the other from Inhambane in the north, were to converge on Gungunhana's capital, at Manjacaze just beyond the Limpopo.

On 8 September 1895, the southern column was attacked at a place called Magul, by a 6,000-man force under the command of Maguigane, Gungunhana's war chief. But, once again, the attackers were Tonga. Apparently, a Gaza Nguni *impi* was present in the area but was never committed to battle. Warned well in advance by cavalry scouts of the approach of the enemy, the Portuguese had plenty of time to get ready for the assault. They built a *zeriba* or thorn bush barrier around their square, and strung barbed wire around the perimeter. This may be the first time that barbed wire was used for defensive purposes by a European army.[73] Charging forward in the traditional "cow horns" formation, the *impi* of the "Nguniized" Tonga launched attack after attack on the Portuguese square. But, although both Portuguese machine guns broke down, the Kropatscheks would allow the Tonga to come no closer to the square than 200 metres and in the end they were obliged to abandon the field. Enes was overjoyed at the news of the victory. Magul, he said, completed the process Marracuene had begun. A mere 600 "white cocks" and Angolan troops had soundly beaten an enemy force ten times its size. And while the African dead could be counted in the hundreds, only five men in the Portuguese force had been killed. The battle marked a clear turning point in the power relationship between the Portuguese and the Gaza Nguni.[74]

It was now the turn of the northern column. Just before dawn on 7 November 1895, African scouts burst into the Portuguese camp, near the lake of Coolela a few miles from the king's kraal at Manjacaze, shouting that "the impi of Gungunhana" was near. The king, all hope gone of being rescued from disaster by "other white men", had finally consented to commit the Gaza Nguni *impi*. The inevitable Portuguese square numbered 557 Europeans and some 500 African auxiliaries; Gungunhana's army was later thought to have fielded between ten and fifteen thousand men. This long awaited Armaggedon proved to be something of an anticlimax. Douglas Wheeler recounts what happened.

> Some eight mangas [divisions] charged the Portuguese lines in the classic Zulu half-moon or 'horn of the bull' formation and at one point came within yards of breaking the European lines. But the traditional fighting machine, with little training in the use of their [some 3,000] rifles, was mowed down by the Portuguese rifle and machine gun fire. The firing lasted only forty minutes, and within an hour the power and prestige of the Lion of Gaza [Gungunhana] was hopelessly undermined.[75]

The Portuguese suffered some 45 casualties, while the losses of the *impi* ran into thousands. Colonel Rodrigues Galhardo, the Portuguese commander, fresh from the *métropole*, thought the battle resembled a "cotillion".

With the Gaza Nguni army in flight, Galhardo's soldiers marched on the royal kraal and, finding it empty, on 11 November burned it to the ground. Although Gungunhana was still at large, it was felt that he was too discredited to be a threat. Besides, rumour had it that he had escaped across the border into South Africa, to his friends, the English. For António Enes and most of the Generation of 1895, the war was over. Enes returned to Portugal. One of his officers, however, the aristocratic cavalryman Joaquim Mousinho de Albuquerque, had remained behind as military governor of the new province of Gaza. On 12 December 1896 he learned that Gungunhana had not fled the country after all, but had taken refuge in a small village just three days' march away called Chaimite.

The village was a sacred spot to the Gaza Nguni, being the final resting place of their founding father, Soshangane, the grandfather of Gungunhana. Mousinho de Albuquerque now set out to capture the king, and after a forced march of only two days through the heart of enemy country, entered Chaimite.

> Albuquerque entered the village of about thirty huts and, protected by the African troops outside the palisade around the huts, he met no resistance as he sought the chief. Gungunhana's bodyguard had rifles but did not use them as Albuquerque went up to Gungunhana, pushed him to the ground, and told him he was no longer chief of the Shangana [Gaza Nguni] but a coward. . . . In the enclosure the Africans beat their shields with their assegais to applaud the Lion's final degradation before Albuquerque.[76]

But this was not Gungunhana's "final degradation". He was put in irons and, with his wives, transported by steamship to the coast. In March 1896 they were embarked for Portugal, where the king was conveyed through the streets of Lisbon in a Roman-style triumph. Later, he would be transferred, minus his wives, to final exile on the island of Terceira in the Azores. He would die there, baptized Reinaldo Frederico Gungunhana, on 23 December 1906.

His captor, Mousinho de Albuquerque, would go on to be fêted as the greatest Portuguese hero of modern times, and to become a cult figure during the fascist dictatorship of António Salazar. But the remaining years of his African career were not happy ones. He was not a success as High Commissioner in Mozambique and his campaigns against the other recalcitrant African peoples of Mozambique were somehow never as brilliant as his capture of the Lion of Gaza had been. He returned to Portugal still a hero, but rendered virtually unemployable by his arrogance and undisguised contempt for his civilian superiors. "On the afternoon of January 8, 1902, Mousinho committed suicide on a Lisbon streetcar by shooting himself twice in the head".[77]

The first Italo-Ethiopian war

Introduction

"Among the great nations of Europe", writes Italian historian Nicola Labanca, "Italy was the one with the smallest and least productive 'colonial empire'. Leaving aside Germany, whose empire lasted from 1884 to 1918, Italy was also the power that held onto its overseas possessions for the shortest period of time". Despite this, Labanca asserts, the period of Italy's emergence as an imperial power, poorly documented and understudied though it is, constitutes one of the most important phases of the nation's history.[78]

For Ethiopia, the main object of Italy's imperial attentions during the 1880s and 1890s and again in the 1930s, there is no ambiguity about the legacy of Italian imperialism. It was her confrontations with Italy that made Ethiopia a nation-state and carved out a place for her in Africa and the world. The great victory of Ethiopian arms over an Italian invasion force at the battle of Adowa in 1896 not only spared Ethiopia the fate of most of the rest of Africa, writes Ethiopian historian Bahru Zewde, but represented a counter-current to the sweeping tide of colonial domination in Africa [as a whole] . . . The racial dimension was what lent [Adowa] particular significance. It was a victory of blacks over whites. [Adowa] thus anticipates by almost a decade the equally shattering experience to the whites of the Japanese victory over Russia in 1905.[79]

Why did Ethiopia survive?

"How did it happen that Ethiopia, as the only old state in Africa, preserved its independence throughout the era of European colonization?" This question, posed by Sven Rubenson, a Swedish historian of nineteenth-century Ethiopia, remains one of the central questions in modern Ethiopian historiography and, indeed, one of the key questions in the historiography of imperialism in Africa as a whole.[80]

Ethiopian survival used to be explained largely as a function of the country's rugged topography. This view, dear to Arnold Toynbee among others, emphasized "the virtual impregnability of the highland-fastness" as the principal factor in "the survival of [Ethiopia's] political independence in the midst of an Africa under European domination, the survival of her Monophysite Christianity in the borderland between Islam and paganism".[81] This line of argument has few supporters today. While accepting that Ethiopia's rugged terrain favours the defence, more recent scholars have made the interesting observation that this has had surprisingly little influence on the development of the Ethiopian style of warfare, which has been overwhelmingly attack-oriented. "Because of the element of chivalry in their military traditions, the Ethiopians did not normally engage in guerrilla warfare", notes Rubenson, nor did they show much interest in building the kinds of fortification that might have turned their difficult topography into a real advantage. In any case, the notion that the mountainous terrain ever really functioned as a barrier to invading armies appears, upon closer examination, to be a myth. The rugged landscape failed to stop Muslim armies from conquering over half of the Ethiopian kingdom in the sixteenth century; it failed to hold up the British invasion of 1868; and the Italian army traversed some of Ethiopia's most moun-tainous country on its way to the battle of Adowa.[82]

More important to Ethiopia's survival than any material resource was its people's strong sense of cultural and spiritual identity and their willingness to take up arms to safeguard it. This sense had been nurtured over centuries by the struggles to preserve their Orthodox Christian faith against Muslim invaders from the Sudan and the Red Sea coast enclaves held by, first, the Turks, and later the Egyptians.

As well as this sense of spiritual identity, Ethiopians had a well-developed feeling of cultural solidarity. This translated into something that more closely approximated to European-style nationalism than anything found elsewhere in Africa. This nationalism found its highest expression in the country's ancient Christian monarchy, an institution which had been recognized by the European powers since the Middle Ages. This gave Ethiopia a considerable edge over other African polities in its dealings with European nations.

What really saved Ethiopia from falling under colonial rule was the determination with which this heritage of national consciousness, "international recognition", and political/diplomatic skill was developed to meet the new challenges.[83]

The battle of Adowa[84]

No textbook on modern European history, and certainly none on African history, fails to note that the first victory won by less-developed, coloured peoples over the armies of a Western power was the Ethiopian defeat of an Italian army at Adowa in 1896. Few textbooks, even on African history go on, however, to explain what happened at Adowa or why.

There can be no doubt that the Ethiopian victory at Adowa was a significant event not only in African, but also in European history. The rout of the Italians demonstrated to Africans and other colonized peoples that Western soldiers were not invincible. Adowa reminded Italians that their country was poor and weak compared to the other European imperial powers. This heightened an already strong sense of national inferiority in Italy and helped prepare the ground for the coming of Benito Mussolini and his fascist movement, which promised a revival of Italian greatness on the scale of the old Roman empire. The "shame" of Adowa made key sectors of the Italian population, and especially the army, extremely receptive to fascist calls for "revenge" and a reassertion of Italian greatness through imperial expansion.

Background to defeat

The Italian army that marched to defeat at Adowa was relatively large by the standards of nineteenth-century African warfare and, at just over 20,000 men, slightly smaller than Kitchener's host at Omdurman. But the qualities that made Kitchener's army so formidable were sorely lacking in its Italian counterpart. The force that Gen. Baratieri led at Adowa, it must be remembered, was not a professional army like the British; Italy, in fact, was the only European nation to use conscripts to fight its African wars. This posed problems, as John Gooch has observed.

> Overseas war was an intermittent activity for which the [Italian] army was entirely unsuited. A conscript army lacked the hardihood, experience and professionalism which was necessary to tackle colonial wars. The Italian officer corps, unlike its French or British counterparts, was not trained to fight foreign wars. . . . The army fought poorly overseas because it lacked expertise, flexibility and a thorough knowledge of its opponents.[85]

But, as Gooch goes on to point out, the Italian politicians and soldiers who set Baratieri's army on its course to disaster, did not believe that its fighting men needed to be prepared "down to the last gaiter button" in order to defeat their African enemies. Instead, the decision-makers took refuge in "an exaggerated sense of European superiority", a belief that the Italian edge in firepower (an illusion, as we shall see) and the innate martial prowess of the Italian soldier, lineal descendant after all of the Roman legionaries, was sure to bring victory. These were dangerous myths, writes Nicola Labanca, because they served to excuse Italian officers from undertaking anything like serious planning for the campaigns in East Africa. There were no plans worthy of the name for the campaign of 1895–6 which led to Adowa, according to Labanca, only the "Roman myth" and the "myth of the cannon".[86]

Preliminaries to battle

The battle of Adowa was the climax of a 250 km penetration into Ethiopia by an Italian army under the command of General Oreste Baratieri, the governor of the Italian colony of Eritrea. Baratieri had begun withdrawing his army northward in the direction of Eritrea in February 1896, under pressure from a large Ethiopian army under the personal command of the Ethiopian emperor, Menelik II, and his wife, the Empress Taytu. The goal of the Ethiopian force was presumably to reconquer Eritrea, but this would have been beyond its capacities, as we will see. A more reasonable aim would have been to harry the Italians back into Eritrea.

Adowa is in Ethiopia's Tigray province, some 200 km from the Red Sea. Baratieri, the Italian commander, had moved his army from fortified positions westward to intercept the Ethiopian line of march. By 13 February, his army had occupied high ground some 48 km east of Adowa in sight of the Ethiopian army. On the eve of the battle, Baratieri commanded just over 20,000 men – about half of them Eritrean *ascaris* and Tigrayan irregulars. The three brigades of Italian infantry present, some of whose units had only just arrived from Italy, included soldiers from elite units such as the *Bersaglieri* (sharpshooters) and the *Alpini* (Alpine troops).

Baratieri's Italian infantry carried new Vetterli magazine-fed repeating rifles, while the *ascaris*, like indigenous troops in all the European armies, were equipped with the cast-off weapons of the national army, in this case single-shot Vetterli breechloaders. The Italian force fielded 56 artillery pieces, almost all of them slow-firing mountain guns.

Menelik's army, meanwhile, far outnumbered the Italian force, with at least 100,000 men, some 70,000 of whom carried repeating rifles, many of them bought from the French. The rest comprised a force straight out of the Middle Ages, armed with swords, spears, and buffalo-hide shields. Menelik had 46 cannon, fewer than the Italians, but most of them were quick-firing Hotchkiss guns, again provided by the French. Some of the Ethiopian cannon were served by Russian artillerymen, originally sent to Ethiopia to help fend off the Muslims who surrounded the centuries-old Christian kingdom on every side. Most, however, were served by gunners from the kingdom's own artillery corps, which had been functioning since the 1870s, when the Ethiopian army had made its big haul of Egyptian cannon. Menelik's army also fielded a number of machine guns.

The battle which now followed was brought on in part by food shortages on both sides. By 28 February, Italian rations had been cut in half and Baratieri was predicting that food would run out altogether by 2 or 3 March. The Ethiopian army's great size made it impossible for it to be provisioned locally. Some Ethiopian soldiers were away foraging – some a considerable distance away – when the battle of Adowa began on 1 March.

Nonetheless, both sides sought to avoid battle. Three times Baratieri

4. Battle of Adowa, 1 March 1896

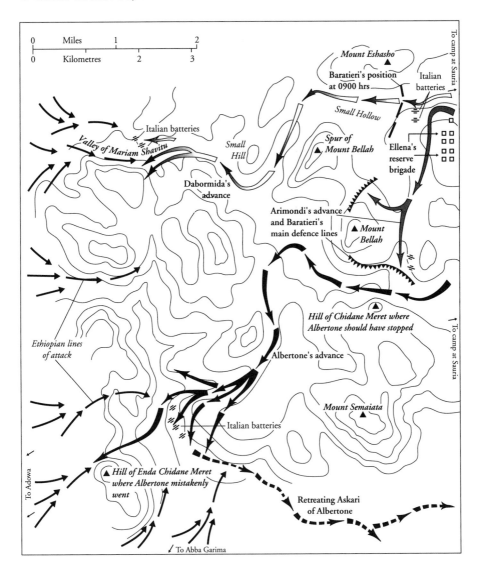

ordered retreat, only to cancel the order each time. Menelik foresaw heavy losses if he attacked the Italian positions, and hoped that by manoeuvring he might be able to draw Baratieri out of his fortified camp. The day before the battle, 29 February – 1896 was a leap year – the Ethiopian king was considering breaking camp.

The battle

Meanwhile, on the same day an informal council of war in the Italian camp resulted in a decision to attack. The commander-in-chief had proposed two options to his brigade commanders – either to sit tight or to retreat – only to find that three of the four favoured neither of these. Brigade commanders Dabormida, Arimondi, and Ellena wanted to attack. General Arimondi expressed contempt for the enemy. The Ethiopians were less numerous than was claimed, he said. There couldn't be more than 50,000 of them. Besides, they were timid and effeminate and incapable of organizing themselves to fight a battle. General Albertone, the fourth brigade commander, favoured sitting tight. A retreat would waste two months of campaigning and open the way to Eritrea. In any case, Menelik's army was on the verge of breaking up, he said.

But Baratieri was also under strong pressure from Rome to attack. On 25 February, he had received a telegram from Italian Prime Minister Francesco Crispi stating:

> This is a military phthisis [wasting disease, e.g. tuberculosis], not a war: small skirmishes in which we always find ourselves facing the enemy with inferior numbers; a waste of heroism without success. . . . We are ready for any sacrifice to save the honor of the army and the prestige of the monarchy.

This, with suggestions from his brigadiers that further retreat might be interpreted as cowardice, convinced the unwilling Baratieri to order an attack. That night at 9pm three brigades – those of Albertone, Arimondi, and Dabormida – moved out, followed at 10.30 by Ellena's reserve brigade. It was apparently Baratieri's plan to occupy high ground midway between his base and the main Ethiopian camp by daybreak. Here he hoped to use his artillery to advantage against the superior enemy.

Thanks to poor maps and communications problems, however, the Italian units managed to get separated on the night march. Albertone's *ascari* brigade ended up occupying a hill 5 km beyond where it was supposed to be and greeted the morning, isolated and exposed to enemy attack. Dabormida's brigade, meanwhile, had wandered far off to the right. By the time shooting commenced around 6am, Albertone on the left flank and Dabormida on the right were out of contact with each other and with headquarters. A wide gap had opened between them which Arimondi's advancing brigade might have filled, but it had got tangled up with Albertone's brigade upon setting out, had halted to let Albertone's men pass, and was not as far forward as it was supposed to be when the shooting began.

The Ethiopians were not taken by surprise. Cavalry scouts had spotted Albertone's *ascaris* on the move and galloped back to spread the alarm. King Menelik's field commander, Ras Mekonnen, came directly from church services to observe the Italian advance. He quickly saw that the three Italian lead columns were widely separated and ordered an attack. The first shot was fired at 6.10am. "Thus began the greatest and bloodiest colonial battle of the century."[87]

The Ethiopians first pinned Dabormida's brigade in place and then delivered a furious assault on Albertone's *ascaris*. For four hours they sent wave after wave of attackers against the Italian mountain guns and the rifle fire of the Eritreans. Around 9am the heavily outnumbered *ascaris* began to retreat, then, with the appearance of even more Ethiopian troops on the field, the retreat became a rout.

Albertone's retreat allowed the Ethiopians to descend *en masse* on the Italian troops in the centre, who had no idea what had happened to Albertone, or Dabormida for that matter, until fleeing *ascaris* from Albertone's wrecked brigade began appearing on their flanks. The brigades of Arimondi and Ellena now came under attack, and Baratieri's headquarters was virtually surrounded. In the midst of the action, the commander lost his pince-nez and had to be led about from place to place on a mule. By noon, realizing that the battle was lost, he ordered a general retreat.

This left Dabormida's brigade isolated on the Italian right and surrounded by enemy troops. Between 1 and 3pm they fought off successive attacks, looking for help that never came. Then, with ammunition running low and fresh Ethiopian troops on the field, a retreat was ordered. The brigade retired in good order, with successive battalions fighting to the last man to cover the withdrawal of the main force. But with the rest of the Italian army now in flight, the escape route for the dwindling survivors of Dabormida's brigade soon closed. Very few of his men came out of the battle alive.

The butcher's bill

Of the 100,000 Ethiopians who fought at Adowa, an estimated 7,000 were killed and 10,000 were wounded. Many of the wounded died in the aftermath of the battle for lack of medical attention. Of the 10,600 Italians who fought at Adowa, 289 officers and 4,600 soldiers were killed, 500 were wounded, and 1,900 taken prisoner. The Eritrean and Tigrayan *ascaris*, meanwhile, lost some 2,000 dead and 1,000 wounded; 1,000 were taken prisoner. In some ways, the dead *ascaris* were the lucky ones. Many of the Eritrean and Tigrayan prisoners, considered traitorous subjects by Menelik and his court, had their right hands and left feet cut off. The prisoners were marched off to Addis Ababa, 500 miles away. Many died *en route*. The survivors were ransomed by the Italian government later in the year.

The legacy of Adowa

Adowa, writes Nicola Labanca, was "one of the most tragic battles in recent European history". Baratieri's army suffered 50 per cent casualties, far higher than those suffered by participants in any other major battle of the nineteenth century. Eylau, the greatest bloodletting of the Napoleonic era, cost the French army casualties of 33.8 per cent, and its losses at Waterloo were just under 30 per cent. "*Macello, carneficina, strage* [butchery, slaughterhouse, slaughter] are the words which recur in the memoirs of the [Italian] combatants" at Adowa.[88]

News of the defeat led to riots in several Italian cities that forced the Crispi government from office. The new government, believing that the public was tired of foreign adventures, opened negotiations with King Menelik. On 26 October 1896, a treaty was signed in Addis Ababa settling the boundaries of Italy's Eritrean colony and nullifying the Italian claim to a protectorate over Ethiopia, which had done so much to set the stage for the tragedy of Adowa.

The returning prisoners of war, and their comrades-in-arms who had been fortunate enough to escape death at Adowa, shared an experience that few other colonial campaigners had known. This experience, Nicola Labanca has written, did not vary according to what unit these veterans had served in or what part of the battlefield they had fought on.

> It was the realization that their belief in their superiority over the "blacks" was an illusion ... A whole swaggering ethos of white conquest was shattered before the very eyes of soldiers who saw thousands of human lives snuffed out in a few hours in a strange and hostile land with no possibility of defence, who succumbed before a people who had been reduced to "semi-savages" in their eyes, who were beaten by an African army depicted right up to the eve of battle as disorganized, poorly armed and incapable of formulating a strategy.[89]

This experience might have been the beginning of a wisdom denied to other, less "fortunate" European imperial powers, but this was not to be. It was, instead, the beginning of a desire for revenge which would culminate in the fascist invasion and conquest of Ethiopia in 1935. The man who would lead this campaign of retribution, the fascist dictator Benito Mussolini, was thirteen years old in 1896. Years later, he would claim that his "whole imagination was engaged" by the tragedy of Adowa so that his "being laboured" for revenge and the restoration of Italian honour.[90]

For victorious Ethiopians, on the other hand, 1 March henceforth would be celebrated as "Adowa Day", the country's national holiday. Adowa would be seen as a victory not only for Ethiopia, but for all of Africa, a development foreseen by Emperor Menelik in a circular to European governments in 1891 protesting against Italian encroachments on his kingdom.

> Ethiopia having existed for fourteen hundred years as a Christian island surrounded by a sea of pagans, I do not intend to listen quietly when governments from distant lands say they will divide up Africa. I trust that God, who has protected Ethiopia until this day, will henceforth protect and increase her, and I have no fear that He will divide her and give her away to other nations.[91]

We should remember, however, that not everyone in Africa looked to Menelik's Ethiopia to be the leader in the struggle against imperialism: the Oromo peoples to the south of Shoa, who were subjected to a particularly brutal conquest by Menelik's armies in the aftermath of Adowa, did not; nor did the Somalis. I.M. Lewis, the British historian of modern Somalia, writes that

> Having defeated a European army (the Italians at Adowa in 1896), [Ethiopia] not only survived the scramble for Africa but gained from it, participating directly in the partition of Somalia and other territory almost as an equal partner . . . If Ethiopia thus entered the modern African stage with all the attributes for playing the leading role, it could not readily dispense with the expansionist dynamic enshrined in its traditional political structure . . . The creator of modern Ethiopia, Emperor Menelik, had in the nineteenth century participated directly with Britain, France and Italy in the dismemberment of the Somali nation and its division into five colonial territories.[92]

The presence of Eritrean *ascaris* and Tigrayan irregulars side by side with the Italians at Adowa should also alert us to another of the major facts of modern

Ethiopian history – the antipathy between the northern peoples, the Eritreans and Tigrayans, and the southerners, the Shoans from the region around Addis Ababa, into whose hands the Ethiopian monarchy had passed in the 1880s. The hostility stems in part from religion, since the Eritreans and at least part of the Tigrayans are Muslims, while the Shoans are Christians. But, in addition, the Shoans were seen as relative upstarts, since for most of its long history Ethiopia had been ruled by northern kings. To the Eritreans and Tigrayans, the Shoans were "country cousins". The most important event in recent Ethiopian history – the three-decade-long civil war which has just ended – featured the same cast: Eritreans and Tigrayans versus the Shoans. Except this time the "country cousins" lost.

The Sudan, 1896–8

Rise of Mahdism

The year 1881 of the Western calendar coincided with the close of the thirteenth century of the Muslim calendar, and it was widely believed in the Sudan that, with the dawn of the new century, God would send a Mahdi, or saviour, to end oppression by the Egyptians, who had re-established control over the Sudan in the 1830s, and to purify the Muslim faith of secular excrescences imposed upon it by the westernized Egyptians and Ottoman Turks. The man who stepped forth to declare himself the Expected Mahdi, Muhammad Ahmad bin Abdallah, was 40 years old, the son of a Nile boat builder and already a holy man of some repute in the valley of the White Nile. As he began to gather disciples about him at his retreat in remote hills west of the Nile, the Mahdi declared that the purpose of his coming forth was to deliver the people of the Sudan from oppression by the Egyptians and their allies among the religious establishment of the Sudan. The westernized state system created by the Turks and imposed on the Sudan by their Egyptian lackeys would be thrown down, he promised, and replaced by a revived *sunna*, the Koran-based community of believers formed by the Prophet Muhammad in the early days of the faith.[93] Because of this, the *Mahdiyya*, the movement launched by the Mahdi in the Sudan, has been seen as a proto–nationalist upheaval, along the lines of the jihad of Abd el-Kader in Algeria a half-century before. Both Sudanese and Western historians have identified the *Mahdiyya* as the beginning of a long struggle to achieve Sudanese independence which bore fruit in the 1960s.

Later, however, the Mahdi would announce that victory over the Egyptians was only the first step in a jihad that was destined to transform the whole Muslim world. This has encouraged some observers to see the Mahdi as the paladin of an Islam that appeared to be increasingly embattled by Christian imperialist powers. In the Balkans and the Middle East the Ottoman Empire of the Turks was reported to be on the verge of collapse. Muslim peoples in the Indian subcontinent and Central Asia were being brought under the rule of the British and Russians. Closer to home, the Muslim peoples of the western Sudan were in the process of being subdued by the French. In Egypt a revolt against the British, in which revivalist Islam had played a role, was crushed in 1882. The *Mahdiyya*, then, has been seen in some circles as a response to Islam's international peril as well as a reaction to developments within the Sudan itself.

It should be stressed, however, that, although he could be said to have accomplished more than they did in the way of state-building and resistance to Western power, this Mahdi was not a Muslim divine and statesman of the stamp of Abd el-Kader or al-Hajj Umar. He was not a *hajji*; he never made the pilgrimage to Mecca. He was not born into the religious elite as his Algerian and Tukolor counterparts had been, nor had he received the kind of formal education which they had. The Mahdi is clearly the most plebeian of the great Muslim resistance leaders of nineteenth-century Africa. Samori, who came from bourgeois stock, was closest to Muhammad Ahmad in origins, although far more cosmopolitan in outlook. When the Mahdi spoke of his jihad as a power for the deliverance of Islam, he was very likely thinking of his own Sudan, a vast land, it must be remembered, and, perhaps, of Egypt. He knew little of the outside world.[94]

However, like Abd el-Kader and Umar, the Mahdi realized early on that military force was crucial to the achievement of his religious agenda. And, like them, he turned out to be a more than passable military strategist. Like Umar's *talaba*, the religious disciples of the Mahdi, the *ansar*, formed the nucleus of his army (and gave their name to it). The primary mission of this army was to expel the Egyptians from the Sudan. This was accomplished in three stages, which came to a close just before the Mahdi's death in a typhoid epidemic in 1885.

The first stage was the capture in 1882 of the main Egyptian military base west of the Nile, at El-Obeid. This was a critical event in the development of the *ansar*. Their first attack on the fortress, "wild, unorganized charges of men armed with swords, spears and sticks", was repulsed by defenders behind thick walls armed with modern Remington rolling-block rifles. On the advice of his second-in-command and eventual successor, the

Khalifa Abdallahi, the Mahdi revised his strategy and undertook a siege of El-Obeid, which ended in success. And, like Abd el-Kader, al-Hajj Umar and Samori, once having learned through bitter experience how devastating European weapons of war could be, the Mahdi recognized the need to turn part of his army into a modern infantry force equipped with Western firearms.

> This force was known as the *jihadiyya* and was in fact largely recruited from [Egyptian] government troops . . . [black soldiers from the Nubas and southern Sudanese tribes] who had been captured in battle by the Ansar . . . Thus the Mahdist army now included, besides the ill-disciplined tribal levies with their primitive weapons, a nucleus of trained troops, armed with firearms and continuing under the Mahdi the life of professional soldiers which they had learned under the Egyptians.[95]

This may be the moment to re-emphasize the importance to the military history of Africa of the black Sudanese soldier, yet another of the continent's "martial races". The professional core of the Mahdist *ansar*, these soldiers also comprised the best units of the Egyptian army that marched into the Sudan with General Kitchener in 1896. It was a rock-hard stand by Kitchener's Sudanese battalions under General Hector MacDonald that clinched the battle of Omdurman for the British against the Mahdists in 1898. Finally, black Sudanese troops were the elite of the German *Schutztruppe* in Tanganyika up to the First World War.

In the second phase of the campaign to drive the Egyptians out of Egypt, the *jihadiyya*, placed under the command of Abu Anja, one of the Mahdi's best generals, quickly proved its value. When British Colonel William Hicks invaded the Sudan at the head of an Egyptian army of 8,500 men in November 1883, it was stopped by "a murderous fire" from the *jihadiyya*. Although its three squares bristled with machine guns and artillery, Hicks's force was surrounded and wiped out at the battle of Shaykan. The victory was the product of the Mahdi's careful planning.

> He allowed the country and climate to fight for him; he waited with serene patience until exactly the right moment, and then struck with devastating force. If only the Mahdists had continued to follow these same tactics, admirably suited to desert warfare, in their later campaigns, their results might have been very different.[96]

In 1884, following Hicks's catastrophic defeat, the British and Egyptians, who still held the Nile and the city of Khartoum at the confluence of the Blue and White Niles, decided to pull out of the Sudan. The decision was made in London as part of a general retrenchment of empire. The person sent to extricate the British and Egyptians from the Sudan was General Charles George Gordon, better known as "Chinese" Gordon for his earlier exploits as a soldier and propagator of the Christian faith in China. Gordon, who had subsequently seen service as governor of Equatoria province in the extreme south of the Sudan, was one of the most famous public figures of his day in Britain and a particular favourite of Queen Victoria. He was what a later generation would have called a "muscular Christian", the kind of man who went forth to civilize the heathen with a pistol in one hand and the Bible in the other. His job was to wind up the British presence in the Sudan but he dithered inexplicably in Khartoum and got himself and his small native army besieged. After 317 days under siege, as efforts by a British army under Lord Wolseley to relieve the city stalled, Khartoum was taken by storm. Aware of Gordon's immense popularity in Britain, the Mahdi had offered to spare his life as the siege lines tightened. He was furious when Gordon's head was brought to him in seeming triumph after the Mahdists' final assault on Khartoum.[97] The death of "Chinese" Gordon was soon made known to a stunned Britain, and an aggrieved Queen Victoria was not alone in vowing that his death would not go unavenged.

Vengeance would wait, however, for over ten years. Retribution was not by itself reason enough for adopting a policy of intervention in the Sudan. Other, more important, considerations had to become manifest before a British government would feel obliged to adopt a "forward policy" in the area. Those considerations gradually surfaced over the decade following Gordon's death. What finally convinced the British government to reconsider its Sudan policy was the mounting evidence of French intentions to occupy the region. Other imperial rivals also had made threatening noises about taking the Sudan, but they do not seem to have been taken as seriously. The Germans in Tanganyika, Leopold in the Congo, and the Italians as part of their designs on Ethiopia, had all asserted vague claims to the Nile valley, but only France seemed prepared to take action to buttress its claims.

Push came to shove in 1896, with the spectacular Ethiopian victory over Italy at Adowa. Britain had set up the Italians as their proxies in the Horn of Africa and had hoped for an Italian victory in order to counter French influence at the Ethiopian court. She now concluded that the Sudan lay open to a Franco-Ethiopian invasion. British suspicions were not far wrong; French officials in Addis Ababa did propose just such a venture to the Ethiopian king, Menelik II.

Britain now reasoned that the Sudan had to be defended – not because the region itself was valuable, but because controlling it guaranteed a "defence in depth" of the Suez Canal and the life-line to India, Britain's "jewel in the crown". The canal passed by Egypt, and it had been decided some time earlier that for this reason Egypt had to be British. If Egypt had to be British, so, too, did the Sudan, Egypt's back door and the source of the Nile which made Egypt prosperous. In 1896, the year of Adowa, a British-trained army was formed in Egypt for the purpose of reconquering the Sudan. When it finally marched south, the new Anglo-Egyptian army would be commanded by Major-General Horatio Herbert Kitchener, a veteran of the Indian Army and of the earlier fighting in the Sudan. Kitchener took the title of *Sirdar*, an Indian term for "leader". In the Sudan, meanwhile, the death of the Mahdi in 1885 had brought to power his second-in-command and chosen successor, the Khalifa Abdullahi.

Kitchener of Khartoum

Kitchener's reconquest of the Sudan would not be a whirlwind affair, the sort of campaign Wolseley might have waged. Kitchener was an engineer and knowledgeable enough of the Sudan and the "Dervishes" to know the price for being rash. Thus, two and a half years would pass before the Sudan would be recovered and Gordon's death avenged. Kitchener's progress south was slow and methodical. As his army marched, Egyptian workers laid track for a Sudan Military Railway alongside the Nile. Gunboats were brought along as well, which had to be dismantled at every cataract in the Nile and then reassembled. In early June 1896 the Anglo-Egyptian army crossed over into the Sudan. On 7 June at Firket in northern Sudan the *Sirdar* defeated a Mahdist army sent to turn him back and went on to reconquer the province of Dongola, next to the Egyptian frontier.

Over two years of railway building and steamboat disassembly and reassembly would remain before Kitchener and his army would see the site of Gordon's martyrdom. The deeper the army went into the Sudan the more worried Kitchener became about the size and composition of his force. Despite its superb equipment and the logistical marvel he had created with his railway and steamboat service, the *Sirdar* feared that his army might not be up to the task ahead of it. It needed reinforcements, he felt, particularly British reinforcements. He had only four British battalions; the majority of his troops were Egyptian and Sudanese infantry. The closer the army got to Khartoum, the more nervous Kitchener became. Could his soldiers be trusted? After all, most of them *were* Muslims, like the Mahdists. The anxious general wired London for reinforcements for his British battalions. He received an additional infantry brigade and a regiment of cavalry. On April 1898 after a hard-fought battle against a Mahdist force sent to block his approach at Atbara, on the Nile to the north of Khartoum, Kitchener wired for and received an additional British brigade. The advance was resumed in early August, and by the end of the month the Anglo-Egyptian-Sudanese army was approaching Omdurman, the Mahdist capital across the river from Khartoum. The *khalifa* made no further effort to block Kitchener's advance, but was seen to be assembling a large army in the vicinity of Omdurman. The two armies would fight the first day of the battle of Omdurman on 1 September 1898. On that day the 23-year-old reporter–soldier Winston Churchill was out ahead of Kitchener's army with a scouting party from his unit, the 21st Lancers. Thomas Pakenham, in his book *Scramble for Africa*, wrote that Churchill was

> staring through his binoculars like a racegoer at the moment when the horses come under starter's orders. What a spectacle, he wrote later, "Never shall I see such a sight again . . . I was in great awe." There, only four miles away across the ribs of the sandy plain, lay the Khalifa's Omdurman, a low straggling line of mud walls, crowned by the white, egg-shaped dome of the Mahdi's tomb. . . . In front of the mud walls, breasting the low ridge, like the Norman army marching into battle on the Bayeux Tapestry, the Khalifa's army was marching swiftly towards him. Perhaps there were 50,000 spearmen, swordsmen and riflemen concentrated on a front only four miles wide, under hundreds of wildly waving banners. "The whole side of the hill seemed to move," wrote Churchill later, "and the sun, glinting on many hostile spear-points, spread a sparkling cloud."

Marching to meet the Khalifa's host, but cut off from their view by Jebel Surgham, the hill at Churchill's back, was Kitchener's army, composed of six brigades of British, Egyptian and Sudanese infantry, some 25,000 men in all. Pakenham continues

> It was not merely the spectacle that held Churchill spellbound, it was the marvellous anachronism that struck him, from his godlike view-point on the black hill. Who would ever again see two great armies, two great worlds, marching into collision on a battle-field a few miles square: Kitchener's industrial world of the twelve-pounder and the

5. The Battle of Omdurman

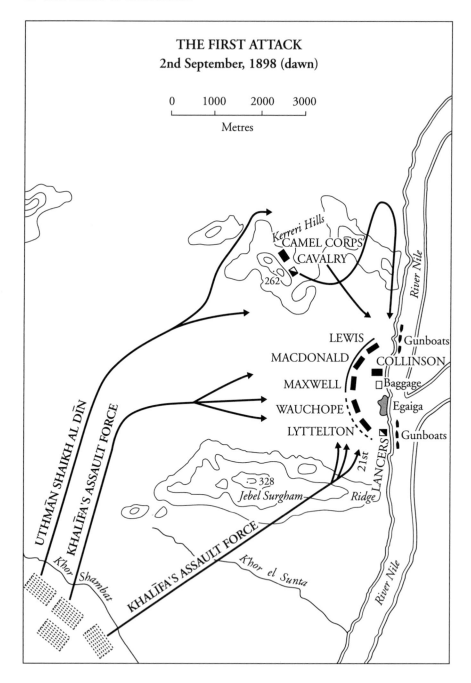

THE FIRST ATTACK
2nd September, 1898 (dawn)

5. The Battle of Omdurman

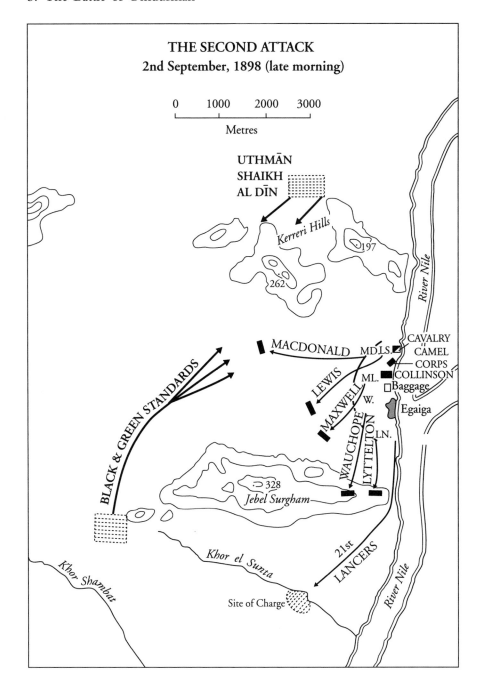

THE SECOND ATTACK
2nd September, 1898 (late morning)

Lee-Metford magazine rifle, against the Khalifa's world of the spear, the banner, and the patched jibbah?

These are splendid word-pictures, but they sacrifice accuracy for colour. The Khalifa's army was not quite as medieval as Churchill and Pakenham have portrayed it. The Mahdists carried some 15,000 shoulder arms into battle at Omdurman, a few less than one for every two soldiers. There were plenty of muzzle-loaders, and some Remingtons and Martini-Henrys, many of them poorly maintained. Barrels had been allowed to become rusty or clogged, and firing pins were covered with dust or dirt. Many soldiers had shortened the barrels of their rifles to make them easier to carry, with calamitous effects on their accuracy and range. Nor was there any tactical sense of how these weapons might best be employed. The riflemen were no longer formed into separate units, as the old *jihadiyya* had been, but were mixed in with the spearmen and swordbearers. It was at once obvious that the function of the riflemen was not to kill the enemy, but to provide cover for the spear and sword carriers, enabling them, like Zulu warriors, to come to grips with the enemy at close quarters. To accomplish this, the volume of fire was more important than accuracy. Like the Ashanti musketeers of the 1870s, Mahdist soldiers fired from the hip, standing or running, not from the shoulder (firing from a prone position was considered cowardly).

Although the Mahdists had good cannoneers (Egyptians captured in earlier battles) and eight modern Krupp guns, artillery played almost no role in their battle plan. Part of the problem was that the *Khalifa's* officers saw cannons as siege, not anti-personnel, weapons. Besides, there were few shells for the big guns and most of those were locally-made and substandard. The rounds produced a loud bang, but little else. The Mahdists also possessed several machine guns – Gatlings, Gardners and Nordenfelts captured from Hicks's column in 1883 – but none of these found their way to the battlefield, for lack of ammunition and trained crews to serve them.

Fighting on the first day was limited to British shelling of the city of Omdurman. The tomb of the Mahdi was among the targets demolished by the British gunners, who were giving a trial run to a new high explosive called lyddite. In the meantime, Kitchener's infantry had built a *zeriba* around their camp and tucked in for the night. About an hour before dawn, cavalry patrols reported that the Mahdist army was on the move and was headed straight for the British camp. Here at some length is Thomas Pakenham's account of the battle that followed:

> Within half an hour [the Mahdists'] flags and spears broke the skyline over the black hill to the southwest. . . . The first phase of the battle was so unequal that it seemed more like an execution. Two divisions

of the Khalifa's army ... put their faith in Allah and charged straight at the British camp. They wore the holy uniform of the patched jibbah (plus, in some cases, chain mail). They advanced in an enormous crescent, brandishing their spears and their texts from the Koran, and chanting, like the muezzin from the minaret, "La Illah illa'uah was Muhammad rasul Allah" ("There is but one God and Muhammad is his Prophet"). The shells knocked holes in their lines, but the holes were soon filled. From 2,000 yards the British infantry started volley-firing with their smokeless Lee-Metfords. Still the Dervishes came on steadily, now running, now walking. The Maxims then joined in. At 800 yards' range the Egyptian and Sudanese battalions followed with their Martini-Henrys, firing black powder. ... Within a few years, the battle formations at Omdurman would seem hard to credit. British infantry were firing volleys shoulder to shoulder, with the front rank kneeling and the rear rank standing, just as redcoats had fought at Waterloo. But out in the open desert the Mahdists had met a death that was modern enough. There they lay, as the smoke cleared, shot and mangled, 2,000 men at least in crumpled heaps. Thousands more were retreating, wounded. Not a single man had survived to reach the British firing line before the Sirdar's voice was heard shouting, "Cease fire! Please! Cease fire. What a dreadful waste of ammunition!"[98]

Most readers, even those whose knowledge of it is limited to scenes from the film *Four Feathers*, are unlikely to be surprised by the foregoing account of the battle of Omdurman. It is a variation on what has become the standard Western version of the battle and, as such, it is desperately in need of updating in the light of impressive new evidence from the other side of the battle line. To begin with, as Ismat Zulfo has convincingly argued, the Mahdist strategy for the second day of the battle of Omdurman was not as mindless as it has been made to appear. Although his generalship left a great deal to be desired, the *Khalifa* did have a plan for the battle that went well beyond the headlong charge recounted by Pakenham and others. The *Khalifa's* design has been obscured in Western accounts of the battle by the tendency to treat the two Mahdist divisions that attacked Kitchener's lines and the two divisions which stayed hidden behind Jebel Surgham as separate entities. In fact, they were intended to work together to spring a gigantic ambush on the British army.

One of the two divisions that moved in the direction of the British lines in the early morning of the second day of battle had veered off to the north without trying to engage the enemy. The second division, by contrast, marched directly at the British. It was not, however, the intent of the *Khalifa* that this second division should itself try to come to grips with the enemy. Its role was, rather, to try to draw Kitchener's army out from behind its *zeriba*, so that, strung out on the plain, its artillery in movement, lured away from the protection of the deadly fire of the armed steamers in the river, it could be attacked by the remainder of the Mahdist force, the division that had veered off to the north and the two divisions concealed behind the Jebel Surgham.

On the face of it, this was a sound enough battle plan. It went awry, according to Zulfo, not because it was badly conceived but because of "the Khalifa's fatal miscalculation of the enemy's firepower [and] his insufficiently detailed knowledge of the enemy". The last point first. The Mahdists had not reconnoitred the ground before attacking the British and had no real sense of their position. They had not realized, for example, how close the infantry was to the protecting fire of the steamboats in the Nile. Secondly, the Mahdist leadership had not understood that the *Sirdar's* army was unlikely to leave the security of its *zeriba* to grapple with the attacking formation so long as it could pick it apart with volley fire at 2,000 yds and rely upon machine gun fire to finish the job should the survivors be foolish enough to perservere. "The nub of the problem was leadership", wrote Zulfo. All of the good generals were dead or engaged elsewhere.[99]

The second great fallacy in the traditional account of Omdurman is that the battle is made to end with the slaughter of the Mahdists outside the *zeriba*. What happened after this, when Kitchener's army left the shelter of its *zeriba* and moved in the direction of Omdurman, is probably more important than the first phase of the engagement.

Having repulsed the attack on his left and centre with great loss to the enemy, the *Sirdar* appears to have thought the battle was over and, eager to avoid a street fight for Omdurman, tried to put his troops between the enemy and the capital. This meant marching his army across the front of the Mahdist force, the Black and Green Standard divisions, lurking behind the Jebel Surgham heights. This large force, it should be recalled, had not been committed to the earlier battle and was still fresh. There is some doubt about whether or not Kitchener knew the Black and Green Standard divisions were present. If he did know, writes a prominent historian,

> he took a serious military risk in marching his army across the front of an undefeated enemy and exposing it to the peril of a flank attack. At best, it is clear that Kitchener misjudged the situation and underesti-

mated the courage and fighting power of his opponents. He thought he had already won the battle; in fact, he had won only the first phase.[100]

Kitchener managed to avoid disaster as the attacks upon his strung-out divisions were not co-ordinated. The Black and Green Standards had been expected to go into the attack together, but failed to do so, giving their target, MacDonald's Sudanese brigade, time to set up. The third Mahdist assault force, the division that had passed in front of Kitchener's position earlier in the day, only arrived on the battlefield when the other two Mahdist divisions had already been beaten off. Wreathed in smoke from their Martini-Henry black-powder rifles, MacDonald's troops held firm against assaults from three different directions. Still, it was a close-run affair. After the battle was over, it was discovered that the Sudanese had an average of only two rounds a man left. Writes the Sudanese historian, Ismat Zulfo,

> The soldiers of the Sudanese battalions were the heroes of the [British] side. It was MacDonald's brigade that saved the situation and bore the brunt of a three-pronged attack from the Khalifa's army, from three different directions within the course of half an hour, without yielding an inch.

After the battle, Winston Churchill offered his own kind of homage to the Sudanese soldier of MacDonald's brigade: "To the faithful loyalty of a dog, he added the heart of a lion. He loved his officer, and feared nothing in the world."[101]

The many thousands of Mahdists dying and wounded on the battlefield received no aid from the British, who simply turned their backs and marched away. This gives an indication of the depth of feeling in the ranks about the death of Gordon. Kitchener quickly took control of Omdurman, and two days later summoned delegates from every unit attached to his force to attend a religious service in what was left of Gordon's palace in Khartoum across the Nile. The tomb of the Mahdi was desecrated and a rumour began to make the rounds to the effect that the *Sirdar* had had his skull made into a drinking cup. When the Queen heard about this, she sternly ordered Kitchener to give up his grisly trophy. Whether the rumour was actually true or the invention of one of the *Sirdar's* troopers will probably never be known.

The defeat at Omdurman for all practical purposes put an end to the *Mahdiyya*. The *Khalifa* escaped to the west with a small band of followers and would remain at large until 1899, when he was killed.

Fashoda

Background

In the months following the British victory at Omdurman, what remained of the Mahdist army was harried from pillar to post in the Sudan, until the whole region had been pacified and brought firmly under what was called "the Anglo-Egyptian condominium". But hunting down the remaining Mahdists was not the only task now facing Kitchener. He also had – quite unexpectedly – to deal with the French.

The confrontation on 18 September 1898 between British and French forces at Fashoda on the upper Nile some 500 miles south of Khartoum is the classic symbol of the "Scramble for Africa" and of the risks it posed for international peace. The meeting at Fashoda of Major Jean-Baptiste Marchand of the French marines and General Horatio Herbert Kitchener of Her Britannic Majesty's Anglo-Egyptian army was the culmination of several years of dreams of conquest, marching and countermarching armies, and diplomatic manoeuvring. The dreams, some fantastic to the point of madness, included the British one, personified by the Anglo-South African millionaire and imperial politician Cecil Rhodes, of a solid bloc of British territory from the southern tip of Africa to the north, "from Cape to Cairo"; and the French dream of a continuous belt of French territory from Senegal on the Atlantic across the Sudan to the Red Sea. But dreaming was not confined to Frenchmen and Britons. Leopold, King of the Belgians, feudal ruler of the Congo Free State, had dreamed of extending his sway from the Atlantic across the Congo basin and then northeast to the Red Sea. The Germans and Italians had indulged more modest dreams. The Germans, who were already in possession of Tanganyika in East Africa, had wished to control the nearby Great Lakes district and with it the headwaters of the Nile. The Italians, who had ensconced themselves in Eritrea on the Red Sea, had nourished plans to control neighbouring Ethiopia and beyond it the Nile valley. Those plans had received a setback in 1896, when the Ethiopians defeated the Italian army at Adowa, but they had by no means been abandoned.

Somehow, the fantastic schemes all came to centre on the region of the headwaters of the White Nile and, ultimately, on an obscure village in the southern Sudan: Fashoda.

By the time Kitchener and Marchand met at Fashoda in September 1898, however, their two countries were the only real contestants left in the field. The Germans had dropped out of the running and the Italians, as we have seen, had been forced to the sidelines. This left King Leopold, who remained a contender almost down to the final gun. His armed force in the Congo, the *Force Publique*, had assembled a large army to march into the valley of the upper Nile and claim it for him. At the last moment, however, the army's African troops had mutinied, killed their Belgian officers, and taken to the bush. This effectively eliminated Leopold from the upper Nile sweepstakes.

The long march

Kitchener and Marchand had begun marching toward the rendezvous at Fashoda from opposite corners of Africa at roughly the same time. Kitchener had been first off the mark in March 1896. It had taken the Anglo-Egyptian army under his command until September 1898, two and a half years later, to bring the Mahdi's army to bay at Omdurman. This had been due largely to the *Sirdar's* insistence on building a railroad parallel to his line of march, and on bringing a flotilla of gunboats over the cataracts of the Nile.

Marchand, meanwhile, had begun his march in June 1896 from the port of Loanga in Gabon on the Atlantic coast, but, whereas Kitchener had some 25,000 troops under his command, Marchand left Loango with only ten French officers and 200 *Tirailleurs Sénégalais*. The young and impetuous Marchand had been told by Paris that he should limit the size of his army. A larger force might spark resistance among the African peoples across whose lands he would have to march on his 2,500-mile trek to the upper Nile and, besides, would not be needed.

Marchand's march on Fashoda was being co-ordinated by the French Foreign Ministry with a descent on the upper Nile valley from the opposite direction by a Franco-Ethiopian force led by a French nobleman, Marquis Charles de Bonchamps. This would help to even up the odds. The French government also expected that Marchand would be welcomed with open arms by the followers of the Mahdi, who would see his troops as allies against the advancing Anglo-Egyptian army. If this strategy was to be successful, Marchand first had to get to Fashoda, 2,500 long miles away across some of the most treacherous terrain in Africa. The marine officer did not make it any easier on himself, his men, or their numerous African porters by taking along tons of trade goods, cases of guns and ammunition, crates of wine and champagne from Paris, and a steamboat, which had to be dismantled periodically along the way. Despite this immense impedimenta and the long delays caused by floods, droughts or mass desertions by overworked porters, the French column managed to straggle into Fashoda before Kitchener got to Omdurman. Its arrival on 10 July 1898 was not auspicious. The last 500 miles had in some ways been the worst part of the long trek. Fashoda is located on the edge of the *sudd*, the trackless papyrus swamp which covers much of the southern Sudan. Marchand's force and its vast paraphernalia had to be transported through this morass in canoes. The steamboat, the "Faidherbe", had got lost and came puffing in to Fashoda over a month later.

Worse was to follow. The Franco-Ethiopian force under Bonchamps was nowhere to be seen when Marchand arrived. In fact, Bonchamps had made it to the Nile rendezvous as planned, but had been obliged to turn back, his soldiers starving and the officers down with fever. Nor were the Mahdists happy to see Marchand and his men. On 25 August, as Kitchener's army was on the last leg of its march on Omdurman, Marchand's little band was attacked by a force of between 1,200 and 1,500 Mahdists. The attackers descended on Marchand's outpost in rowing boats towed by two of "Chinese" Gordon's old steamboats, with the apparent aim of making an amphibious landing. Fortunately for Marchand and his *tirailleurs*, there was some advance warning.

Like Kitchener's British troops at Omdurman a few days later, they enjoyed the advantage of carrying magazine rifles with an accuracy well beyond the range of the enemy's weapons. The boats never got near the shore. When the flotilla beat a retreat to the north later in the day, over half the Mahdist attackers were dead or dying.

Kitchener meets Marchand

On 18 September 1898 Kitchener arrived at Fashoda with some 1,500 troops, including a company of Cameron Highlanders, a fleet of gunboats, Maxim guns and artillery. Speaking in proper but heavily accented French, the *Sirdar* informed Marchand that he was trespassing on land which belonged to Egypt, and must leave. The marine major replied that the upper Nile region had been vacated by the Egyptians over a decade earlier and thus no longer belonged to them. Kitchener replied that he had not come to debate the fine points of international law. "I cannot argue these points", the great man said, "but I would suggest you consider the preponderance of the force at my disposal". Marchand, perhaps braver than he was prudent, replied: "Until we receive orders to retire we shall not haul down our flag but are ready to die at our posts". Kitchener closed the interview by remarking, "But this situation could lead to war".

Their unpleasant duty done, the two men allowed the better side of their natures to shine through. Kitchener invited Marchand and his officers aboard his "flagship" for a round of lukewarm whiskies-and-sodas. That afternoon, it was the turn of Marchand and his staff to entertain the British. Being French, the first thing they had done upon arriving at Fashoda in June was to lay out an herb and vegetable garden, plant flowers, and scrounge chickens from the local population. Now the French officers could proudly show Kitchener around their flower garden and offer him fresh vegetables and roast capon, washed down with the champagne they had themselves transported all the way from the Atlantic coast. It was all very convivial, but when the British departed the next day, they left behind a detachment of 600 Sudanese soldiers and a warning that they would return and that it would be preferable if Marchand were not still there when they did.

To the brink of war

The fate of the southern Sudan now passed from the hands of the soldiers into those of the diplomats. It was perhaps fortunate for the cause of world peace that France was embroiled in a serious domestic crisis when the news of the confrontation at Fashoda reached the newspapers in Europe. The crisis, which seemed to threaten the very existence of the French Third Republic, was the famous Dreyfus Affair. Had it not been for this domestic political crisis, France and Britain might well have gone to war over Fashoda. As it was, the diplomatic duel which followed on the heels of the meeting at Fashoda between Kitchener and Marchand pitted two of the cleverest and most nationalistic politicians in Europe – Prime Minister, Lord Salisbury and Foreign Minister, Théophile Delcassé. Salisbury came of one of Britain's oldest aristocratic families; his ancestor, Robert Cecil, had served as foreign secretary to Queen Elizabeth I, back in the late sixteenth century. He was determined that the Anglo-Egyptian Sudan, as it was to become known, should remain under British control. His interest was purely strategic. The Anglo-Egyptian Sudan lay on the flank of the Red Sea link in the crucial lifeline to British India; to allow it to fall into other hands would invite the breaking of that lifeline.

The French Foreign Minister, Delcassé, was not an aristocrat like Lord Salisbury. He came from a small provincial town and had started out as a journalist. He felt equally strongly that France should control the headwaters of the Nile. There was, to begin with, that dream of a continuous belt of French territory from the Atlantic to the Red Sea. In addition, Delcassé, like many of his colleagues in the French government, still resented the way the British had pushed France out of Egypt in the 1870s. He believed the French had more of a right to be in Egypt than the British. Had Bonaparte not brought the blessings of the French Revolution – "liberty, equality, and fraternity" – to Egypt in the waning years of the eighteenth century? Hadn't the great Egyptian modernizer, Mehemet Ali, turned to France for advice and technical assistance in the 1830s and 1840s? Was it not France who had built the Suez Canal? After all this, to concede to Britain the control of the Suez Canal company and, hence, its influence in Egypt – and this the result of a British bribe to the Egyptian ruler! – was intolerable and could not be accepted as final.

Britain and France came close to war in the closing months of 1898. At one point French troops were actually entrained for the Mediterranean ports. Salisbury replied by ordering the mobilization of the Royal Navy and of its reserve fleet in order to intercept any movement of French troops to Africa. This, together with the worsening of the domestic political crisis in France, led Delcassé to step back from the brink of war.

In fact, all this opened the way to a diplomatic revolution in Europe: the transformation of the Anglo-French rivalry into the Anglo-French *Entente* or alliance in 1904. The crux of this alliance was the settling of differences in Africa, Britain receiving a free hand in Egypt and France in Morocco.

Conclusion

In their classic study, *Africa and the Victorians: the Official Mind of Imperialism*, Gallagher and Robinson remark that:

> At first sight there is a certain absurdity about the struggle for Fashoda. The massive advance of Kitchener's army took two and a half years, and it ended by browbeating a few men marooned by the side of the Nile. There was a strange disproportion between ends and means. . . . A still deeper absurdity seemed to lie in the French speculation about damming the river and in the labours of the British to stop them. Even Marchand himself came to see that the scheme was hare-brained, for it turned out that there was no stone within miles of

6. Africa after the scramble, 1912

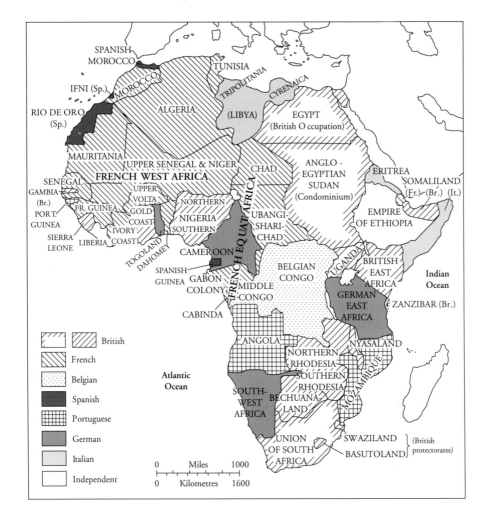

Fashoda. To this extent, the great rivalry for the Upper Nile was based on a myth. The greatest absurdity of all might seem to be that for two months two great powers stood at the brink of war for the ownership of the sudd and desert of the Upper Nile.[102]

Chapter Five

Ominous portents, 1898–1914

Introduction

There is a more "modern" feel to the colonial wars in Africa after 1900. To begin with, they are on a grander scale. The era of "small wars" appears to be over. It is true that Lugard's conquest of Northern Nigeria in 1902–3 and the suppression of the 1905–6 rising in German East Africa were both accomplished with small numbers of troops, but the overall thrust of the period is toward the employment of relatively large armies, almost on the scale of European warfare. The Second Boer War, at the very outset of the period, was the biggest war yet waged in Africa, involving some 440,000 British and colonial troops on one side and just under 90,000 Boers on the other.[1] (These figures do not include the many Africans employed in both armed and unarmed capacities by the two sides.) In Libya, Italy found herself obliged to commit 100,000 troops to what had been originally thought of as an "easy" conquest. This was nearly three times the number projected by the Italian general staff at the outset of the war in 1911.[2] The French, finally in 1914, had 74,800 troops under arms in Morocco, compared with only 3,000 when their invasion of the country had begun in 1907.[3]

Part of the reason for this is that the technological gap, so prominent a decade earlier, appears to have narrowed somewhat. Again, the Fulani armies faced by Lugard in Northern Nigeria and the various African tribes involved in the Tanganyika rebellion, neither of which possessed much in the way of firearms, are exceptions to this trend. The Boers, of course, are the prime example of the tendency toward better insurgent armament. Their mounted infantrymen were equipped with up-to-date magazine rifles which they knew how to use with devastating effect. The Boers were also one of the few enemies faced by European armies in Africa who possessed artillery. Reminiscent of the Boers were the Herero and Nama peoples of South West Africa, who also fought as mounted infantry. They were generally as

185

well armed as the Boers and were equally proficient marksmen, as the Germans who fought them in the 1904–7 war were quick to attest.

More important than improved armament, however, is the change in African strategy and tactics. The trend is decisively away from the murderous set-piece battles of the past and in the direction of guerrilla warfare. The Boers in the third phase of the 1899–1902 war, the Herero and Nama, the Libyans and the Moroccans, all waged guerrilla war, which goes a long way toward an explanation of why the European armies engaged in Africa during this period were so large. Despite the forces arrayed against them, the guerrillas enjoyed considerable success. The Boers tied down a huge British army, which, in the end, was forced to employ draconian tactics, much criticized at home and abroad, to overcome them. The Italians were still trying to "pacify" the Libyan hinterland when they entered the First World War in 1915; the "pacification" of Libya would only be completed under the Fascist regime in 1932. The French invasion of Morocco, begun in 1906, followed a similar course. The last Moroccan guerrilla band surrendered to the French in 1934.

The European powers employed what earlier generations of colonial soldiers might have considered extraordinary means to overcome their guerrilla opponents. There were technological innovations, but they seem rather mundane. Italian troops in Libya were the first to use aircraft in warfare, mainly for reconnaissance but sometimes for bombardment as well.[4] The French in Morocco appear to have invented the staff car, and were among the first to find a military use for dirigibles (for observation).[5] Some of the other changes in the way colonial wars were waged during this period, however, foreshadow the techniques of total war employed later in the century.

In order to crush the Boer guerrillas, the British confined some 154,000 Boer men, women and children and 107,000 "black Boers' – African labourers and servants in Boer employ – in what soon became known as "concentration camps".[6] The high death rates among the camp inmates, the vast majority of whom were civilians, shocked public opinion in many parts of the world. Even more ominous (and, unfortunately, much less publicized) were the "labour camps" set up by the Germans to accommodate Herero and Nama survivors – soldiers and civilians alike – of the 1904–7 war in South West Africa. Although there may not have been a conscious policy to this end, the result of confining sick and malnourished Africans in these poorly-equipped facilities, without proper nutrition and medical attention, was to turn the labour camps into "death camps."

There was also a greater tendency among European soldiers in Africa during this period to contemplate "extermination" of their enemies as a way of bringing conflicts to an end. The best known example of this is German General Lothar von Trotha's notorious 1904 "extermination" proclamation to the Herero people, which will be discussed below. Trotha's proclamation, eventually countermanded by the Kaiser under pressure from his ministers, was the centrepiece of the debate on colonial repression which dominated the 1907 general elections in Germany.

If German atrocities in Africa failed to attract much international attention at this early date, the misdeeds of their Italian allies in Libya did not. In October 1911 Arab and Turkish forces launched a surprise attack on Italian troops at a place called Sciara Sciat on the outskirts of Tripoli. In the course of fierce fighting, a large number of Italian prisoners were massacred by Arab soldiers. After the enemy attack was beaten off, the Italians vented their anger at the fate of their captured comrades by carrying out a massacre of their own. The Italian reprisals aroused international protests and led to calls for a ceasefire and mediation of the dispute between Italy and Turkey.

Less well known is the insistence of Lord Lugard, High Commissioner of the Protectorate of Northern Nigeria, on the "annihilation" of the rebellious population of the Northern Nigerian village of Satiru in 1906.[7] Lugard's West African Frontier Force

> emptied its magazines into the mob of peasants armed with hoes and hatchets, shooting them down as if they were vermin. Lugard later estimated that his men had killed 2,000 of them without loss to themselves. Prisoners were executed, their heads cut off and put on spikes. Then the village was razed to the ground, and the Sultan [of Sokoto] pronounced a curse on anyone who tried to rebuild Satiru or cultivate its fields.[8]

The slaughter and atrocities were sufficiently shocking to British officialdom "in the know" (which did not include the Colonial Office) that the Deputy High Commissioner for Northern Nigeria wrote to a correspondent that "It would be worth Leopold of Belgium's while to pay ten thousand pounds to get hold of what we know about this."[9]

The Second Boer War, 1899–1902

As noted above, the Anglo-Boer wars fall only partly within the parameters of this book. Although no general account of the Second Boer War will be attempted here, some comment is clearly required on those aspects which help to shed light, by way of comparative analysis, on warfare in Africa generally during the period of imperial conquest. There is also room for extended discussion of black African involvement in what has for so long been erroneously described as a "white man's war".

Two myths persist concerning the nature of the Second Boer War. The first holds that the conflict was the last of the "gentlemen's wars", the second that it was a "white man's war". The first of these myths was called into serious question relatively early, during the war itself in fact, as evidence emerged concerning the high death rates among civilians in British concentration camps, the use of "scorched earth" tactics to deprive Boer commandos of food and shelter, and the summary executions of Boer irregulars by British troops. The second myth has had a longer run. Until quite recently, most historians have accepted that a tacit agreement was reached between Boer and Briton at the beginning of the conflict to confine black South Africans to non-combatant roles in the war and that both sides observed this right to the end. The doyen of South African historians, Leonard Thompson has, for example, written that both sides "refrained from involving the African peoples of South Africa in their fighting, except as unarmed servants and scouts and, on the British side, as guards. Bitterly though the war was fought, it was a 'white man's war.'"[10]

This myth has been effectively exploded by the research of Peter Warwick, whose book *Black people and the South African War, 1899–1902* (1983) demonstrates extensive involvement of armed Africans on both sides during the war. In addition to over 100,000 black South Africans who were employed by the British as scouts, spies, guards, servants and couriers, "At least 10,000 and possibly as many as 30,000 blacks were fighting with the British army as armed combatants by the end of the war" (pp. 4–5; 25). Despite an almost pathological fear of placing guns in the hands of Africans, the heavily outnumbered Boers also seem to have tried to recruit black warriors to serve in their army towards the end of the war (p. 26).

The events of the Second Boer War cast into bolder relief the shortcomings of African strategies of armed resistance to European invasion. In the first phase of the war, the Boers, despite some early spectacular successes, pursued what would eventually prove to be a losing strategy: one strikingly similar to that employed by a number of African armies before and afterwards. Mobility was the big Boer advantage over the British, in that it enabled them to elude confrontation and fight only at times of their own choosing. This clearly pointed to guerrilla warfare as the proper strategy for the Boers. Indigenous African armies, such as those of the Zulus, the Tukolors, the Gaza Nguni, and the Mahdists, enjoyed the same advantage, but like the Boers at the outset of the second South African war, too often threw it away in order to fight set-piece battles or conduct prolonged sieges. Even Samori had a fatal fascination with sieges. The Boers, to their credit, were flexible enough to realize the folly of this and to take steps to convert to guerrilla warfare. Up to that point, however, it was only their modern firearms and superb marksmanship, combined with generally incompetent British leadership, that saved the Boers from the fate of their African counterparts. Their decision to besiege the British garrisons at Kimberley, Ladysmith and Mafeking, for example, was as unwise as Samori's decision to lay siege to France's ally Tieba at Sikasso. Like Samori, the Boers lacked the numbers to carry on long sieges or to ward off relieving armies. And like the Ethiopians, they lacked the heavy artillery to bring sieges to an early conclusion.

Northern Nigeria campaign, 1899–1906

Introduction

The year 1898 saw a monumental changing of the guard in Nigeria, as chartered company rule came to an end with the purchase by the British government of the rights and properties of the Royal Niger Company of Sir George Taubman Goldie for £850,000. So passed into the hands of the state not only Southern Nigeria but also the company's somewhat specious claims to Northern Nigeria. The takeover also brought under government control the Royal Niger Constabulary (RNC), the company troops who had for so many years kept the peace in Southern Nigeria after their fashion. The company's men eventually would be incorporated into the new West African Frontier Force (WAFF), created in 1897 at the behest of the Colonial Secretary, Joseph Chamberlain, to vie with the French for control of the hinterlands of the Gold Coast and the Central Sudan. The WAFF would become the instrument of imperial conquest of the man now appointed to lead it, the old Africa hand and *bete noire* of the French, Frederick Lugard.[11]

Goldie's Royal Niger Company had made its exit from the Nigerian scene in a blaze of martial activity. In a whirlwind campaign in January–February 1897, its constabulary had invaded and conquered the southwestern emirates of Nupe and Ilorin on the southwestern edge of the Sokoto Caliphate. The RNC's victory was a portent of things to come that should have set off loud alarm bells in the Caliphate, whose tributary states the fallen emirates were. The Nupe army, which fielded some 30,000 men, was smartly defeated by a force of just over 1,000 African troops and 32 European officers and NCOs. The margin of victory was the superior armament – seven artillery pieces and six Maxim guns – and fire discipline of the RNC troops.

So confident was Goldie after the victory in Nupe that he marched on neighbouring Ilorin with a force of only 320 African infantry and 22 Europeans. Artillery support was reduced to two guns, and only four Maxims were taken along. Moreover, the men only carried ten days' rations. Although victory was gained in the end, the Ilorin campaign, whether through over-confidence or poor scouting, almost ended in disaster. Again, there were lessons here for Sokoto. The Ilorin army had tried to lure the RNC force into an ambush while it was still in marching columns, but impatient cavalry had sprung the trap too soon, giving the company soldiers time to form into a square. Nonetheless, the horsemen had come dangerously close to scattering the RNC troops. "They waited too long and lost their opportunity", wrote a British officer who was present at the engagement. "If the charge had been made whilst the square was still unformed and the carriers were hastening up from the rear, the result would have been disastrous".[12]

Lugard in command

In 1899, Lugard was promoted Brigadier-General and appointed British High Commissioner for Her Majesty's new Protectorate of Northern Nigeria. The title was grand, the responsibilities immense, and, as was typical of the early days of colonial rule, the operating budget was small. In all, the High Commissioner could count upon a budget of some £88,000 to administer a territory of some 300,000 square miles inhabited by perhaps 24 million people. He was also short of manpower. His civilian staff consisted of less than 100 people, who were eventually to be spread around the residencies and other facilities throughout the region. To impose his will he had the troops of the WAFF, some 200 European officers and, at most, 3,000 African infantrymen. These limitations do not, however, seem to have persuaded Lugard to adopt a policy of restraint in relations with the Sokoto Caliphate.

Although the British government was anxious to maintain friendly ties to the Caliphate and, in fact, cautioned Lugard and other officials in the region to refrain from activities that might lead to hostilities, Lugard seems to have been determined from the time of his appointment to bring the Caliphate under direct British rule, by force if necessary. Like most of the colonial captains, from "Père" Bugeaud in the 1840s to Wolseley in the 1870s and the *officiers soudanais* and Kitchener in the 1880s and 1890s, Lugard believed that the enemy could not be made to co-operate unless they had first been crushed.

Even after 1900 the Colonial Office would have preferred peaceful penetration, but Lugard was determined to found the British title on the right of conquest. Accordingly, he forced the pace several times and succeeded in presenting the Colonial Office with faits accomplis.[13]

Lugard had the good fortune to fall upon the caliphate at a time of serious internal crisis. The emirate of Kano, one of the most important in the Sokoto confederation, was wracked by civil war. Local mahdis cropped up here and there, a sure sign that all was not well. Some of these holy men had been encouraged by the presence of the Sudanese mahdist adventurer, Rabih Zubair, who had overthrown the neighbouring state of Bornu and announced his intention to "liberate" the Sokoto Caliphate as well. Although these problems remained for the most part local in their impact, their overall effect was to weaken the emirates directly involved, and to keep the capital constantly on tenterhooks as one crisis succeeded another.

Lugard and the WAFF would not find the Caliphate well prepared for war. There had been some desultory mid-century attempts to purchase Western arms and create a force of trained and disciplined musketeers capable of manoeuvre. A few artillery pieces had been acquired over the years. But rearmament had not been undertaken quickly enough, so that, as the war for Northern Nigeria opened in 1902, the Caliphate would face its enemies with an armed force that looked very much like the one that confronted Usuman dan Fodio and his *jihadis* a century earlier.

It is true that, as the threat of war with the British grew, the leaders of the Caliphate did make some last-minute efforts to obtain modern armament and Western military expertise. But by then, as Joseph Smaldone has demonstrated, it was too late.

> The important point is that between 1897 and 1903 the nascent revolution in military technology, army organization, and techniques of warfare that was occurring in the emirates was forcibly suppressed. The process of military modernization which had begun only a few decades earlier was interrupted by the Brussels Act, and then abruptly terminated by British conquest. The failure of this revolution is to be attributed to events and circumstances beyond the domain and control of the Sokoto Caliphate: the closure of the firearms supply from the north, European regulation of the trade in modern rifles, and British military occupation.[14]

The pretext for Lugard's invasion of the Caliphate was the murder of a British official and the friendly reception accorded to the murderer by the ruler of Kano. But other, overarching justifications were presented to the

Colonial Office: the response of the emirates to Lugard's 1900 proclamation of the Protectorate had ranged from silence to hostility; slave raiding continued to thrive in the Caliphate; the masses of the Caliphate were oppressed by their government and would welcome liberation by British forces.

The ensuing campaign has been described by an unhappy Nigerian historian as a "triumphal procession" for the British, which "illustrates the pathetic futility of West Africa's traditional war machinery in the modern world".[15] These judgments are too harsh. While it is clear that, for the most part, the forces of the Caliphate were no match for Lugard's WAFF, there were some surprises along the way and, in the end, an honourable conclusion at least for the Caliph and his army.

The "surprises" that the WAFF experienced along the way of its "triumphal procession" suggest how the Caliphate might have mounted a more effective resistance, had it been able to acquire more modern armament and undertake a more concerted approach to the defence of the emirates.

The first surprise occurred in 1901, on the eve of the war, during a punitive expedition against the emirate of Admamawa by a WAAF column under the command of Colonel T.L.N. Morland, one of Lugard's closest associates. Having repulsed a series of cavalry charges, the WAAF square advanced on the city of Adamawa, outside the walls of which the troops of Emir Zubeiru had drawn up for a last stand.

The square went into the attack, only to be met by a well-aimed burst of grapeshot from two cannon, at a range of only thirty yards. Over fifty men went down and the square was for a time on the verge of disintegration. This was easy to understand: it would be one of the very few times the WAFF would have to face artillery fire in the whole of its pre-First World War experience. However, the square's British officers were able to rally the men and rush the guns before they could be reloaded. The gunners who had so stunned the British square were veterans of the wars in the Western Sudan, Tukolor soldiers who had followed Ahmadu Seku into exile in the Caliphate in the 1890s.

The two centrepieces of Lugard's offensive were the attacks on the great commercial centre of Kano and the capital of the Caliphate at Sokoto. Knowing that London was extremely nervous about getting deeply involved in a war in Northern Nigeria after having only just finished with the unpleasantness in South Africa, Lugard planned to begin his attacks on the two states before informing the Colonial Office. That way, he reasoned, it would be more difficult for the government to stop him. He could argue, Archinard-like, that the prestige of Britain would suffer if her troops were suddenly withdrawn while on campaign. His plans were upset, however, by a journalistic "scoop". The Reuters wire service had learned of the impending campaign against Kano and Sokoto, and the story had appeared in the British newspapers. This produced angry telegrams from the Colonial Office demanding to know why it was being kept in the dark and calling upon the High Commissioner to abandon his plans for attacking the two emirates. Lugard now proceeded to produce a detailed defence of his actions, after which he sent off the troops without informing his superiors in London. The next thing they heard from Lugard was the news that Kano, then Sokoto, had fallen to the WAFF.

Great Kano, surrounded by walls 11 miles in length, 30 to 50 feet high and some 40 feet thick at the base, was a formidable target. To take it, Lugard dispatched a somewhat larger force than usual, 722 infantrymen under 24 officers, supported by four Maxims and four 75 mm guns. Defence of the city was not helped by the fact that the emir of Kano, Aliyu, chose this moment to leave for Sokoto with a large part of his army, ostensibly to pay homage to the new Caliph, Attahiru II, and pray at the grave of his mother. Although the British artillery had some difficulty breaching the walls of Kano, in the end a breach was made, and infantry stormed through and occupied the city. The fall of Kano had a predictably depressing impact upon the people of those parts of the Sokoto Caliphate who were still free from alien rule. And nowhere more so than in the capital city of Sokoto itself, Lugard's next and last objective.

Opinion was divided in Sokoto about how to deal with the British, who, after the fall of Kano, were understood to be about to march against the city. Some members of the Caliph's entourage wanted to make peace, arguing that the fate of Kano made it clear that resistance would only lead to death and destruction. Another group called for armed resistance. A third party, which included the Caliph, called for a mass exodus of the people of the caliphate rather than suffer rule by the infidels. At this stage it was unclear whether the retreat being proposed was intended to be a strategic withdrawal or a *hijra* to some distant site where a new polity might be formed free of British influence.

As there was no agreement on what course to take, the government decided to prepare to resist the impending British attack. The city walls were repaired and "people engaged in prayers for their success as well as in the making of charms against bullets."[16] But, perhaps to avoid the kind of devastation Kano had suffered by giving battle from within her walls, the Caliph ignored the counsel of his advisors and ordered the army of Sokoto to await Lugard's column on the plain outside the city.

The British attack came on 15 March 1903. The WAFF expedition comprised 656 African riflemen under the command of 25 European officers and five NCOS. Fire support was provided by four Maxims and four 75 mm cannon. The supplies and equipment for this force were brought forward by an incredible 595 carriers, 195 of whom were artillery and Maxim gun bearers. The battle which now took place outside the walls of Sokoto lasted about ninety minutes. As the WAFF column neared the city, "hordes of horsemen and footmen armed with swords, spears, old guns and bows and arrows appeared, charging the square over and over again, only to be mown down by machine gun and carbine fire."[17] The Caliph, seeing that further resistance would be futile, fled to the east with what remained of his army. The British force proceeded to occupy a largely empty capital city.

The Colonial Office, however, was not happy with this spectacular victory. Indeed, upon his return to headquarters some weeks later, Lugard found himself being chastised by London for attacking Kano and Sokoto without authorization. In a reply worthy of his near contemporary, Colonel Archinard of Western Sudan fame, Lugard, in effect, told his superiors that, as the man on the spot, he was in a better position than they to decide what strategy to pursue. He went on to suggest that they had allowed themselves to be panicked by sensationalist reporting in the press about the danger of a long and bloody war resulting from his attack on the emirates.

As far as Lugard was concerned, the war for Northern Nigeria was now over. The Caliphate's great market town, Kano, and its capital, Sokoto, had fallen almost without a fight. A new caliph had been named and, although the previous occupant of the throne was still at large, it was assumed that he had little support and could safely be ignored. Lugard returned to England. But the war was not over and the deposed caliph was not the forlorn figure of straw Lugard had depicted. In mid-May 1903, after Lugard's departure, the Deputy High Commissioner, William Wallace, informed the Colonial Office that the situation in Northern Nigeria had become very threatening.

> The people appear to rise en masse at the Sultan's [Caliph's] call: men, women and children leaving their towns and villages deserted to follow him, thus showing a fanaticism which I, for one, never for a moment thought they possessed.[18]

Contrary to Lugard's earlier reports, the Caliph, Attahiru, seems to have been widely respected and popular with his subjects, and to have enjoyed a considerable reputation as a warrior. The Caliph had called upon his people to join him in undertaking a "strategic withdrawal" from the now "polluted" emirates. His aim was not, as some observers did and still do assume, to lead a traditional Muslim *hijra* to escape from infidel rule. Rather, his plan was to make a last stand on Bima Hill near the town of Burmi, the most sacred ground in the Sokoto Caliphate. "It occupies a place not dissimilar to Avalon in the Arthurian legends of Britain [in] Fulani folklore and legend".[19]

That the resistance now being mounted under the leadership of the Caliph was a serious matter was brought home to a WAFF patrol under the command of Captain D.W. Sword, which on 13 May 1903 found itself surrounded outside the walls of the town of Burmi. Sword's 130-man force was pursuing the Caliph's army when it came under attack and was ultimately forced to withdraw with 43 per cent casualties. Most of the losses came from arrow wounds, as Sword kept his square within 80 yards of the city wall for two hours, afraid to retire for fear the enemy would penetrate his formation.

The Caliph was finally brought to bay outside Burmi on 27 July 1903. The battle now fought was the most hotly contested engagement of the war. It raged on from eleven in the morning until six in the evening, when British artillery and Maxim guns succeeded in silencing the last enemy redoubt, the "King's Palace" and the mosque inside the walls of Burmi. The resistance had been led by the Caliph in person. He was killed along with his two sons and 90 members of his entourage in the early stages of the fighting. His death marked the final defeat of the Sokoto Caliphate and the end of resistance to British rule in Northern Nigeria.

Joseph Smaldone underscores the irony in the events which had just occurred.

In retrospect, it is ironical that in some ways the military situation had come full circle in the hundred-year history of the Sokoto Caliphate. The Caliphate had emerged after 1804 by a strategy of piecemeal but rapid conquest; its original armies were composed principally of infantry; its tactical formation was the "square"; it depended on firepower to overcome the shock power of enemy cavalry; and its ruling class was ethnically distinct from the subject population. By 1903 the situation was similar in these respects but the Caliphate was now the victim of defeat. Britain also imposed its military control by a strategy of piecemeal but rapid conquest; its armed forces consisted of infantry; its tactical formation was the "square"; it relied on firepower to overcome the shock effect of enemy cavalry, and the new imperial regime was dominated by an ethnic minority.[20]

"Pacification" of German South West Africa, 1904–7

Introduction

In the early years of the twentieth century, Germany's African empire was rocked by major revolts in its two largest colonies, South West Africa (1904–7) and Tanganyika (1905–6). Both uprisings stemmed from mistreatment of the African population by German settlers, and from opposition to government policies that threatened to undermine traditional African economies. African involvement was massive in both rebellions and was met by measures considered extreme even by the standards of colonial Africa. There emerged from the repression of these revolts a "Black Legend" of German colonialism that would provide a plausible rationale for the takeover of Germany's colonies by the Western allies in the aftermath of the First World War.

The uprising of the Herero and Nama peoples against German rule in South West Africa should spark interest among students of military history on account of its sheer audacity. On the face of it, these two poor pastoral peoples had no business throwing down the gauntlet to the western world's most powerful army. Yet, in the opening rounds of the war, it was the poor pastoralists who most often won. The methods eventually employed by the Germans to counter the guerrilla warfare of the Hereros and Namas and to force their surrender should also be of interest, since they foreshadow some of the practices of total war and of the counter-insurgency strategies used later in the century.

The Herero rising

The rebellion in South West Africa began in January 1904. It is hard to avoid the conclusion that the root cause of the upheaval was the particularly vicious racism of the German settlers. A missionary contended that

> The real cause of the bitterness among the Hereros toward the Germans is without question the fact that the average German looks down upon the natives as being about on the same level as the higher primates (baboon being their favorite term for the natives) and treats them like animals. The settler holds that the native has a right to exist only in so far as he is useful to the white man. It follows that the whites value their horses and even their oxen more than they value the natives.[21]

196

Opinion in Germany was often not much more enlightened. When Matthias Erzberger, the spokesman of the Catholic Centre Party in the Reichstag, told the deputies that Africans had souls just as white people did, he was met by jeers from the right side of the chamber.[22]

The African population was also driven to desperation by what they saw as the destruction of their way of life. Increasingly, they were being forced off the land and obliged to work as labourers on German ranches or in the small settler towns. In part, this was due to a series of devastating natural events: a cattle disease that wiped out many of their herds, malaria and typhoid epidemics and an invasion of locusts. But it was also true that this was the role that had been cast for the Hereros by the German colonial government, responsive to the demands of the settlers for labour. Once they had been driven from their land, much of which had been bought up by Germans, there would be no going back to the pastoral life of their ancestors.

Before going to war, the leader of the Hereros, Samuel Maherero, had tried to enlist allies among the other African peoples of the colony, particularly the formidable Nama people to the south. He had written to his counterpart, the leader of the Nama people, Hendrik Witbooi, to ask him to transcend the old tribal rivalries between Herero and Nama and fight together for Africa.

> All our obedience and patience with the Germans is of little avail for each day they shoot someone dead for no reason at all. Hence I appeal to you, my Brother, not to hold aloof from the uprising but to make your voice heard so that all Africa may take up arms against the Germans. Let us die fighting rather than die as a result of maltreatment, imprisonment or some other calamity. Tell all the Kapteins [chiefs] down there to rise and do battle.[23]

The message did not reach Witbooi. Mahaherero had given it to the chief of another tribe, the Rehoboth, to pass on to the Nama leader but he had, instead, turned it over to the Germans. This, together with the fact that the Nama proceeded to honour an earlier agreement with the Germans to provide scouts for them, dramatically illustrates the formidable obstacles that faced African leaders who tried to mount a common front against the Germans in South West Africa. That the Nama should have waited until the Hereros were on their knees before coming into the war against the Germans was a catastrophe for the cause of African resistance in the region. Writes Horst Drechsler, "It was nothing short of a tragedy that the Herero and Nama took up arms successively rather than simultaneously against the hated German yoke".[24]

The outbreak of the Herero–Nama War in German South West Africa on 12 January 1904 caught the colonial authorities by surprise. Most of South West Africa's small *Schutztruppe* force, under the command of the governor, Colonel Theodor von Leutwein, was absent in the south of the colony when the first attack came. It was a strategic blow against the railroad connecting the capital, Windhoek, and the port of Swakopmund. For weeks those among the 5,000 German settlers lucky enough to make it to one of the garrison towns had only militia, a handful of regulars and 85 marines from the gunboat "Habicht" to protect them. But the Hereros, who were redoubtable guerrilla fighters, lacked the experience and weaponry to assault fortified places defended by machine guns. This gave the government in Berlin time to rush out reinforcements. Shocked at the poor showing in the Reich's first major war since 1870, the government also decided to shake up the command structure in South West Africa.

The débâcle to date, and indeed the revolt itself, was blamed on Governor Leutwein, whose presumed leniency toward the Hereros had emboldened them to rise up. On orders from Kaiser Wilhelm II himself, military command was given to General Lothar von Trotha, one of Germany's rare veteran colonial officers. Trotha had commanded the suppression of a rebellion by the Hehe tribe in Tanganyika in 1896, and had led the German contingent in China during the Boxer Rebellion. He was also a man who could be counted on to be firm with the Hereros. The general made this clear in a letter to Governor Leutwein after his arrival in South West Africa.

> I know the tribes of Africa. They are all alike. They only respond to force. It was and is my policy to use force with terrorism and even brutality. I shall annihilate the revolting tribes with streams of blood and streams of gold. Only after a complete uprooting will something emerge.[25]

Governor Leutwein had been proposing negotiations with the Hereros, arguing that, with reinforcements arriving, the Germans would be able to bargain from strength and thus bring the revolt to an end. Killing all the Hereros, as the military seemed to be proposing, would be suicidal for the colony, which could only prosper if it had a ready labour force. The colony's settlers were of the same mind. General Trotha proved unsympathetic to these arguments. The Hereros had to be crushed.

Although reinforcements continued to stream in from Germany, along with plentiful supplies of arms and ammunition, General Trotha faced serious problems in implementing his war plan. The biggest problem was logistical. The German army, like most European armies, relied heavily upon railways to move troops and supplies.

This dependence on the railroad seriously compromised the mobility of the forces in the field. Artillery, machine guns, and rapid-fire rifles gave the Germans overwhelming superiority in firepower, but it was purchased at a high cost, for it tied the German soldier to a bulky, slow-moving, and highly vulnerable supply train, without which their weapons were useless.[26]

South West Africa had only one railway line, from Swakopmund on the coast to the capital at Windhoek in the centre of the country, but, by the time of Trotha's arrival on the scene, the main Herero army had moved to the northeastern part of the country, far from the railway. The general sought to resolve this dilemma by building a new rail line from Swakopmund northeast to Otavi, on the edge of the Waterberg plateau some 570 km from the coast, where the Hereros had taken refuge. Work was actually begun on the rail line, but was then held up for so long by a strike of Italian labourers working on it that it never contributed to the German offensive.

By August 1904 most of the Hereros had taken refuge on the Waterberg plateau, just to the west of an extension of the Kalahari desert called the Omaheke sandveld. Exactly why they had decided to move *en masse* on to the plateau and remain encamped there is not clear. One suggestion is that their earlier victories over the Germans had emboldened the Hereros to seek an Armageddon, which they believed they could win.[27] Perhaps a more reasonable explanation is that this pastoral people with its huge herds of cattle and large numbers of dependents was simply tired of running and wished to make a stand.

In any case, the Hereros' decision to stand fast gave Trotha and his army the opportunity it needed to slowly move up its supplies and concentrate its forces. It also gave them the chance to formulate a strategy for the oncoming fight, which was, it became clear, to envelop the Herero position on the plateau on three sides, leaving an exit open to the east. When Leutwein was first told of this plan, he criticized Trotha for giving the Hereros a chance to escape. Perhaps he was not ruthless enough to see what Trotha had in mind. What the general did, following the bombardment of the Herero positions by his 32 artillery pieces, was to push the 8,000 Herero fighters, with twice as many women and children in tow, off the plateau and on through the gap to the east into the Omaheke sandveld. This waterless expanse, around 200 miles wide, separated the British protectorate of Bechuanaland from South West Africa. In early August pursuing German troops made sure the last waterhole was sealed off, and then constructed a series of manned posts around the perimeter to make sure the Hereros could not make their way back. The clear intention was that they should perish in the sandveld. Nevertheless, the Hereros were able to survive in the desert and make their way back through the German lines in sufficient numbers that, on 2 October, 1904 General Trotha felt it necessary to issue a formal proclamation to them.

> I, the great general of the German troops, send this letter to the Herero People. Hereros are no longer German subjects. They have murdered, stolen, they have cut off the noses, ears and other bodily parts of wounded soldiers and now, because of cowardice, they will fight no more. . . . All the Hereros must leave the land. If the people do not do this, then I will force them to do it with the great guns. Any Herero found within the German borders with or without a gun, with or without cattle, will be shot. I shall no longer receive any women or children. I will drive them back to their people or I will shoot them. This is my decision for the Herero people.
> Signed: the Great General of the Mighty Kaiser[28]

The general felt compelled to clarify these orders to his soldiers, so an additional message was read out to them explaining what was meant by shooting women and children. Trotha explained that

> the shooting of women and children is to be understood to mean that one can shoot over them to force them to run faster. I definitely mean that this order will be carried out and that no male prisoners will be taken, but it should not degenerate into killing women and children. This will be accomplished if one shoots over their heads a couple of times. The soldiers will remain conscious of the good reputation of German soldiers.[29]

Trotha's proclamation and the strategy it announced shocked the German chancellor, Count Bernhard von Buelow, who finally prevailed upon an unwilling Kaiser to order the general to revoke it and offer to accept the surrender of the Hereros. Although the cable ordering him to rescind his proclamation arrived bearing the Kaiser's signature, Trotha reacted with bad grace. For a time he refused to comply, but in the end events were to force his hand. The day after he had issued his annihilation order in October, the Witbooi Nama, led by their chief, Hendrik Witbooi, had declared war. Trotha now had more than the Hereros to worry about. The Nama, though fewer in number than the Hereros, were even more formidable guerrilla fighters. It would eventually take a force of some 70,0000 German troops, seven times the number who fought at the battle of the Waterberg, to get to grips with with the elusive Nama and ensure the final defeat of the Hereros.

But why had Hendrik Witbooi waited until this late date – with the Hereros on their last legs, dying by the thousand in the Omaheke desert, or liable to be killed on sight if they managed to make it back to Hereroland – to go to war with the Germans? In military terms, his decision makes no sense. There was little he could do to help the Hereros. The number of German soldiers in the country was growing every day, and he could count on no more than 1,500 riflemen.

Hendrik Witbooi had chosen to take up arms against the Germans (to "put on the white feather", the Nama war emblem) because he and his people had finally seen the writing on the wall. His men, who had served as scouts for the Germans, had seen how the German soldiers treated the Hereros, and had been shocked at the evident German intention to exterminate them. They had concluded, not unreasonably, that when the Germans had finished with the Hereros, it would be the turn of the Nama. The Nama scouts had deserted the *Schutztruppe* and returned home to tell Hendrik Witbooi what they had seen. And so the 80-year-old chief of the Nama sent the following message to his fellow chiefs.

> I have now stopped walking submissively and will write a letter to the [German] Captain saying that I have put on the white feather and that the time is over when I will walk behind him . . . The Savior himself will now act and He will free us through His grace and compassion.[30]

At first the Nama, masters of guerrilla warfare that they were, carried all before them. German settlers in Namaland were killed, and German soldiers invariably failed to catch the marauders who had killed them. When the numbers of German soldiers became too great to cope with, and all the trails were blocked and the scarce waterholes under surveillance, Witbooi and his mounted men and their families disappeared into the Kalahari desert, where no German soldiers could follow them. Meanwhile, the German troops, ill-prepared for the kind of fighting that was being required of them, began to fall sick. Some died of malaria, and many more of typhus. His failure to bring the Nama to heel eventually discredited Trotha, who was now ordered home. But the departure of the general was not intended to indicate that the authorities had decided to negotiate rather than fight. Indeed, more German troops were poured into the colony. Nama losses began to mount, and on 29 October 1905 Hendrik Witbooi was killed in a skirmish with the Germans. The Nama now accepted German terms and began to lay down their arms.

In the case of the Hereros Trotha's policy of extermination had come very close to succeeding. About half of the tribe had been driven into the sandveld and half again had died there. Of the ones who somehow managed to filter back into the colony, many were killed by German patrols, and now many of those who had survived were to be sent to labour camps, where even more would die.

> For sick people to be sent to labour camps was a death sentence. Work was heavy (dragging railway trucks by hand), food meagre, medical supplies non-existent. By 1907 the Germans reported that *over half* the 15,000 Herero and 2,000 Nama prisoners had died in the camps. Worst of all were conditions on Shark Island, a windswept rock off Luederitzbuch (Angra Pequena), where Hendrik Witbooi's gallant band and other Nama prisoners were sent in September 1906, in flagrant violation of the terms of their surrender. Within seven months, 1,032 out of 1,732 had died of cold and ill-treatment . . . Others were dying, and all but a tenth were crippled. When the census was taken in 1911, only half the Nama estimated a decade before (9,800 out of 20,000) and less than a quarter of the original number of Herero (15,000 out of 80,000) were found to have survived the war.[31]

A postscript: the Maji–Maji rebellion, 1905–6[32]

The African rebellion against German rule in Tanganyika sprang largely from resistance to the colonial government's policy of forcing peasants to give up subsistence agriculture to grow cotton for export.

From the point of view of African resistance, two developments are of interest. The first was the major role played in the uprising by religion, in this case the cult of a snake spirit called Hongo. The leading figure in the cult and, in a sense, the spiritual leader of the revolt itself was the spirit medium, Kinjikitile Ngwale. He emerges as a prophet who called upon all the various peoples of Tanganyika to unite to expel the Germans. His goal seems to have been an essentially conservative one. He wished to be rid of the Germans so as to return to the "golden age" he believed had existed before their arrival. Nevertheless, because of his message of unity against the enemy, Kinjikitile has been acclaimed as the forefather of Tanzanian nationalism. But Kinjikitile, and the other spirit mediums who joined his cult, also told the people that they could provide them with a "war medicine" that could turn German bullets to water. The medicine, called "maji-maji", consisted of water ("maji" in Swahili), castor oil and millet seeds. Magic of this sort was, of course, a fairly common feature of African resistance movements. Religious figures in the Tukolor empire, the Congo and the Barue kingdom of Mozambique, for example, also claimed to possess the ability to turn European bullets to water.

Although Kinjikitile was captured by the Germans and executed early in the rebellion, this did nothing to halt its spread. In less than a month all of the southern part of Tanganyika was up in arms, and the movement was beginning to expand to the north. But the failure of the rebels to capture German outposts – the failed siege of Mahenge in August 1905 is an example – began to slow the momentum.

What finally turned the tide for the Germans, however, was not failed sieges or battlefield victories. They had too few troops for this, and because of the fighting going on concurrently in South West Africa, there were few reinforcements to be had. The German governor, Graf von Goetzen, had no more than 800 *askaris*, with a handful of European officers, to police the entire colony. The only reinforcements available, as it turned out, were 100 marines. The strategy the Germans adopted was one that had been practiced only sporadically in Africa since the days of Bugeaud's *razzias* in Algeria: starving the enemy into submission. It was, however, a strategy that would gain in popularity as the twentieth century wore on. In October 1905 three German columns marched south, where the main centres of resistance lay, burning villages and destroying crops as they went. Leaders of the rebellion were caught and hanged. By June 1906 the "Maji-Maji" revolt was over. The starvation strategy had been remarkably effective. Famine killed some 250,000–300,000 Africans, according to a leading source – ten times the number of people who had taken up arms.[33]

Perhaps half of the Vidunda and Matumbi tribes and three-quarters of the Pangwa, peoples of the southern highlands, had died in the famine. But victory through famine was also an inexpensive strategy. Repression in South West Africa had cost £20 million. Governor von Goetzen achieved victory for only £2 million.

When the famine ended the survivors returned to a country which was almost unrecognizable. Miambo forests had begun to take over the maize fields and cotton plots, and soon these forests gave sanctuary to rhino, buffalo and elephants. In due course, the hills of Ungindo, once teeming with people, became the largest game park in the world.[34]

To the shores of Tripoli (1911–12)[35]

Introduction

The Italians had had their eye on Libya for some time. It had always been Italy's consolation prize in the rush for colonies in Africa. "No, you can't have Tunisia," Bismarck and the British had told the Italians when the French occupied Tunisia in 1881, "but Libya is yours for the taking". The Italians, of course, had not wanted Libya just then, but Tunisia – there was a large Italian colony there and a great deal of Italian capital had been sunk into the country – but powers greater than Italy had decided otherwise. France was to have Tunisia to keep her mind off Alsace-Lorraine.

In the final analysis, for those who believed Italy had to have an empire, Libya was better than nothing. Of course, Libya already had an owner (apart, that is, from its inhabitants) – the Turks of the Ottoman Empire – but this did not discourage Italian expansionists. Libya had once been known as Cyrenaica and had been a vital part of the Roman Empire and home to an important colony of Roman settlers. Surely this gave Italy a stronger claim to the region than the Turks, whose ancestors were still wandering the steppes of Central Asia when Libya was a prosperous Roman colony. Italian imperialists soon were referring to Libya as Italy's "fourth shore" (*quarta sponda*) and highly-coloured accounts of the plentiful and fertile farmland to be found there began circulating in the land-hungry Italian south.

In November 1884 operational plans had actually been drawn up to land 30,000 Italian troops in Libya, but the invasion scheme had been abandoned a month later when Italy was offered the Red Sea enclave of Massawa by Britain. (Interestingly, the Italian armed forces did not bother to draw up new plans for the occupation of Massawa, but simply put the new name on the old Libyan operational plan and used that instead.[36]) For the next 25 years, then, Italian attention would be focused on East Africa, with the results we have seen.

Italian interest in Libya revived in the decade prior to the First World War. The main impetus came from domestic politics. The centrist government of Premier Giovanni Giolitti hoped to outflank a growing right-wing nationalist current in the country by indulging in an expansionist venture of its own. The Libyan operation might have the added value of winning nationalist support in parliament for a government bill in favour of universal manhood suffrage. It was rather like the Bourbon expedition to Algiers in reverse. But the target chosen, Giolitti's advisors cautioned, had to be one whose seizure would not greatly concern the other powers. Clearly, the *irredenta*, the "unredeemed" territory still in Austrian hands in the Alps to the north was out of bounds, as was Morocco, which the French were preparing to occupy. There was not much likelihood, however, of wide international protest about the despoliation of the unloved Turks. Especially if the conquest went smoothly and was over quickly.

Invasion

The invasion of Libya was well planned. The 1884 operational plan had been updated periodically, most recently on the eve of the invasion. As it turned out, however, the plan was based on certain highly questionable assumptions.

First, it had been decided after some debate that the large Arab population of Libya was not likely to take part in the fighting against Italian forces and could safely be ignored. The assumption, shortly to be proved erroneous, was that the Arabs, oppressed as they were by their Turkish overlords, would welcome Italian "liberation", or at the very least remain neutral. The idea that the Arabs might make common cause with the Turks on religious grounds seems to have been dismissed by the Italian general staff.

Secondly, it was assumed by the planners that Turkish opposition would not be heavy. Italy's military attaché in Istanbul assured Rome that Turkey was already heavily committed in the Near East and in the Balkans and would not be in a position to offer much resistance in Libya. Intelligence reports indicated that there were only 5,000–6,000 Turkish troops in Libya, most of them in Tripoli, the capital. It was expected that this handful of troops would resist just long enough to uphold their honour and would then march off for home through Egypt. The possibility that the Turks might, instead, retreat into the desert and wage a guerrilla war does not seem to have been discussed.

The army learned in early September 1911 that the invasion of Libya was going ahead and began making the necessary preparations. Orders were drafted and efforts made to assemble the matériel necessary to equip an expeditionary force. Troops were called up on 23 September and two days later the navy was mobilized. On 27 September an ultimatum was presented to the Turks, giving them 24 hours to turn over the Libyan coastal region, Cyrenaica and Tripoli and its environs, to Italy. The Turks refused, and the Libyan War of 1911–12 was on.

An Italian expeditionary force of just under 45,000 men set sail for the shores of Tripoli under the command of General Carlo Caneva. Tripoli, however, was already in Italian hands when the soldiers arrived, having fallen almost without a struggle to a landing brigade of sailors and marines. The main task of the army over the next two weeks was to secure the city of Tripoli against the possibility of a Turkish counterattack. Although the Turkish garrison had disappeared before the first Italian troops landed, and it could be assumed that they had fled the country, no chances were taken. The oasis surrounding Tripoli was occupied and a defence perimeter 5 km-deep drawn around it. To the west and south, where the oasis faded into desert, trenches were dug and barbed wire strung. To the east, however, the Italian positions fronted onto an Arab quarter called Sciara Sciat, and here no attempt was made to erect defences. During this initial period of the occupation every effort was made to convince Italy and the rest of the world of the truth of one of the assumptions underlying the invasion, that the Arabs of Libya welcomed deliverance from their Turkish oppressors. Relations between the expeditionary force and the local population were described as a "happy partnership".[37]

On 23 October, this illusion was rudely shattered. A joint force of Turks and Arabs launched attacks all along the Italian defence perimeter. The main thrust, however, hit the part of the line which was weakest, the unfortified section opposite the Arab quarter of Sciara Sciat. After fierce fighting, the attackers were beaten back, but not before some 250 Italian soldiers captured at Sciara Sciat were taken to a Muslim cemetery and killed. While the Turkish and Arab dead numbered thousands, Italian losses were also unacceptably high: 500 dead and 200 wounded.

Having chosen to believe that the Arabs were estranged from their Turkish overlords, the joint Turkish–Arab assault took the Italian high command completely by surprise. The other ranks, who had been told that they had nothing to fear from the Arabs, were shocked and outraged at what had happened.

> Officers and men were ignorant of Arabs and Berbers, and saw in their resistance to conquest and fearlessness of death evidence of their *bestialità*. Panic, and a desire to inflict reprisals on a native populace which had apparently betrayed them, led to a brief orgy of summary executions in which hundreds – perhaps thousands – of Arabs were shot.[38]

The Italian reprisals stirred international protests. In order to avoid the possibility of outside intervention and a settlement by arbitration which would surely fall far short of Italian goals, the Giolitti government was now forced to escalate the war. Troop levels were increased, until Italy had nearly 100,000 men in Libya. Plans were made to occupy the rest of Tripolitania, which would be officially placed under the Italian flag, and to occupy Turkish islands in the Aegean and blockade the Turkish mainland. The campaign into the Tripolitanian interior was launched, towns were taken, but the anticipated enemy capitulation failed to take place.

The rest of the war was a stalemate in the desert between an Italian army that lacked the resources and will power to carry the fight into the interior, and a Turkish-Arab force that held the initiative but was too weak to break through the Italian defences. On the sea, the Italian navy tried to lure the Turkish fleet out of the Dardanelles into a general engagement, and, when this failed, contented itself with occupying a number of Turkish islands, including Rhodes.

Fortunately for Italy, the Turks were in an even tighter spot than she was. Their troops in the Libyan desert had not been paid for months, and were falling sick and running short of water. Besides, Turkey had a number of looming crises in the Balkans to contend with. In Lausanne in the summer of 1912, peace terms were finally agreed. Italy was given Libya and agreed to leave the Aegean islands once Turkish troops had departed from North Africa. Since the Turks did not evacuate their troops from Libya until the end of the First World War, Italy held on to the Aegean islands.

Italy had survived what would soon be known as Phase One of the war in Libya; she had not won a victory. Her army had failed to defeat the enemy in the field, even though it was equipped with the latest military hardware, including aircraft. And while the Turks had submitted to the loss of Libya – officially, at least – the Libyan people themselves were unwilling to accept a transfer to a new set of masters, especially Christian ones. The guerrilla warfare in the desert was resumed despite the Lausanne accords, and would continue on well into the interwar period.

Part of the problem for Italy was the difficulty of getting her conscript army to adjust to fighting an anti-guerrilla war in the desert. No training for this kind of warfare had been provided before the troops left; common soldiers had been given only a fleeting and inaccurate idea of the nature of the population they would find in Libya and the enemy they would have to fight. As far as transporting the army to Libya, the planning had been handled well enough, but once the troops had come ashore, it seems to have foundered. Having confidently assumed that the Turks would simply melt away and that the Arab population would be friendly, the general staff had made no further operational plans.

The war was costly both in lives and money. Some 4,000 Italian soldiers died in combat, from wounds or disease; another 5,000 were wounded.[39]

The war cost just over one billion lire – about half of Italy's total annual revenue. The Libyan adventure drained the nation's defence forces at home of men, rations, ammunition, horses and other supplies. Almost all the infantry machine gun sections ended up in Africa. When the First World War broke out, there were still 50,000 Italian troops in Libya. "Before 1911 Italy had been militarily weak on one continent", wrote John Gooch, "after 1912 she was weak in two".[40]

Chapter Six

Legacies

Legacies to military theory and practice

Small wars theory

The colonial wars in Africa gave rise to the concept of the "small war," described by one of its most famous practitioners, General Sir Garnet Wolseley, as warfare against "uncivilised nations." The classic manual for waging war in the colonies, Colonel C.E. Callwell's *Small wars: their principles and practice*, was first published by the British government in 1896 and reprinted three times, the last time in 1914. The concept of the "small war," now much refined and rechristened "low intensity conflict", still excites controversy among military theorists.

An artillery officer with extensive colonial experience, Callwell had a broad understanding of the requirements for European success in small wars. Experience taught him that these wars usually fell into one of three categories: (a) wars of conquest; (b) interventions to crush uprisings; and (c) campaigns to wipe out an insult (a Victorian category that would probably find few adherents today).

Although European armies possessed a considerable technological edge over their "savage" opponents, Callwell knew that victory in small wars was far from automatic. Superior technology meant that Europeans usually enjoyed a tactical advantage in battle, but, often, the more important strategic edge lay with the enemy. African or Asian opponents could control the pace of war by refusing to give battle or by adopting a strategy of guerrilla warfare. European armies faced with inevitable logistical problems in the field and uneasy and impatient politicians at home, desperately needed to find some quick way to bring the enemy to battle and to fight and win a decisive victory.

Technology did not always provide the answer, Callwell believed. Most foes were quick to devise ways to neutralize technology, either by copying it or by finding the strategic or tactical means to render it ineffective. What Europeans needed most in order to win was superior discipline, tactics and morale. Technology could play a role; as an artillery officer, Callwell understood the value of firepower. But technology – firepower – was only effective when it was married to organization.

Beyond this, however, Callwell was adamant that Europeans could not abandon the strategic high ground to their enemies in colonial warfare. Armies needed to know what they were fighting for, what the goal of their campaign was. And they needed to know what was required to finally force their enemy to come to terms. What was it that the enemy prized so much that he would surrender rather than see it lost or destroyed? Once you knew the answer to that question, and had fashioned a strategy that would allow you to strike the enemy where he was weakest, victory was in your grasp.

But, reasonable as these precepts might sound, they sometimes pointed colonial soldiers in directions that were, in the long term, counterproductive. The desperate need to bring the enemy to battle before the food or ammunition ran out, or before the minister of war decided to recall the troops, often provoked Western armies into adopting strategies of attrition: destroying enemy crops and homesteads, running off herds, burning villages. This approach inevitably boomeranged, producing resentful and sullen subjects, and destroying resources vital to the progress of the colony. Callwell, however, enthusiastically endorsed attrition as a strategy for winning small wars. Forbearance and pity were lost on "savages", he believed; they only responded to, and understood, force.

Callwell also rendered a disservice to posterity by maintaining that the ideal soldier for fighting small wars was the cavalryman. Mounted men, he believed, gave European armies an edge in mobility and, besides, cavalry wielding the *arme blanche* frightened "natives". Callwell's recommendations and the presumed lessons of the Second Boer War helped restore cavalry to a prominent place on European battlefields, at the very time that machine guns and heavy artillery were rendering them obsolete.

Callwell's preferences to the contrary, the African wars restored light infantry to its traditional role as a mobile striking arm, the ideal instrument, in fact, for waging colonial operations and anti-guerrilla warfare.

These shortcomings, however, do not detract from the relevance of Callwell's ideas on fighting unconventional wars. Indeed, with the end of the Cold War and the rapid increase in "low-intensity conflicts" around the world, his concerns seem prescient. The debate in his day between those who put their faith in the Maxim gun and those who believed sound strategy was the answer finds an echo in our own time in the controversy between technological determinists and those who believe that conflicts are basically political and cultural, and thus not susceptible to technological solutions.

At a time when low-intensity conflicts are becoming almost banal in their frequency, military commanders could do far worse than turn to Callwell's *Small wars* for sustenance. Callwell offers, for example, the eminently sound advice that commanders

> must realize that every insurgency assumes a different complexion given the circumstances – political, ideological, cultural, and geographic – which shape it. It remains to the commanders to define what they wish to achieve, to determine "what the enemy prizes most," and to remember that technological superiority in no way relieves them of the obligation to craft a viable strategy. . . .[1]

Practice of warfare

The African colonial wars had some negative effects upon the profession of arms in Europe. Generals who made names for themselves in the "small wars" in Africa were not always the best choices for command in the "big war" of 1914–18. Venerable military practices such as the hollow square, volley firing, and reliance upon cold steel to decide battles, gained a new lease on life in Africa, with dire consequences for infantrymen in the First World War. We have already noted the unfortunate resurrection of the cavalry as a result of its role in the Boer War of 1899–1902.

France's imperial wars spawned semi-autonomous colonial armies – the *Armée d'Afrique* (along with the Foreign Legion) in North Africa, the *Armée Coloniale* (marines) in West Africa – who disliked, and were disliked by, the metropolitan army; who had long been alienated from political regimes at home; who had their own ideas on colonial government, economic development, and relations with indigenous peoples. In 1958, this long-strained relationship between France and its colonial soldiers snapped, leading to army revolt in Algiers against a government in Paris it rightly believed was preparing to abandon "*Algérie Française*" to the Algerians.

Africans also learned some military lessons from the colonial wars. The most important of these was already being applied in the decade before the outbreak of the First World War, as African rebels from Morocco to Somalia turned their backs on the bloody pitched battles of the past and embraced guerrilla warfare. In succeeding years, European armies would find it increasingly difficult to cope with this new strategy of resistance.

Legacy to European politics

The major and most obvious consequence of the colonial wars in Africa was, of course, a spectacular increase in the territory, population and resources at the disposal of the European imperial powers. Indeed, Germany, Belgium and Italy made their entry on to the imperial stage by way of their new African holdings. But, with the new imperial gains in wealth and power came new imperial responsibilities: new lands to be administered and guarded, new subjects to try to understand, to police and manipulate.

The carving up of Africa seemed to many to confirm Western claims of racial, cultural and technical superiority, to provide reassurance that notions of the "white man's burden", the *mission civilisatrice*, were not just elitist, racialist fantasies, but real tasks imposed upon Western civilization by virtue of its manifest global hegemony. But there was another side to this coin. The wholesale subjugation of African populations, often with appalling indifference to human suffering, fostered a political backlash in some quarters. Revelations of brutality and misrule in the African colonies helped stoke the fires of anti-imperialism in France, Germany and Britain. Engaged writers such as Lucien Descaves and Paul Vigné d'Octon in France used African settings for their anti-militarist and anti-colonial novels.

Her African colonial conquests emboldened France to look more and more to her empire to sustain her claims to greatness. It could provide her with an international Francophone cultural community, an exclusive trade zone based on the franc, an African *Force noire* to compensate for a French army kept smaller than Germany's by a stagnant metropolitan birthrate. This reliance upon her empire made its break-up after The Second World War doubly traumatic for France.

The Boer War would have profound consequences for Britain and her empire. Her costly victory over the Boers dissuaded Britain from further intervention in the affairs of the white settler regimes in Africa and elsewhere. This all but abandoned the political field in South Africa to the

Afrikaner Nationalists, with consequences whose effects are only now being corrected. This hands-off attitude also encouraged the emergence of white supremacist governments in Kenya and Southern Rhodesia, whose removal was only accomplished following long and bloody struggles by their African populations.

Legacy to Africa

Before independence

What the immediate future held in store for Africa in military terms was expanded horizons for the soldiers of its colonial armies. Black and North African soldiers, for example, served in large numbers in the various theatres of the First World War. Those who served in the French colonial armies saw duty not only in Togo and Cameroon but also at Gallipoli, in the Balkans and on the Western Front. In all, some 845,000 "natives" served under the *tricouleur* during the 1914–18 war, including 181,000 *Tirailleurs Sénégalais*. West Africans serving under the Union Jack fought in Cameroon, while some 50,000 East Africans, including 35,000 troops of the King's African Rifles, fought the Germans in East Africa. Another one million Africans saw service as carriers for the British in East Africa, where they suffered extraordinarily high casualties from gunfire, disease and overwork. Deaths may have reached ten per cent of the total, or 100,000 men.[2] African soldiers also fought in East Africa in World War I in the German, Belgian and Portuguese forces.

World War II found African soldiers even further afield. After helping to defeat the Italians in Ethiopia in 1940, the King's African Rifles were sent to Burma to fight the Japanese. They served mainly as carriers. All together, some 166,000 African troops served Britain outside Africa during the Second World War. Around 141,000 black and North African soldiers served in the French forces during the Second World War. West African troops were stationed in France at the beginning of the war and took part in the unsuccessful defence of the *métropole* in 1940. Many of them spent the rest of the war in German prison camps. Later, African troops in French service found themselves back in Europe, after having participated in the defeat of the *Afrika Korps* in Tunisia. French West African, Algerian and Moroccan troops fought for France in Italy, but when Free French forces took part in the liberation of France, their black soldiers were left behind. This *blanchiment* of the Free French forces was carried out under orders from

General Charles de Gaulle. Some have argued that De Gaulle did not want to give Frenchmen the impression that they were being liberated by colonials, rather than by themselves. Others have contended that this was done to avoid friction with the Americans, who thought the racial mixing in the French army might have a negative impact on their own segregated army.

In the postwar era, African soldiers played an important part in Europe's colonial wars in the Third World. Some 15,000 West and North African soldiers fought for France in Indochina, and more than twice as many served the *métropole* in the Algerian war. Although eventually nothing came of it, Britain apparently also had plans to create a permanent manpower reservoir for overseas service among its West African forces. This kind of thinking was particularly prevalent in the wake of the independence of India, which had for so long been the main source of colonial troops for intervention abroad. Needless to say, foreign service of this sort ended with African independence in the 1960s.

Resistance and nationalism

One of the themes of the new historiography of the wars of imperial conquest has been to emphasize the point that the historical memory of resistance to conquest and of uprisings against colonial rule has been a prime ingredient in African nationalism. Michael Crowder wrote in 1971 that

> Where the heroes of European histories of this period are [the French-men] Archinard, Galliéni, Dodds [the Englishmen], Lugard, Garnet Wolseley and [the Portuguese] Texeira Pinto, those of the African are Samori [Guinea], Bai Bureh [Sierra Leone], Lat Dior [Senegal], Nana of Ebrohimic [Niger Delta], Behanzin [Dahomey] and Attahiru Ahmadu [Northern Nigeria]. Battles are seen not in terms of the success of the conquerors but of the prowess of the defeated leaders in the face of overwhelming odds. And these battles, fought only seven or eight decades ago, are still vivid in oral tradition.[3]

Crowder's examples, drawn from the colonial wars of West Africa, could be multiplied for southern, eastern, and central Africa, as Terence Ranger has shown. In Tanganyika, the national liberation movement took as its heroes two victims of German repression. The first was the Wahehe leader Mkwawa, whose spear-toting warriors defeated a German column armed with machine guns in 1891. After the British took over Tanganyika after the First World War, a District Officer observed that "Today all Wahehe idealize Mkwawa. This may be because he actually beat the white man in battle."[4]

The second resistance hero we have already met – the spirit medium Kinjikitile, who sought to unite all of the peoples of Tanganyika to drive out the Germans in the Maji-Maji Rebellion of 1905–6.

Finally, a somewhat more homely example to re-emphasize the point of historical continuity between the resistance movements of the past and modern consciousness: it concerns the Embu people of Kenya, who were badly beaten by the British in 1906, forced to give up their weapons and forbidden to carry any weapons in the future. A Kenyan scholar wrote sixty years later:

> [T]he memories of 1906 remain fresh, in fact, at the feeder road leading to Ngoiri Primary School, built on the scene of the surrender of the weapons, there is a sign board on which is written the words: "Return our Shields and our Spears." The sign board was planted there in 1963 on Kenya's Independence Day.[5]

Africa's dubious inheritances

Legacy of the colonial military

Along with traditions of armed resistance, modern Africans also inherited military institutions founded during the colonial era. This has been a much less happy legacy. Whereas pre-colonial African armies enjoyed strong ties to the societies and political systems from which they sprang, and indeed were often indistinguishable from them, this was not the case with the colonial armies. European colonial powers tried to separate their African soldiery as much as possible from the surrounding populace. This was thought necessary because the main mission of colonial troops in Africa was to maintain order, a task that would have been greatly complicated by identification between the soldiers and indigenous society.

The colonial powers achieved the separation they sought by drawing their recruits from the marginal ethnic groups of their colonies, usually smaller, more remote rural tribes who were likely to have little rapport with the more sophisticated urban or coastal peoples among whom they were stationed. In the Gold Coast, for example, the British recruited their enlisted ranks from the poor, illiterate rural tribes in the far north of the country, rather than from the better educated, more cosmopolitan Fante or Ashanti of the south.

The French followed similar policies in their colonies. In Chad, for example, the colonial government succeeded in dividing the African population by recruiting troops almost exclusively from among the animist black population of the south rather than from among the Muslim Arab population of the north. Naturally, these recruits from remote, marginal areas were also more likely to be amenable to the kind of iron discipline imposed in colonial armies.

Another divisive tactic was to recruit officers from one part of the country and other ranks from another. In Nigeria, for example, the other ranks came from the north and the officers from the south.[6] Yet another tactic to separate soldiers from the populace was that of stationing troops from rival ethnic groups in one another's territories.

The only imperial power that did not promote ethnicity in its colonial army was Belgium. In the *Force Publique* in the Congo, a deliberate policy of multi-ethnicity was followed in order to minimize the chances of mutiny. Each battalion of the *Force Publique* had to include members of at least four ethnic groups; presumably this sort of ethnic mix would discourage solidarity in the ranks. An unintended consequence of this policy was that the *Force Publique* was practically the only genuine national institution in the Congo at independence in 1960.[7]

Finally, the whole ethos of colonial military service – long-term enlistment (often up to twenty years), the stress on loyalty and unquestioning obedience, the identification with one's regiment – tended to foster a strong sense of identification with the imperial power.

The indigenous population often met the indifference of the troops with suspicion and in some cases outright hostility. African colonial armies, wrote Pierre van den Berghe, "were often regarded by the local population with deep distrust, as hated tools of the white conqueror".[8] Military service in colonial armies has tended to divide citizens of the new independent states of Africa. The Algerian *harkis* who fought for the French in the Algerian War are considered traitors by many of their fellow citizens. Veterans who fought for France in the *Tirailleurs Sénégalais* are often regarded the same way in modern West Africa.

The armies inherited by the newly independent African nations were little changed from what they had been under colonial rule. This tended to put the armed forces at odds with civilian governments, whose primary aim was to foster a spirit of national unity. Amii Omara-Otunnu, a Ugandan historian, explains how the recruitment policies of the army worked to undermine democracy in his country.

> [T]he colonial policy of drafting groups from "racial", geographical and religious backgrounds different from the people among whom they were to be deployed . . . later led to the emphasis on ethnicity in the army. After Independence this began to be subject to the individualistic opportunism of Ugandan leaders, and the practice of recruiting troops on ethnic and linguistic criteria has now become entrenched.[9]

It was, of course, the "practice of recruiting troops on ethnic and linguistic criteria" which, more than anything else, paved the way to power in Uganda for the dictator Idi Amin Dada. His power base was his own Kakwa tribe, a marginal Muslim group which had been a favorite target of British recruiters in colonial days.

After independence, far from abating, the military's hostility to civil society has in many cases increased. This has contributed as much as anything else to the seemingly endless cascade of military *coups d'état* in Africa since independence. One of the most pressing (and daunting) tasks of contemporary African governments is somehow to restore the symbiosis between armies and the people that existed before the imperial conquest. This challenge has been effectively summarized by Claude Welch, one of the more perceptive observers of the post-independence African military scene.

> African governments must carry out a significant revision of the patterns of civil-military relations inherited from colonial rule, lest the political power exercised by the armed forces continue to grow unabated. For example, these governments should convert their armed forces into more representative reflections of their societies, and find ways in which the military can be used as instruments of national integration. Perhaps most important, the governments must find effective means to institutionalise civilian control, lest the military establishments of individual states become praetorian guards, arrogating to themselves a disproportionate share of national revenue and political power.[10]

Cult of violence

Africa's problem with armed violence, however, perhaps lies deeper than the alienation of its soldiers. It may be a problem which also afflicts much of the civilian population. There is some evidence that one of the legacies of the colonial era was the widespread internalizing of the belief that, in Chairman Mao's phrase, "power grows out of the barrel of a gun". As J.M. Lee has observed,

> Successful leadership in Africa at all levels seems to express itself often in a quasi-military manner. Men have personal followings which behave like private armies. The word "power" itself has become a symbol to conjure with.[11]

Lee, however, is talking about a legacy from white rule which is all about how to win and hold on to political and, perhaps, social power. African sociologist, Ali Mazrui, believes that the cult of violence so prominently on display in many parts of Africa today is part of an attempt by African males to heal the deep psychological wound caused by colonial rule. Masculine virtues like virility and martial valour were linked in pre-colonial society, he argues, and that connection was severed under European hegemony. The warrior's self-reliance in pre-colonial Africa was reduced to dependency under colonial rule. The colonial powers recruited some African males to serve in their armed forces, while the rest of the male population was disarmed and ordered to keep the peace. Thus, for most of the African male population, says Mazrui, "Colonialism and Christianity not only demilitarised but demasculated Africa". This was a powerful blow, both socially and psychologically, from which post-colonial Africa has yet to recover, he concludes.[12]

Since independence, efforts to reclaim a warrior tradition for African males have led to the lionization of martial figures such as Idi Amin Dada in Uganda or Jean-Bedel Bokassa in the Central African Republic. The cult surrounding the memory of Shaka in South Africa is another example.[13]

These are problematical developments, as Mazrui admits.

> The warrior tradition in Africa is far from being as yet dominant once again, but there are signs of an important resurrection. As a reaction and rebellion against dependency, this wears the face of proud promise. But as an initiation into the culture of violent valour, the resurrection of the warrior tradition in African political culture also carries its own special hazards. As Africa seeks to consolidate its manhood, and recovers its adulthood, it must also remember to conserve its humanity.[14]

Mazrui's remarks about a "culture of violent valour" bring us to a related topic, Frantz Fanon's notion, first articulated in the late 1950s when the Algerian war of independence was raging, that Africans could only effectively decolonize themselves if they employed the same violence against their former colonial masters as was used against them in the wars of imperial conquest. In arguing in this way, in his book *The wretched of the earth*, for example, Fanon seemed to be making the point that those Africans who had achieved independence without fighting for it were only half-liberated. What made this argument so compelling in some quarters, and in Algeria perhaps more than anywhere else, was the fairly widespread feeling that the level of violence employed by the Europeans, first to conquer Africa and now to hang on to it, had been, and was, excessive. Here the Africans were not thinking only of the enormous firepower unleashed on the continent, although this was certainly in their minds, but also of the almost universal belief among European conquerors that Africans had to be beaten and beaten soundly in battle before they could be made amenable to European rule. But, often, all those who took in what Fanon said, and acted upon it, were doing, consciously or not, was emulating their tormentors and enshrining violence as a regenerative force. Throughout their history, with the possible exception of the armies of Shaka Zulu, Africans had observed limits to the use of violence, sometimes even substituting ritual and symbol for physical force. It is not clear that Africans understand those limits any more. If they do not, this may be the saddest of all the unhappy legacies of the wars of imperial conquest.

Notes

Preface

1. C. Townshend (ed.), "Preface", *The Oxford illustrated history of modern war* (Oxford: Oxford University Press, 1997).
2. Oliver & Fage, *A short history of Africa*, 6th edn (London: Penguin, 1988), p. 177.
3. First published in 1961, this influential book was reprinted seven times before a new edition was brought out in 1981.
4. Robinson, "Non-European foundations of European imperialism: sketch for a theory of collaboration", in *Studies in the theory of imperialism*, R. Owen & B. Sutcliffe (eds) (Harlow: Longman, 1975), p. 119.
5. Boahen, *African perspectives on colonialism* (Baltimore: Johns Hopkins University Press, 1985), p. 46.
6. Hargreaves, "West African states and the European conquest", in *The history and politics of colonialism*, vol. 1 of *Colonialism in Africa, 1870–1914*, L.H. Gann and P. Duignan (eds) (Cambridge: Cambridge University Press, 1969), p. 206.
7. See especially Ranger's articles, "Connexions between 'primary resistance' movements and modern mass nationalism in East and Central Africa", Parts 1 & 2, *Journal of African History*, **9**(3–4), 1968, pp. 437–53, 631–41.
8. Hargreaves, "West African states and the European conquest", p. 216.
9. O'Sullivan, "The Franco-Baoulé war, 1891–1911: the struggle against the French conquest of the central Ivory Coast", *Journal of African Studies* **5**, 1978, p. 331.
10. *African Affairs* **2**, 1970, pp. 329–49.
11. Robert I. Rotberg & Ali Mazrui (eds), *Protest and power in black Africa* (New York: Oxford University Press, 1970), p. xviii.
12. Jauffret's two-volume study should be seen, however, as complementing, not replacing, two books in English which also appeared in the 1980s: Doug Porch's *The march to the Marne: the French army, 1871–1914* (Cambridge: Cambridge University Press, 1981) and Tony Clayton's *France, soldiers and Africa* (London: Brassey's, 1988).
13. Pélissier's books are published on his own press in his hometown of Orgeval, France.
14. See, for example, Axtell's *The invasion within: the contest of cultures in colonial North America* (New York: Oxford University Press, 1985), and Jennings's *Empire of fortune: crowns, colonies, and tribes in the Seven Years' War in America* (New York: Norton, 1988).

220

Chapter One

1. N. Mostert, *Frontiers: the epic tragedy of South Africa's creation and the tragedy of the Xhosa people* (New York: Knopf, 1992).

2. R. Oliver & A. Atmore, *Africa since 1800*, 4th edn (Cambridge: Cambridge University Press, 1994), p. 100.

3. R. Robinson, J. Gallagher, with A. Denny, *Africa and the Victorians: the official mind of imperialism*, 2nd edn (London: Macmillan, 1981), pp. 161–2, and especially R. Robinson, "Non-European foundations of European imperialism", pp. 117–40.

4. For a good summary of this point of view, see Boahen, *African perspectives on colonialism*, pp. 1–14.

5. Perhaps the most authoritative statement of this viewpoint is in H. Brunschwig, *French colonialism, 1871–1914: myths and realities* (New York: Knopf, 1992), pp. 184–5.

6. Curtin et al., *African history: from earliest times to independence*, 2nd edn (Harlow: Longman, 1995), p. 398.

7. Goody, *Technology, tradition and the state in Africa* (London: Oxford University Press, 1971), pp. 36–7.

8. Smith, *Warfare and diplomacy in pre-colonial West Africa* (London: Methuen, 1977), p. 70.

9. L. Mair, *African kingdoms* (Oxford: Clarendon, 1977), p. 66.

10. *ibid.*, pp. 71–2.

11. D. Ross, "Dahomey", in *West African resistance: the military response to colonial occupation* (New York: Africana, 1971), p. 149.

12. *ibid.*

13. R.B. Edgerton, *Like lions they fought: the Zulu War and the last black empire in South Africa* (New York: Ballantine, 1988), p. 24. This view of Zulu martial prowess has also enjoyed a long life. In a 1970 book, *Britain and her army, 1509–1970: a military, political and social survey* (London, Allan Lane), British military historian Corelli Barnett wrote (p. 319) that the Zulus' "martial spirit was kept high by sexual repression, leading to marked irritability vented on the enemy by means of the assegai".

14. A. Donny, *L'Art militaire au Congo* (Brussels: Th. Falk, 1897), p. 10.

15. C.J. Balesi, *From adversaries to comrades-in-arms: West Africans and the French military, 1885–1918* (Waltham, Mass.: Crossroads Press, 1979), pp. 43–5.

16. C. Spring, *African arms and armor* (Washington, D.C.: Smithsonian Institution Press, 1993), p. 32.

17. Smith, *Warfare and diplomacy*, pp. 107–8.

18. Spring, *African arms and armor*, p. 118.

19. I. Knight, *The anatomy of the Zulu army from Shaka to Cetshwayo, 1818–1879* (London: Greenhill, 1995), pp. 179–80.

20. R.A. Caulk, "Armies as predators: soldiers and peasants in Ethiopia c. 1850–1935", *International Journal of African Studies* 11(3), 1978, p. 463.

21. Smith, *Warfare and diplomacy*, pp. 158–9.

22. *ibid.*, p. 157.

23. J.K. Fynn, "Ghana-Asante", in M. Crowder (ed.), *West African resistance*, p. 20.

24. R.B. Edgerton, *The fall of the Asante empire: the hundred-year war for Africa's Gold Coast* (New York: Free Press, 1995), p. 51.

25. *ibid.*, p. 54.

26. Fynn, "Ghana-Asante", pp. 25–7; Edgerton, *Fall of the Asante empire*, pp. 51–5. The

authoritative source on Ashanti firearms imports is R.A. Kea, "Firearms and warfare on the Gold and Slave Coasts from the sixteenth to the nineteenth centuries", *Journal of African History* **12**(2), 1971, pp. 185–213.

27. Edgerton, *The fall of the Asante empire*, p. vi.

28. J. Smaldone, *Warfare in the Sokoto Caliphate: historical and sociological perspectives* (Cambridge: Cambridge University Press, 1977), p. 32.

29. Ritter, *Shaka Zulu: the rise of the Zulu empire* (London: Longmans, Green, 1955), p. 41.

30. The best source on the tactics of the Zulu *impi* is Ian Knight's recent *Anatomy of the Zulu army* (London: Greenhill, 1995) which takes into account much new research.

31. Knight, *Anatomy of the Zulu army*, p. 33.

32. D.R. Morris, *The washing of the spears: a history of the rise of the Zulu nation under Shaka and its fall in the Zulu War of 1879* (New York: Random House, 1965), p. 60.

33. J. Keegan & A. Wheatcroft (eds), *Who's who in military history from 1453 to the present day*, 3rd edn (London: Routledge, 1996), p. 272.

34. S. Rubenson, *The survival of Ethiopian independence* (London: Heinemann, 1978), pp. 30–1.

35. The 1867–8 campaign receives colourful if somewhat dated treatment in D. Chandler, "The expedition to Abyssinia, 1867–8", in *Victorian military campaigns*, B. Bond (ed.) (London: Hutchinson, 1968), pp. 105–59.

36. H.G. Marcus, *A history of Ethiopia* (Berkeley: University of California Press, 1994), pp. 72–6.

37. J. Dunn, "'For God, Emperor, country! The evolution of Ethiopia's nineteenth-century army'", *War in History* **1**(3), 1994, p. 284.

38. Dunn, "'For God, Emperor, and Country'", pp. 290–1; R.A. Caulk, "Firearms and princely power in Ethiopia in the nineteenth century," *Journal of African History* **13**, 1972, pp. 624–7.

39. Caulk, "Firearms and princely power," p. 626.

Chapter Two

1. C.R. Boxer, *The Portuguese seaborne empire, 1415–1825* (New York: Knopf, 1969), p. 50.

2. L.L.C. Faidherbe, *Le Sénégal. La France dans l'Afrique Occidentale* (Paris: Hachette, 1889), p. 140.

3. K.R. Andrews, *Trade, plunder and settlement: maritime enterprise and the genesis of the British Empire, 1480–1630* (Cambridge: Cambridge University Press, 1984), p. 114.

4. Meredith, *An account of the Gold Coast of Africa: with a brief history of the African Company* (London: Longman, Hurst, Rees, Orme and Brown, 1812), pp. 103–4.

5. C.R. Boxer, *Four centuries of Portuguese expansion, 1415–1825: a succinct survey* (Johannesburg: Witwatersrand University Press, 1961), p. 27.

6. P.D. Curtin, *Death by migration: Europe's encounter with the tropical world in the nineteenth century* (Cambridge: Cambridge University Press, 1989), p. 8, Table 1.1.

7. R. Oliver & A. Atmore, *The African Middle Ages, 1400–1800* (Cambridge: Cambridge University Press, 1981), pp. 82, 90–1, 104–5.

8. Boxer, *Portuguese seaborne empire*, pp. 50–1.

9. G.V. Scammell, *The first imperial age: European overseas expansion c. 1400–1715,* 2nd edn (London: Routledge, 1991), p. 83; Boxer, *Portuguese seaborne empire*, pp. 301–2.

10. R.J. Hammond, "Uneconomic imperialism: Portugal in Africa before 1910", in *The history and politics of colonialism, 1870–1914*, vol. 1 of *Colonialism in Africa, 1870–1960*, p. 359.

11. D.R. Headrick, *The tools of empire: technology and European imperialism in the nineteenth century* (New York: Oxford University Press, 1981), pp. 142–4, 146.

12. Robinson, "Non-European foundations of European imperialism", p. 126.

13. Kanya-Forstner, "A final comment on the value of Robinson and Gallagher", in *Imperialism: the Robinson and Gallagher controversy*, W.R. Louis (ed.) (London: Franklin Watts, 1976), p. 231.

14. Brunschwig, "French expansion and local reactions in Black Africa at the time of imperialism (1880–1914)", in *Expansion and reaction*, H.L. Wesseling (ed.) (Leiden: Leiden University Press, 1978), p. 117.

15. See, for example, L.C. Barrows, "The merchants and General Faidherbe: aspects of French expansion in the 1850s", *Revue française d'histoire d'outre-mer* **61**(223), 1974, pp. 236–83; M.O. McLane, "Commercial rivalries and French policy on the Senegal River, 1831–1858", *African Economic History* **15**, 1987, pp. 39–67; and C. Coquery-Vidrovitch, *Brazza et la prise de possession du Congo, la mission de l'Ouest africain 1883–1885* (Paris: Mouton, 1969).

16. Kanya-Forstner, *The Conquest of the Western Sudan: a study in French military imperialism* (Cambridge: Cambridge University Press, 1969), pp. 10–15.

17. M. Clark, *Modern Italy, 1871–1982* (Harlow: Longman, 1984), p. 6.

18. Labanca, *In marcia verso Adua*, p. 51.

19. Wehler, "German imperialism: Robinson and Gallagher and Bismarck's colonial policy", in *Imperialism: the Robinson & Gallagher controversy*, p. 208.

20. Oliveira Marques, A.H. de, *History of Portugal*, vol. 2, *From empire to corporate state* (New York: Columbia University Press, 1972), pp. 72–4, 110–14.

21. Stengers, "King Leopold's imperialism", in *Studies in the theory of imperialism*, pp. 248, 262.

22. Global figures on German troop strength in 1900 come from Paul Kennedy, *The rise and fall of the Great Powers: economic change and military conflict from 1500 to 2000* (New York: Random House, 1987), p. 203, table 19. Data on the size of the German colonial army in Africa were taken from J.S. Herron, *Colonial army systems of the Netherlands, Great Britain, France, Germany, Portugal, Italy and Belgium* (Washington, D.C.: Government Printing Office, 1901), pp. 115–18. There were no soldiers, only police, in Germany's other African colony, Togo.

23. Monteil, *De Saint-Louis [Sénégal] à Tripoli, par le lac Tchad, voyage à travers du Soudan et du Sahara accompli pendant les années 1890–91–92* (Paris: Alcan, 1895), p. 1. Quoted in vol. 2 of Jauffret, *Parlement, gouvernement, commandement*, p. 778.

24. Algeria was, of course, an exception since from 1870 onward, as it was considered a department of France. In 1873, the *Armée d'Afrique*, which had conquered Algeria in the 1840s and then remained there as a permanent occupation force, was designated the Nineteenth Corps of the French metropolitan army and given the mission of invading Sicily and southern Italy in case of war with the Triple Alliance. A. Clayton, *France, soldiers and Africa*, p. 24.

25. J. Stengers, *Combien le Congo a-t-il coûté la Belgique?* (Brussels: Acadeémie Royale des Sciences Coloniales, 1957), p. 330.

26. J. Iliffe, *Africans: the history of a continent* (Cambridge: Cambridge University Press, 1995), pp. 1, 3.

27. H. Strachan, *European armies and the conduct of war* (London: George Allen & Unwin, 1983), p. 88.

28. J.J. Texeira Botelho, *Historia militar e politica dos Portugueses em Moçambique de 1833 aos nossos dias*, 2nd edn (Lisbon: Centro Tip. Colonial, 1936), pp. 452, 460.

29. Curtin, *Death by migration*, pp. xiii, 159.

30. Minute by Deputy Adjutant General Schomberg, Royal Marines, to Sanitary Report by Staff Surgeon, H. Fegan, Royal Navy, HMS "Active", 31 December 1873. Carton "Ashantee War, 1873–4", File No. 11 "Ashanti Battalion, 1873", Archives, Royal Marine Museum.

31. *ibid.*, Horse Guards to Admiral Seymour, Royal Navy, 23 December 1873.

32. E. Fraser & L.G. Carr-Laughton, *The Royal Marine Artillery, 1804–1923* (London: Royal United Service Institution, 1930), vol. 2, p. 553.

33. Donny (ed.), *L'Art militaire au Congo*, p. 32.

34. Herron, *Colonial army systems*, p. 42.

35. Killingray, "Colonial warfare in West Africa, 1870–1914," in *Imperialism and war*, J.A. De Moor & H.L. Wesseling (eds) (Leiden: Brill, 1989), p. 146.

36. Mangin, *La force noire* (Paris: Hachette, 1910), pp. 175–6.

37. Quoted in M. Michel, *Galliéni* (Paris: Fayard, 1989), p. 119.

38. M. Michel, *La mission Marchand, 1895–9* (Paris: Mouton, 1972), p. 34.

39. Ditte, *Observations sur la guerre dans les colonies: organisation-exécution. Conférences faites à l'Ecole Supérieure de Guerre* (Paris: Lavauzelle, 1905), pp. 40–1.

40. Jauffret, *Parlement, gouvernement, commandement*, vol. 2, p. 1131.

41. L.H. Gann & P. Duignan, *The rulers of British Africa, 1870–1914* (Stanford, Cal.: Stanford University Press, 1978), p. 84.

42. On these two forces, see A. Haywood and F.A.S. Clarke, *The history of the Royal West African Frontier Force* (Aldershot: Galen & Polden, 1964), and H. Moyse-Bartlett, *The King's African Rifles, a study in the military history of East and Central Africa, 1890–1945* (Aldershot: Gale & Polden, 1956).

43. L.H. Gann & P. Duignan, *The rulers of German Africa, 1884–1914* (Stanford, Cal.: Stanford University Press, 1976), p. 118.

44. G.F.H. Berkeley, *The campaign of Adowa and the rise of Menelik* (New York: Negro Universities Press, 1969), pp. 373–4.

45. *ibid.*, pp. 70–1.

46. Azevedo Coutinho, *A campanha do Barue em 1902* (Lisbon: Tip. da Livraria Férin, 1904), pp. 61–2.

47. Herron, *Colonial army systems*, p. 131.

48. Jauffret, *Parlement, gouvernement, commandement*, vol. 2, p. 653ff.

49. Labanca, *In marcia verso Adua*, pp. 175–8; Labanca, *Il Generale Cesare Ricotti e la politica militare italiana dal 1884 al 1887* (Rome: Stato Maggiore dell'Esercito, 1986), p. 191.

50. Bond (ed.), *Victorian military campaigns*, p. 16.

51. A.J. Marder, *The anatomy of British sea power: a history of British naval policy in the pre-dreadnought era, 1880–1905* (New York: Knopf, 1940), pp. 248–9.

52. Grosser Generalstabs, *Die Kaempfe der deutschen Truppen in Suedwestafrika auf Grund*

amlichten Materials bearbeitet von der Kriegsgeschichtlichen Abteilung I des grossen Generalstabs, vol. 2 (Berlin: Mittler und Sohn, 1907), p. 300.

53. D. Porch, *The march to the Marne*, p. 134.

54. Gann & Duignan, *The rulers of German Africa*, pp. 108, 112-3.

55. R.J.B. Bosworth, *Italy, the least of the Great Powers: Italian foreign policy before the First World War* (London: Cambridge University Press, 1979), p. 21.

56. Pélissier, *Naissance de Mozambique*, vol. 1, p. 140.

57. A.J. Telo, *Economia e imperio no Portugal contemporaneo*, (Lisbon: Edições Cosmos, 1994), p. 150.

58. H.L. Peterson (ed.), *Encyclopedia of firearms*, 3rd edn (New York: E.P. Dutton, 1967), p. 187.

59. Gann & Duignan, *Rulers of British Africa*, p. 79.

60. *ibid.*

61. *ibid.*, p. 113n. On the appearance of the Gatling gun in the Ashanti campaign, see A. Lloyd, *The drums of Kumasi: the story of the Ashanti wars* (Harlow: Longman, 1964), p. 97.

62. C. Balesi, "West African influence on the French army of World War I", in *Double impact: France and Africa in the age of imperialism*, G.W. Johnson (ed.) (Westport, Conn.: Greenwood, 1985), pp. 96, 103 n16.

63. R. Ford, *The grim reaper: the machine-gun and machine-gunners* (New York: Sarpedon, 1996), pp. 63-4.

64. A. Enes, *A guerra de Africa em 1895 (memorias)*, 2nd edn. (Lisbon: Edições Gama, 1945), p. 359.

65. D.J.M. Muffett, *Concerning brave captains: being a history of the British occupation of Kano and Sokoto and of the last stand of the Fulani forces* (London: André Deutsch, 1964), p. 114.

66. J. Laband, *Kingdom in crisis: the Zulu response to the British invasion of 1879* (Manchester: Manchester University Press, 1992), p. 82.

67. Clowes, *The Royal Navy: a history from the earliest times to the death of Queen Victoria* (London: Sampson, Low, Marston, 1903), vol. 7, p. 463.

68. P. Kennedy, *The rise and fall of British naval mastery* (Atlantic Highlands, N.J.: Ashfield Press, 1983), p. 166.

69. T. Ropp, *The development of a modern navy: French naval policy, 1871–1904*. S.S. Roberts (ed.) (Annapolis, Md.: Naval Institute Press, 1987), p. 141.

70. *ibid.*, p. 157.

71. *ibid.*, pp. 142-3.

72. Gann & Duignan, *Rulers of German Africa*, p. 110.

73. Boahen, *African perspectives on colonialism*, pp. 56-7.

Chapter Three

1. G. Hardy, *Faidherbe* (Paris: Editions de l'Encyclopédie de l'Empire Français, 1947), pp. 24-7.

2. Kanya-Forstner, *Conquest of the Western Sudan*, pp. 8–9.

3. C.-A. Julien, *La conquête et les débuts de la colonisation (1827–1871)*, vol. 1 of *Histoire de l'Algérie contemporaine* (Paris: Presses Universitaires de France, 1964), pp. 184–5.

4. J. Ruedy, *Modern Algeria: the origins and development of a nation* (Bloomington: Indiana University Press, 1992), p. 66.

5. Julien, *La conquête*, pp. 48–9.

6. P. Guiral, "L'opinion marseillaise et les débuts de l'entreprise algérienne (1830–1841)", *Revue historique* **154**(1), 1995, pp. 9–34.

7. B.G. Martin, *Muslim brotherhoods in nineteenth-century Africa* (Cambridge: Cambridge University Press, 1976), pp. 47–8.

8. Julien, *La conquête*, p. 182.

9. M. Emérit, *L'Algérie à l'époque d'Abd-el-Kader* (Paris: Larose, 1951), p. 148.

10. C.H. Churchill, *The life of Abd el Kader, ex-Sultan of the Arabs of Algeria* (London: Chapman & Hall, 1867), p. 28.

11. B.G. Martin, *Muslim brotherhoods*, p. 62.

12. R. Oliver & A. Atmore, *Africa since 1800*, 5th edn (Cambridge: Cambridge University Press, 1994), p. 48.

13. Iliffe, *Africans: the history of a continent*, p. 166. According to Thomas Pakenham, *The Boer war* (New York: Random House, 1979), pp. 607–8, 356, 693 imperial and 82, 742 colonial troops fought for Britain in the 1899–1902 war.

14. Julien, *La conquête*, pp. 129–30, 171, 181.

15. A.T. Sullivan, *Thomas-Robert Bugeaud, France and Algeria: 1784–1849: power, politics and the good society* (Hamden, Conn.: Archon Books, 1983), pp. 84–5.

16. D. Porch, "French colonial forces on the Saharan rim", in J.C. Bradford (ed.), *The military and conflict between cultures: soldiers at the interface* (College Station, Tex.: Texas A&M University Press, 1997), p. 165.

17. G. Hardy, *Histoire sociale de la colonisation française* (Paris: Larose, 1953), p. 108. Quoted in C. Harrison, *France and Islam in West Africa, 1860–1960* (Cambridge: Cambridge University Press, 1988), p. 15.

18. J. Gottmann, "Bugeaud, Galliéni, Lyautey: the development of French colonial warfare," in E.M. Earle (ed.), *Makers of modern strategy: military thought from Machiavelli to Hitler* (Princeton: Princeton University Press, 1971), p. 235.

19. Callwell, *Small wars: their principles and practice*, 3rd edn (Lincoln, Neb.: Univ. of Nebraska Press, 1996), p. 188. The index to *Small wars* contains 73 references to Abd el-Kader, Algeria and Bugeaud.

20. Sullivan, *Thomas-Robert Bugeaud*, p. 81.

21. Gottmann, "Bugeaud, Galliéni, Lyautey", pp. 236–7.

22. Julien, *La conquête*, p. 194.

23. S.T. Ross, *From flintlock to rifle: infantry tactics, 1740–1866* (London: Cass, 1996), p. 163.

24. Sullivan, *Thomas-Robert Bugeaud*, pp. 81–2.

25. Kanya-Forstner, *Conquest of the Western Sudan*, p. 8.

26. Idéville, H., comte d', *Le Maréchal Bugeaud d'après sa correspondance intime et des documents inédits, 1784–1849* (Paris: Firmin-Didot, 1882), vol. 3, pp. 155–6.

27. Julien, *La conquête*, p. 175.

28. Quoted in *ibid*.

29. Sullivan, *Thomas-Robert Bugeaud*, pp. 164, 166.

30. Jauffret, *Parlement, gouvernement, commandement*, vol. 2, p. 881.

31. Quoted in D. Porch, "Bugeaud, Gallieni, Lyautey", in P. Paret (ed.), *Makers of modern*

strategy: from Machiavelli to the nuclear age (Princeton: Princeton University Press, 1986), p. 380.

32. Julien, *La conquête*, pp. 320–1.

33. Sullivan, *Thomas-Robert Bugeaud*, pp. 126–9.

34. Julien, *La conquête*, p. 223.

35. *ibid.*, p. 473 *passim*.

36. Fanon, *The wretched of the earth* (New York: Grove Press, 1963), p. 94.

37. W.B. Cohen, "Imperial mirage: the Western Sudan in French thought and action", *Journal of the Historical Society of Nigeria*, **7**(3), 1974, pp. 417–45.

38. J.L.A. Webb, "The trade in gum arabic: prelude to French conquest in Senegal", *Journal of African History*, **26**, 1985, pp. 149–68.

39. Hardy, *Faidherbe*, p. 31.

40. D. Robinson, *The holy war of Umar Tal: the Western Sudan in the mid-nineteenth century* (Oxford: Clarendon, 1985), p. 330.

41. J. Méniaud, *Les pionniers du Soudan avant, avec et après Archinard, 1879–1894* (Paris: Société de publications modernes, 1931), Vol. 1, p. 61.

42. Hardy, *Faidherbe*, p. 31.

43. Pasquier, "L'Influence de l'expérience algérienne sur la politique de la France au Sénégal (1842–1869)", in *Perspectives nouvelles sur le passé de l'Afrique noire et de Madagascar*, C.-A. Julien (ed.) (Paris: Publications de la Sorbonne, 1974), pp. 282, 284. Faidherbe's own remarks, contained in a 1 October 1858 report to the Ministry of Marine, are quoted in *ibid.*, p. 273.

44. Kanya-Forstner, *Conquest of the Western Sudan*, pp. 31–2.

45. Hardy, *Faidherbe*, pp. 9–14.

46. L. Barrows, "Louis Léon César Faidherbe (1818–1889)", in *African proconsuls: European governors in Africa*, L.H. Gann & P. Duignan (eds) (New York: Free Press, 1978), pp. 52–4.

47. *ibid.*, pp. 82–4; Faidherbe, *Le Sénégal*, p. 93.

48. Sullivan, *Thomas-Robert Bugeaud*, pp. 166–7.

49. J.D. Hargreaves, "The Tokolor empire of Ségou and its relations with the French", in *Boston University Papers on Africa*, J. Butler (ed.) (Boston: Boston University Press, 1966), vol. 2, pp. 131–2.

50. K. Shillington, *History of Africa* (London: Macmillan, 1989), p. 106.

51. There should be no confusion here between the Tijani order of the Sudan, with its radical theology and politics, and the more conservative *Tijaniyya* of North Africa, which had allied with the French against Abd el-Kader in Algeria.

52. M. Hiskett, "The nineteenth-century jihads in West Africa", in *The Cambridge History of Africa*, vol. 5, J.E. Flint (ed.) (London: Cambridge University Press, 1976), p. 156.

53. *ibid.*, p. 158.

54. Martin, *Muslim brotherhoods*, p. 72.

55. B.O. Oloruntimehin, *The Segu Tukulor empire* (New York: Humanities Press, 1972), p. 39.

56. Martin, *Muslim brotherhoods*, p. 82.

57. Faidherbe, *Le Sénégal*, p. 216.

58. J.R. Willis, *In the path of Allah: the passion of al-Hajj Umar: an essay into the nature of charisma in Islam* (London: Cass, 1989), p. 130.

59. Oloruntimehin, *Segu Tukolor empire*, p. 53.

60. *ibid.*, p. 1.
61. Hiskett, "Nineteenth-century jihads", p. 159.
62. Hardy, *Faidherbe*, pp. 64–8.
63. Oloruntimehin, *The Segu Tukulor empire*, p. 32.
64. Robinson, *Holy war of Umar Tal*, pp. 210, 215, 217–18.
65. Y. Person, "Western Africa, 1870–1886", in *Cambridge History of Africa*, Vol. 6, R. Oliver & G.N. Sanderson (eds) (Cambridge: Cambridge University Press, 1985), p. 216.
66. J. Meyer et al., *Histoire de la France coloniale: des origines à 1914* (Paris: Armand Colin, 1991), pp. 486–7.
67. Balesi, *From adversaries to comrades-in-arms*, pp. 5–6.
68. M. Echenburg, *Colonial conscripts: the Tirailleurs Sénégalais in French West Africa, 1857–1960* (Portsmouth, N.H.: Heinemann, 1991), p. 10.
69. H. Wesseling, *Divide and rule: the partition of Africa, 1880–1914* (Westport, Conn.: Praeger, 1996), p. 177.
70. Echenburg, *Colonial conscripts*, pp. 12–14.
71. B.G. Martin, *Muslim brotherhoods*, p. 98; Willis, *Passion of Al-Hajj Umar*, p. 222.
72. I. Wilks, *Asante in the nineteenth century: the structure and evolution of a political order* (Cambridge: Cambridge University Press, 1975), p. 45 (map iv).
73. Fynn, "Ghana-Asante", in *West African resistance*, p. 19.
74. J.M. Perry, *Arrogant armies: great military disasters and the generals behind them* (New York: Wiley, 1996), pp. 102–7.
75. A. Lloyd, *The drams of Kumasi*, p. 57.
76. W.W. Claridge, *A history of the Gold Coast and Ashanti*, 2nd edn. (London: Frank Cass, 1964), vol. 1, p. 529.
77. Wilks, *Asante in the nineteenth century*, pp. 178–9, 691.
78. Quoted in Lloyd, *Drums of Kumasi*, p. 93.
79. J. Lehmann, *All Sir Garnet: a life of Field-Marshal Lord Wolseley* (London: Jonathan Cape, 1964), pp. 164, 171.
80. Wilks, *Asante in the nineteenth century*, p. 323.
81. *ibid.*, pp. 681–2.
82. Edgerton, *Fall of the Asante empire*, pp. 55–6.
83. J. Keegan, "The Ashanti campaign, 1873–4", in *Victorian military campaigns*, pp. 178–9.
84. G. Wolseley, *The story of a soldier's life* (New York: Charles Scribner's Sons, 1903), vol. 2, pp. 257, 264.
85. W.D. McIntyre, *The imperial frontier in the tropics, 1865–1875: a study of British colonial policy in West Africa, Malaya and the South Pacific in the age of Gladstone and Disraeli* (London: Macmillan, 1967), pp. 81, 100.
86. Lehmann, *All Sir Garnet*, p. 163.
87. Lloyd, *Drums of Kumasi*, p. 93.
88. Keegan, "The Ashanti campaign", p. 179.
89. Lehmann, *All Sir Garnet*, p. 165.
90. *ibid.*, p. 9.
91. J. Keegan & A. Wheatcroft (eds), *Who's who in military history*, p. 322.
92. Lehmann, *All Sir Garnet*, pp. 14–15.
93. Keegan & Wheatcroft (eds), *Who's who in military history*, p. 322.
94. Wolseley, *Story of a soldier's life*, p. 261.

95. *ibid.*, pp. 347, 264.

96. Lloyd, *Drums of Kumasi*, p. 76.

97. Wolseley, *Story of a soldier's life*, p. 265.

98. *ibid.*, p. 314.

99. Lloyd, *Drums of Kumasi*, pp. 84–8.

100. Lehmann, *All Sir Garnet*; Lloyd, *Drums of Kumasi*; E.W. Spiers, *The late Victorian army, 1868–1902* (Manchester: Manchester University Press, 1992).

101. Wolseley, *Story of a soldier's life*, pp. 312–13.

102. Keegan, "The Ashanti campaign", pp. 184–6.

103. Lloyd, *Drums of Kumasi*, p. 76.

104. Keegan, "The Ashanti campaign", p. 186.

105. Lehmann, *All Sir Garnet*, p. 186.

106. Unpublished ms., journal of Lt. Parkins Hearle, Royal Marine Light Infantry, pp. 11–12. Archives, Royal Marine Museum, file "Ashantee War, 1873–4", 7/14/9(4).

107. Jauffret, *Parlement, gouvernement, commandement*, p. 821; A. Donny (ed.), *L'Art militaire au Congo*, p. 59.

108. Fynn, "Ghana-Asante", p. 40.

109. Callwell, *Small wars*, p. 475.

110. Lloyd, *Drums of Kumasi*, pp. 81–2.

111. Wolseley, *Story of a soldier's life*, p. 339.

112. Lloyd, *Drums of Kumasi*, p. 114.

113. Lehmann, *All Sir Garnet*, pp. 190–1.

114. Wilks, *Asante in the nineteenth century*, pp. 505–6.

115. Lehmann, *All Sir Garnet*, p. 193.

116. Wilks, *Asante in the nineteenth century*, pp. 508–9.

117. Brackenbury, *The Ashanti war* (Edinburgh & London: Blackwood, 1874), vol. 2, p. 239.

118. Callwell, *Small wars*, p. 354; Lloyd, *Drums of Kumasi*, p. 150.

119. Wolseley, *Story of a soldier's life*, p. 370.

120. Edgerton, *Fall of the Asante empire*, p. 262.

121. Fynn, "Ghana-Asante", pp. 49–50.

122. Keegan & Wheatcroft, (eds) *Who's who in military history*, p. 322.

123. Fynn, "Ghana-Asante", pp. 20, 46–50. For an old-fashioned, Eurocentric but nonetheless sometimes insightful history of the 1900 campaign, see F. Myatt, *The golden stool: an account of the Ashanti War of 1900* (London: William Kimber, 1966).

124. Edgerton, *Fall of the Asante empire*, pp. v–vi.

125. F. Fynney, *The Zulu army and Zulu headmen. Published by direction of the Lieutenant-General commanding* (Pietermaritzburg, April 1879), p. 6. Quoted in J. Guy, "A note on firearms in the Zulu kingdom with special reference to the Anglo-Zulu War, 1879", *Journal of African History*, **12**, p. 561, 1971.

126. Morris, *Washing of the spears*, p. 147.

127. Wolseley to Carnarvon, 12 May 1875, in British Parliamentry Papers, Command 1342-I, vol. 52. Quoted in James O. Gump, *The dust rose like smoke: the subjugation of the Zulu and the Sioux* (Lincoln, Neb.: University of Nebraska Press, 1994), p. 86.

128. J. Martineau, *The life and correspondence of the Right Hon. Sir Bartle Frere* (London: John Murray, 1895), vol. 2, p. 224. Quoted in Jeff Guy, *The destruction of the Zulu kingdom: the civil war in Zululand, 1879–1894* (Harlow: Longman, 1979), p. 48.

129. British Parliamentary Papers, Command 2079:39, Shepstone to Carnarvon, 5 January 1879, p. 55. Quoted in Guy, *Destruction of the Zulu kingdom*, p. 47.

130. Hicks Beach to Frere, 17 October 1878, in British Parliamentary Papers, Command 2200, vol. 52. Quoted in Gump, *The dust rose like smoke*, p. 91.

131. Quoted in C.F. Goodfellow, *Great Britain and South African confederation, 1870–1881* (Capetown: Oxford University Press, 1966), p. 161.

132. Guy, *Destruction of the Zulu kingdom*, p. 50.

133. Laband, *Kingdom in crisis*, p. 46.

134. Smith-Dorrien, *Memories of forty-eight years' service* (London: John Murray, 1925), p. 13. Quoted in Gump, *The dust rose like smoke*, p. 22.

135. Laband, *Kingdom in crisis*, pp. 72–95; Edgerton, *Like lions they fought*, pp. 71–92; Gump, *The dust rose like smoke*, pp. 21–2.

136. Morris, *Washing of the spears*, p. 387.

137. Edgerton, *Like lions they fought*, p. 4.

138. Morris, *Washing of the spears*, p. 387.

139. Laband, *Kingdom in crisis*, pp. 96–114.

140. R. Lock, *Blood on the painted mountain: Zulu victory and defeat: Hlobane and Kambula, 1879* (London: Greenhill, 1995).

141. Knight, *Go to your God like a soldier: the British soldier fighting for empire, 1837–1902* (London: Greenhill, 1996), p. 138.

142. J. Guy, *Destruction of the Zulu kingdom*, p. 69ff.

Chapter Four

1. J.D. Hargreaves, *Prelude to the partition of West Africa* (London: Macmillan, 1963), p. 253.

2. Wesseling, *Divide and rule*, p. 180.

3. Méniaud, *Les pionniers du Soudan*, vol. 1, p. 67.

4. *ibid.*, pp. 115–18.

5. Kanya-Forstner, *Conquest of the Western Sudan*, pp. 61–3.

6. B.I. Obichere, "The African factor in the establishment of French authority in West Africa, 1880–1900", in *France and Britain in Africa: imperial rivalry and colonial rule*, P. Gifford & W.R. Louis (eds) (New Haven: Yale University Press, 1971), p. 447.

7. B.O. Oloruntimehin, "Senegambia–Mahmadou Lamine", in *West African resistance*, pp. 80–110.

8. Prince of Cayor, a state just south of St. Louis in Senegal, who resisted French occupation in the 1860s and 1870s; successive peace treaties with the Tukolor leaders al-Hajj Umar and Ahmadu Seku helped the French to focus their energies on his suppression.

9. Boahen, *African perspectives on colonialism*, p. 57.

10. Michel, *Galliéni*, pp. 109–10.

11. Kanya-Forstner, "Mali-Tukolor", in *West African resistance,* pp. 76–7.

12. D. Grévoz, *Les canonnières de Tomboctou: les Français à la conquête de la cité mythique (1870–1894)* (Paris: L'Harmattan, 1992), pp. 128–66.

13. Person, "Guinea-Samori", in *West African resistance*, p. 112.

14. Quoted in M. Crowder, *West Africa under colonial rule* (Evanston, Ill.: Northwestern University Press, 1968), p. 87.

15. Balesi, *From adversaries to comrades-in-arms*, p. 12.

16. M. Legassick, "Firearms, horses and Samorian army organization, 1870–1898", *Journal of African History* **7**, 1966, p. 98, n11.

17. Méniaud, *Les pionniers du Soudan*, vol. 1, p. 357.

18. Person, "Guinea-Samori", p. 141.

19. J. Ganiage, *L'expansion coloniale de la France sous la Troisième République (1871–1914)* (Paris: Payot, 1968), p. 176.

20. Quoted in M. Crowder, *West Africa under colonial rule*, p. 89.

21. Person, "Guinea-Samori", p. 140.

22. Kanya-Forstner, *Conquest of the Western Sudan*, p. 187.

23. Méniaud, *Les pionniers du Soudan*, p. 63.

24. Legassick, "Firearms, horses, and Samorian army organization", pp. 104–5, 1966.

25. Méniaud, *Les pionniers du Soudan*, p. 149.

26. Wilks, *Asante in the nineteenth century*, p. 304.

27. Person, "Guinea-Samori", p. 138; Person, "Samori and resistance to the French", pp. 107–8. For an entirely erroneous account of the encounter between the *sofas* of "Samory, the fanatical Mahdi" and British troops in 1897, see Haywood & Clarke, *History of the Royal West African Frontier Force*, p. 26.

28. Suret-Canale, "Guinea in the colonial system", in *Essays on African history: from the slave trade to neocolonialism*, J. Suret-Canale (ed.), trans. C. Hurst (London: C. Hurst, 1988), p. 126.

29. Person, "Samori and resistance to the French", p. 111.

30. Quoted in Suret-Canale, "Guinea in the colonial system", p. 126.

31. Crowder, *West Africa under colonial rule*, pp. 88–9.

32. Person, "Samori and resistance to the French", p. 112.

33. Person, "Guinea-Samori", p. 141.

34. Headrick, *Tools of empire*, p. 197.

35. Stengers, "King Leopold's imperialism", p. 249.

36. Stengers, "The Congo Free State and the Belgian Congo before 1914", in *The history and politics of colonialism,* p. 261.

37. Headrick, *Tools of empire*, p. 197.

38. J. Stengers & J. Vansina, "King Leopold's Congo, 1886–1908", in *From 1870 to 1905*, vol. 6 of *The Cambridge history of Africa*, J.D. Fage & G.N. Sanderson (eds) (Cambridge: Cambridge University Press, 1985), p. 334.

39. *ibid.*, pp. 349–50.

40. E.S. Grogan & A.H. Sharp, *From the Cape to Cairo* (London: Nelson, n.d.), pp. 294–5. Quoted in V.G. Kiernan, "Colonial Africa and its armies", in *Imperialism and its contradictions*, H.J. Kaye (ed.) (London: Routledge, 1995), p. 81.

41. F. Flament et al. (eds), *La Force Publique de sa naissance à 1914. Participation des militaires à l'histoire des premières années du Congo* (Brussels: Institut Royal Colonial Belge, 1952), pp. 216–17.

42. *ibid.*, pp. 330–1.

43. Stengers, "The Congo Free State and the Belgian Congo before 1914", p. 267. Although the term "Arab" is incorrect in describing the Free State's opponents in the wars of the 1890s, it has been used so widely for so long in the historical literature I

have decided to retain it here.

44. Stengers & Vansina, "King Leopold's Congo", p. 332.

45. Flament et al., *La Force Publique*, pp. 208–9.

46. H. Brode, *Tippoo Tib: the story of his career in Central Africa, narrated from his own account* (Chicago: Afro-Am Press, 1969), p. 247.

47. Flament et al., *La Force Publique*, pp. 198–9.

48. *ibid.*, p. 200.

49. P. Ceulemans, *La question arabe et le Congo (1883–1892)* (Brussels: Académie Royale des Sciences d'Outre-Mer, 1959), pp. 189–96, 321–58; J. Vansina, *Kingdoms of the savanna* (Madison: University of Wisconsin Press, 1966), p. 241.

50. R. Cornevin, *Histoire du Congo Léopoldville-Kinshasha des origines préhistoriques à la République démocratique du Congo* (Paris: Berger-Levrault, 1970), p. 152.

51. H. Brode, *Tippoo Tib*, pp. 244–7.

52. Flament et al., *La Force Publique*, pp. 207–8, 292.

53. Ceulemans, *La question arabe et le Congo*.

54. S.L. Hinde, *The fall of the Congo Arabs* (New York: Negro Universities Press, 1969), pp. 184, 187.

55. Curtin et al., *African history*, p. 393.

56. R. Pélissier, *Les guerres grises. Résistance et révoltes en Angola (1845–1941)* (Orgeval, France: Pélissier, 1977); D. Wheeler & R. Pélissier, *Angola* (New York: Praeger, 1971), especially chapters 3–4.

57. R. Pélissier, *Naissance de la Guiné: portugais et africains en Sénégambie (1841–1936)* (Orgeval, France: Pélissier, 1989); J. Cunningham, "The colonial period in Guiné", *Tarikh* **6**(4), 1980, pp. 31–46.

58. James Duffy, *Portuguese Africa* (Cambridge, Mass.: Harvard University Press, 1961), p. 231.

59. R. Pélissier, *Naissance du Mozambique*, vol. 1, pp. 85–6.

60. Mousinho de Albuquerque, "O Exercito nas colonias orientais," *Revista do Exercito e da Armada* **1**(2), p. 99, 1893. Quoted in Pélissier, *Naissance du Mozambique*, vol. 1, p. 95.

61. A. Enes, *A guerra de Africa em 1895* (Memorias), 2nd edn (Lisbon: Edições Gama, 1895), pp. 362–3.

62. P.R. Warhurst, *Anglo-Portuguese relations in south-central Africa, 1890–1900* (Harlow: Longman, 1962), pp. 79–80.

63. R.J. Hammond, *Portugal and Africa, 1815–1910: a study in uneconomic imperialism* (Stanford: Stanford University Press, 1966), p. 185.

64. D.L. Wheeler, "Gungunhana", in *Leadership in Eastern Africa: six political biographies*, N.R. Bennett (ed.) (Boston: Boston University Press, 1968), p. 195.

65. Enes, *A guerra de Africa*, p. 567. Quoted in Hammond, *Portugal and Africa*, p. 198.

66. Telo, *Economia e imperio*, p. 150.

67. Pélissier, *Naissance du Mozambique*, vol. 2, p. 624.

68. Rodney, "The year 1895 in southern Mozambique: African resistance to the imposition of European colonial rule," *Journal of the Historical Society of Nigeria* **5**(4), p. 514, 1971.

69. Hammond, *Portugal and Africa*, p. 196.

70. Wheeler, "Gungunhana", pp. 184, 186, 192, 201, 204, 217.

71. J.J Texeira Botelho, *Historia militar e politica*, p. 460.

72. Rodney, "The year 1895 in southern Mozambique", p. 523.

73. Byron Farwell is certainly mistaken in claiming that wire was first used in this way by the Boers at the battle of Magersfontein in December 1899. *The great Boer War* (London: Allen Lane, 1977), p. 103.

74. Enes, *A guerra de Africa*, pp. 354–62.
75. Wheeler, "Gungunhana", pp. 207–8.
76. *ibid.*, pp. 209–10.
77. D. Wheeler, "Joaquim Mousinho de Albuquerque", in *African proconsuls*, p. 439.
78. Labanca, N., *Storia dell'Italia coloniale* (Milan: Fenice 2000, 1994), p. 4.
79. Zewde, B., *A history of modern Ethiopia, 1855–1974* (London: James Currey, 1991), p. 81.
80. Rubenson, *The survival*, p. 1.
81. Toynbee, *A study of history* (London: Oxford University Press, 1934–1961), vol. 2, p. 365. Quoted in Rubenson, *The survival*, p. 1.
82. Rubenson, *The survival*, p. 407.
83. *ibid.*, p. 409.
84. The following overview of the battle of Adowa relies heavily on accounts of the battle given in R. Battaglia, *La prima guerra d'Africa* (Turin: Einaudi, 1958), and A. Del Boca, *Gli italiani in Africa orientale*, vol. 1, part 2 (Rome Bari: Laterza, 1985).
85. Gooch, *Army, state and society in Italy, 1870–1915* (New York: St. Martin's Press, 1989), p. 172.
86. Gooch, *ibid.*; Labanca, *In marcia verso Adua*, pp. 180–1, 191–2.
87. Del Boca, *Gli italiani in Africa orientale*, vol. 1, pt. 2, p. 658.
88. Labanca, *In marcia verso Adua*, pp. 356, 359.
89. *ibid.*, p. 357.
90. Quoted in P. Wright, "Italy's African dream: Part I: the Adowa nightmare", *History Today* **23**(3), 1973, p. 160.
91. S. Rubenson, "Adwa 1896: the resounding protest", in *Protest and power in black Africa*, R.I. Rotberg & A.A. Mazrui (eds) (New York: Oxford University Press, 1970), p. 129.
92. Lewis, *A modern history of Somalia: nation and state in the Horn of Africa* (Harlow: Longman, 1980), p. v.
93. P.M. Holt, "The Sudanese Mahdia and the outside world, 1881–9", *Bulletin of the School of Oriental and African Studies*, **21**, 1958, pp. 276–8.
94. L.C. Brown, "The Sudanese Mahdiya", *in Protest and power in Black Africa*, p. 149.
95. P.M. Holt, *The Mahdist state in the Sudan, 1881–1898: a study of its origins, development and overthrow* (Oxford: Clarendon, 1958), p. 55.
96. A.B. Theobald, *The Mahdiya: a history of the Anglo-Egyptian Sudan, 1881–1899* (London: Longmans, Green, 1957), p. 62.
97. Holt, "The Sudanese Mahdia and the outside world", pp. 280–1.
98. Pakenham, *Scramble for Africa*, pp. 543–4.
99. Zulfo, *Karari: The Sudanese account of the battle of Omdurman*, trans. P. Clark (London: Zed Press, 1980), pp. 161–3, 179–81.
100. Theobald, *The Mahdiya*, pp. 230–1.
101. Zulfo, *Karari*, p. 97.
102. *Africa and the Victorians*, p. 376.

Chapter Five

1. Pakenham, *The Boer war*, p. 607.
2. Brian R. Sullivan, "The strategy of the decisive weight: Italy, 1882–1922," in *The

making of strategy: rulers, states, and war, 2nd edn, W. Murray et al. (eds) (Cambridge: Cambridge University Press, 1995), p. 326.

3. J.-L. Miège, "The French conquest of Morocco: the early period, 1901–1911," in *Imperialism and war*, De Moor & Wesseling (eds), p. 214, Table 3.

4. Labanca, *Storia dell'Italia coloniale*, p. 29.

5. Miège, "The French conquest of Morocco," p. 207.

6. Pakenham, *The Boer war*, pp. 549, 608.

7. Letter, Lugard to Flora Lugard (wife), 9 March 1906. Quoted in M. Perham, *Lugard*, vol. 2, *The years of authority, 1898–1945* (London: Collins, 1960), p. 260.

8. Pakenham, *The Scramble for Africa*, p. 652.

9. R.A. Adeleye, "Mahdist triumph and British revenge in Northern Nigeria: Satiru 1906", *Journal of the Historical Society of Nigeria* 6(2), pp. 205–7, 1972.

10. Thompson, *Oxford History of South Africa* (Oxford: Oxford University Press, 1971), vol. 2, p. 326.

11. Lugard had earned the enmity of the French during the British campaign to establish paramountcy in Uganda in 1892. Never one for subtlety, Lugard had threatened to turn a Gatling gun on Catholic priests during the struggle for power. Uganda's Catholic flock, considered by Lugard to be the main fomenters of resistance to the British takeover, was shepherded by the French order of White Fathers. The incident was played up by the French mass-circulation press.

12. S. Vandeleur, *Campaigning on the Upper Nile and Niger* (London: Methuen, 1898), p. 272.

13. J.E. Flint, "Nigeria: the colonial experience", in *The history and politics of colonialism*, p. 251.

14. Smaldone, *Warfare in the Sokoto Caliphate*, p. 122.

15. A.E. Afigbo, "The establishment of colonial rule, 1900–1918", in *History of West Africa*, vol. 2, J.F.A. Ajayi & M. Crowder (eds) (Harlow: Longman, 1974), pp. 431–2.

16. O. Ikime, *The fall of Nigeria: the British conquest* (London: Heinemann, 1977), p. 203.

17. Lieutenant (later General) F.P. Crozier, quoted in Muffett, *Concerning brave captains*, p. 132.

18. *ibid.*, p. 161.

19. *ibid.*

20. Smaldone, *Warfare in the Sokoto Caliphate*, p. 123.

21. J. Bridgman, *The revolt of the Hereros* (Berkeley: University of California Press, 1981), p. 62.

22. K. Epstein, "Erzberger and the German colonial scandals, 1905–1910", *English Historical Review*, **74**, 1959, p. 637.

23. H. Drechsler, *"Let us die fighting": the struggle of the Herero and the Nama against German imperialism (1884–1915)* (London: Zed Press, 1980), p. 143.

24. *ibid.*

25. Trotha to Leutwein, 5 November 1904, Imperial Colonial Office File No. 2089, pp. 100–102. Quoted in H. Drechsler, *"Let us die fighting"*, p. 154. I have, however, used the much smoother rendering of Trotha's remarks (taken from Drechsler) in Bridgman, *Revolt of the Hereros*, pp. 111–12.

26. Bridgman, *The revolt of the Hereros*, p. 169.

27. *ibid.*, p. 117.

28. *ibid.*, pp. 127–8.

29. *ibid.*, p. 128.

30. *ibid.*, pp. 134–5.

31. Pakenham, *Scramble for Africa*, p. 615.

32. See especially three works by J. Iliffe: *A modern history of Tanganyika* (Cambridge: Cambridge University Press, 1979); "The organization of the Maji-Maji rebellion", *Journal of African History* **8**, 1967, pp. 495–512; and *Tanganyika under German rule, 1905–1912* (Cambridge: Cambridge University Press, 1969).

33. G.C.K. Gwassa, "The outbreak and development of the Maji Maji war 1905–07", Ph.D. thesis, University of Dar es Salaam, 1973, p. 389. Cited in Iliffe, *Modern history of Tanganyika*, p. 200.

34. Pakenham, *The scramble for Africa*, p. 622.

35. The following sources have been helpful to me in preparing this section: A. Del Boca, *Tripoli bel suol d'amore 1860–1922*, vol. 2 of *Gli italiani in Libia* (Rome-Bari: Laterza, 1968); J. Gooch, *Army, state and society in Italy, 1870–1915* (New York: St. Martin's, 1989); F. Malgeri, *La guerra libica* (Rome: Edizioni di Storia e Letteratura, 1970); S. Romano, *La quarta sponda: La guerra di Libia, 1911/1912* (Milan: Bompiani, 1977).

36. Labanca, *In marcia verso Adua*, p. 191.

37. Gooch, *Army, state and society*, p. 141.

38. *ibid.*, p. 142.

39. Romano, *La quarta sponda*, p. 254.

40. Gooch, *Army, state and society*, p. 148.

Chapter Six

1. D. Porch, "Introduction" to Callwell, *Small wars*, pp. xvii–xviii.

2. G.W.T. Hodges, "African manpower statistics for the British forces in East Africa, 1914–1918", *Journal of African History* **19**(1), 1978, p. 115.

3. Crowder, *West African resistance*, p. 2.

4. Quoted in T. Ranger, "Connexions between 'primary resistance' movements and modern mass nationalism in East and Central Africa", Part I, *Journal of African History* **9**(3), p. 443, 1968.

5. Quoted in *ibid.*, p. 140.

6. J.M. Lee, *African armies and civil order* (New York: Praeger, 1969), p. 45.

7. R. First, *Power in Africa* (New York: Pantheon, 1970), p. 78.

8. Quoted in C.E. Welch, "The roots and implications of military intervention", in *Soldier and state in Africa: a comparative analysis of military intervention and political change*, C.E. Welch (ed.) (Evanston, Ill.: Northwestern University Press, 1970), p. 8. Also see A. Ly, *Mercénaires noirs: note sur une forme de l'exploitation des Africains* (Paris: Présence Africaine, 1957).

9. Omara-Otunnu, *Politics and the military in Uganda, 1890–1985* (New York: St. Martin's, 1987), p. 170.

10. Welch, "Continuity and discontinuity in African military organisation", *Journal of Modern African Studies* **13**(2), 1975, pp. 229–48.

11. Lee, *African armies and civil order*, p. 54.

12. Mazrui, "The resurrection of the warrior tradition in African political culture", *The Journal of Modern African Studies* **13**(1), 1975, pp. 68, 71.
13. *ibid.*, p. 68.
14. *ibid.*, p. 84.

Select bibliography

Primary sources

Callwell, C.E. [1906]. *Small wars: their principles and practice*. Introduction by D. Porch. (Lincoln, Neb.: University of Nebraska Press 1996) [London: HMSO].
The Anglo-Saxon world's classic text on colonial warfare.
Ditte, A. *Observations sur les guerres dans les colonies, organisation–exécution. Conférences faites à l'École Supérieure de Guerre* (Paris: H. Charles-Lavauzelle, 1905).
The French Callwell.
Donny, Col. A. (ed.). *L'Art militaire au Congo*. (Brussels: Th. Falk, 1897).
Manual on colonial warfare in the Congo Free State.
Goodrich, C.F. *Report of the British naval and military operations in Egypt, 1882* (Washington, D.C.: Government Printing Office, 1883).
Analysis of key nineteenth-century amphibious operation.
Smith-Dorrien, H. *Memoirs of forty-eight years service* (London: John Murray, 1925).
Survivor of Isandlwana who became general in First World War.
United States. War Department. Adjutant General's Office. Military Information Division. Herron, J. (compiler). *Colonial army systems of the Netherlands, Great Britain, France, Germany, Portugal, Italy, and Belgium* (Washington, D.C.: Government Printing, Office, 1901).
Useful survey of European colonial armies c. 1900; coverage is fullest on Dutch, British and French forces.
Wolseley, G. *The story of a soldier's life*, vol. 2 (New York: Charles Scribner's Sons, 1903).
Indispensable to understanding of 1873–1874 Ashanti War; sheds much light on *mentalité* of European imperial soldiery.

Reference works

Heggoy, A.A. & J.M. Haar (eds). *The military in imperial history: the French connection* (New York: Garland, 1984).

Absolutely indispensable guide to sources.

Higham, R. (ed.). *A guide to the sources of British military history* (London: Routledge, 1972). Dated; must be supplemented by Jordan below.

Jordan, G. (ed.). *British military history: a supplement to Robin Higham's guide to the sources* (New York: Garland, 1988).

Keegan, J. & A. Wheatcroft (eds). *Who's who in military history: from 1453 to the present day*, 3rd edn (London: Routledge, 1996). Useful but some surprising errors and omissions.

Kwamena-Poh, M., J. Tosh, R. Waller & M. Tidy (eds). *African history in maps* (Harlow: Longman, 1982). Standard aid for African history courses; annotated maps.

Porter, A.N. (ed.). *Atlas of British overseas expansion* (London: Routledge, 1991). Exhaustive, up-to-date; black-and-white maps.

Porter, A.N. *European imperialism, 1860–1914* (New York: St. Martin's, 1996). "State of the debate" survey; directed to students.

General studies

Ajayi, J.F.A. (ed.). *History of West Africa* [2 vols] (New York: Columbia University Press, 1972). See chapters by Hargreaves, Person.

Birmingham, D. & P.M. Martin. *History of Central Africa* [2 vols] (Harlow: Longman, 1983).

Boahen, A.A. *African perspectives on colonialism* (Baltimore: Johns Hopkins University Press, 1985). Useful for view of why Africans lost colonial wars.

Curtin, P.D., S. Feierman, L. Thompson & J. Vansina. *African history from earliest times to independence*, 2nd edn (Harlow: Longman, 1995). More than just a popular textbook.

Fage, J.D. & R. Oliver (eds). *c. 1600 to c. 1790*, vol. 4 of *The Cambridge History of Africa* (Cambridge: Cambridge University Press, 1975). Solid, useful for pre-colonial history of major African states.

Flint, J.E. (ed.). *c. 1790 to c. 1870*, vol. 5 of *The Cambridge History of Africa* (Cambridge: Cambridge University Press, 1976). Less helpful than preceding volume.

Foerster, S., W.J. Mommsen & R. Robinson (eds). *Bismarck, Europe, and Africa: the Berlin Africa Conference of 1884–1885 and the onset of partition* (Oxford: Oxford University Press, 1988). See essay by Michael Crowder.

Gann, L.H. & P. Duignan (eds). *Colonialism in Africa, 1870–1960* [5 vols] (London: Cambridge University Press, 1969–75). Tone of series set by editors' defensiveness about Western imperialism; Vol. 1 has essays on European expansion by Brunschwig, Ranger, Stengers.

Gann, L.H. & P. Duignan (eds). *African proconsuls: European governors in Africa* (New York: Free Press, 1978). Chapters on Faidherbe, Galliéni, Mousinho d'Albuquerque.

Gifford, P. & W.R. Louis (eds). *Britain and Germany in Africa: imperial rivalry and colonial rule* (New Haven: Yale University Press, 1967).

Gifford, P. & W.R. Louis (eds). *France and Britain in Africa: imperial rivalry and colonial rule* (New Haven: Yale University Press, 1971).

Hargreaves, J.D. *West Africa partitioned*, vol. I: *The loaded pause, 1885–1889* (London: Macmillan, 1974).

Background to the Scramble.

Iliffe, J. *Africans: the history of a continent* (Cambridge: Cambridge University Press, 1995).

Popular textbook; stresses role of ecology and demographics in African history.

Julien, C.-A. *Les techniciens de la colonisation (XIXe–XXe siècles)* (Paris: Presses universitaires de France, 1946).

Dated, somewhat uncritical, but still useful.

Kea, R.A. Firearms and warfare on the Gold and Slave Coasts from the sixteenth to the nineteenth centuries. *Journal of African History* **12**, pp. 185–213, 1971.

Exhaustive study of role of firearms in rise of Ashanti.

Keegan, J. *A history of warfare* (London: Hutchinson, 1993).

Some interesting pages on Zulus.

Kiernan, V.G. *From conquest to collapse: European empires from 1815 to 1960* (New York: Pantheon, 1982).

Kaleidoscopic but general military history by Marxist critic.

Kiernan, V.G. *Imperialism and its contradictions*, Harvey Kaye (ed.) (London: Routledge, 1995).

See essay on 'Colonial Africa and its armies'.

Meyer, J. et al. *Des origines à 1914*, vol. 2 of *Histoire de la France coloniale* (Paris: Armand Colin, 1991).

Best survey of French colonial history down to First World War.

Murray, W., M. Knox & A. Bernstein (eds). *The making of strategy: rulers, states, and war* (Cambridge: Cambridge University Press, 1994).

See chapter on Italy by Brian Sullivan.

Oliver, R. & J.D. Fage. *A short history of Africa* (Harmondsworth: Penguin, 1962).

Textbook which took view that African resistance was hopeless, anachronistic and counter-productive.

Oliver, R. & G.N. Sanderson (eds). *From 1870 to 1905*, vol. 6 of *The Cambridge history of Africa* (Cambridge: Cambridge University Press, 1985).

Extremely useful compilation; exhaustive bibliography.

Owen, R. & B. Sutcliffe (eds). *Studies in the theory of imperialism* (Harlow: Longman, 1972).

Excellent primer; covers all major European powers.

Pakenham, T. *The Scramble for Africa: the white man's conquest of the Dark Continent from 1876 to 1912* (London: Weidenfeld & Nicolson, 1991).

Sprawling, kaleidoscopic but a good read.

Robinson, R., J. Gallagher & A. Denny. *Africa and the Victorians: the official mind of imperialism*, 2nd edn (London: Macmillan, 1981).

Perhaps most influential book written on imperialism in Anglo–Saxon world since 1945.

Schumpeter, J. *Imperialism and social classes* (New York: Augustus M. Kelley, 1951).

Introduces 'atavism' as major impetus to imperialism; to be read in conjunction with Kanya-Forstner on 'military imperialism'.

Suret-Canale, J. *Afrique noire occidentale et centrale* [3 vols] (Paris: Editions Sociales, 1958–72).

Wide-ranging survey; Marxist perspective.

Suret-Canale, J. *French colonialism in tropical Africa, 1900–45* (London: C. Hurst, 1971).

Translation of parts of afore-mentioned.

Wesseling, H.L. *Divide and rule: the partition of Africa, 1880–1914* (Westport, Conn: Praeger, 1996).

Rather old-fashioned political survey; splendid anecdotes.

Wesseling, H.L. (ed.). *Expansion and reaction* (Leiden: Leiden University Press, 1978).

Useful comparative, cross-cultural approach but uneven.

White, G. Firearms in Africa: an introduction. *Journal of African History* **12**, pp. 173–83, 1971.

Focus on resistance

Ajayi, J.F.A. The continuity of African institutions under colonialism. See Ranger (1968), pp. 189–200, 1968.

Western rule is just a blip on big screen of African history.

Bennett, N.R. (ed.). *Leadership in Eastern Africa: six political biographies* (Boston: Boston University Press, 1968).

Biographies of East African resistance leaders.

Crowder, M. (ed.). *West African resistance: the military response to colonial occupation* (London: Hutchinson & Co., 1971).

Old but still indispensable guide to varieties of West African resistance; nothing like it for rest of Africa.

Crowder, M. 'Many questions – some answers': African resistance in West Africa – a general view. See Foerster et al., pp. 401–13, 1988.

Agenda for future research on African resistance.

Crummey, D. (ed.). *Banditry, rebellion and social protest in Africa* (London: James Currey, 1986).

Explores links between anti-colonial resistance and "social banditry" à la E.J. Hobsbawm.

Davidson, A.B. African resistance and rebellion against the imposition of colonial rule. See Ranger (1968), pp. 177–88, 1968.

Soviet perspective on history of African resistance movements.

De Moor, J.A. & H.L. Wesseling (eds). *Imperialism and war. Essays on colonial war in Asia and Africa* (Leiden: E.J. Brill, 1989).

Comparative, cross-cultural approach; very stimulating.

Denoon, D. & A. Kuper. Nationalist historians in search of a nation: the "new historiography" in Dar es Salaam. *African Affairs* **69**, pp. 329–49, 1970.

See Preface above.

Maddox, G. & T.K. Welliver (eds). *Conquest and resistance to colonialism in Africa*, vol. 1 of *Colonialism and nationalism in Africa: a four-volume anthology of scholarly articles* (New York: Garland, 1993).

Very useful collection on African resistance.

Mazrui, A.A. Postlude: toward a theory of protest. See Rotberg & Mazrui (eds), pp. 1185–96, 1970.

Stretches definition of resistance to limit.

Ogot, B.A. (ed.). *War and society in Africa: ten studies* (London: Frank Cass, 1972).

East African focus.

Ranger, T.O. (ed.) 1968. *Emerging themes of African history. Proceedings of the International Congress of African Historians held at University College, Dar es Salaam, October 1965* (Nairobi: East African Publishing House, 1968).

Collective manifesto of influential "Dar es Salaam" revisionist school, who saw demonstration of connections between resistance and twentieth-century nationalist movements as a main task of scholars of African history.

Robinson, R. Non-European foundations of European imperialism: sketch for a theory of collaboration. See Owen & Sutcliffe (eds) (1995), pp. 117–40, 1995.

More explicit statement of thesis on 'peripheral flux' as stimulant to imperial expansion.

Rotberg, R.I. & A. Mazrui (eds). *Protest and power in Black Africa* (New York: Oxford University Press, 1970).

Chapters by Person on Samori and Rubenson on Adowa.

Chapter One: Africa on the eve of European penetration

Ajayi, J.F.A. & R. Smith. *Yoruba warfare in the nineteenth century* (Cambridge: Cambridge University Press, 1964).

How one African people waged war in pre-colonial era.

Caillié, R. [1830]. *Travels through Central Africa to Timbuctoo and across the Great Desert to Morocco, 1824–1828* [2 vols] (London: Cass, 1968).

Major source of Timbuktu fantasy which mesmerised French.

Chauveau, J.-P. Une histoire maritime africaine est-elle possible? Historiographie et histoire de la navigation et de la pêche africaines à la côte occidentale depuis le XVe siècle. *Cahiers d'études africaines* **26**, pp. 173–235, 1986.

Could Africans have developed navies?

Curtin, P.D. *The image of Africa: British ideas and action, 1780–1850* (Madison, Wisconsin: University of Wisconsin Press, 1964).

Still important for evolution of European imperial *mentalité*.

Dike, K.O. *Trade and politics in the Niger Delta, 1830–1885* (Oxford: Clarendon, 1966).

First major study by African historian in post-independence era.

Eldredge, E.A. *A South African kingdom* (Cambridge: Cambridge University Press, 1993) [on Sotho kingdom].

Goody, J. *Technology, tradition and the state in Africa* (London: Oxford University Press, 1971).

Anthropologist; interesting chapter on pre-colonial warfare.

Hamilton, C. *The "Mfecane" aftermath: reconstructive debates in Southern African history* (Johannesburg/Pietermaritzburg: University of Witwatersrand Press/University of Natal Press, 1995).

Cutting edge research on the origins and impact of explosive rise of Zulu empire.

Hiskett, M. *The sword of truth; the life and times of the Shehu Usuman dan Fodio* (New York: Oxford University Press, 1973).

Kea, R.A. *Settlements, trade and politics in the seventeenth century Gold Coast* (Baltimore: Johns Hopkins University Press, 1982).

Useful for background to Ashanti-British conflict.

Law, R. *The Oyo empire, c. 1600–1836: a West African imperialism in the era of the Atlantic slave trade* (Oxford: Clarendon, 1977).

Law, R. Horses, firearms and political power in pre-colonial West Africa. *Past & Present* **72**, pp. 112–32, 1976.

Mair, L. *African kingdoms* (Oxford: Clarendon, 1977).

Helpful section on pre-colonial African armies.

Martin, B.G. *Muslim Brotherhoods in nineteenth century Africa* (New York: Cambridge University Press, 1976).
Good on Abd el-Kader, al-Hajj Umar.
Smaldone, J.P. *Warfare in the Sokoto Caliphate* (Cambridge: Cambridge University Press, 1977).
Marries history and sociology; insightful.
Smith, R.S. Peace and palaver: international relations in pre-colonial West Africa. *Journal of African History* **14**, pp. 599–621, 1973.
Negotiation a viable alternative to war among African states.
Smith, R.S. *Warfare and diplomacy in pre-colonial West Africa* (London: Methuen, 1976).
The essential text; suggestive for other parts of Africa as well.
Thornton, J. *Africa and Africans in the making of the Atlantic world, 1400–1680* (Cambridge: Cambridge University Press, 1992).
Africans as subjects, not objects, of early modern history.
Uzoigwe, G.N. The warrior and the state in precolonial Africa. *Journal of African and Asian Studies* **12**(1–4), pp. 20–47, 1977.
Guide to an as yet unrealized research agenda.

Chapter Two: The invaders

August, T.G. *The selling of the empire: British and French imperialist propaganda, 1890–1940* (Westport, Conn.: Greenwood, 1985).
More helpful for interwar period.
Bond, B. (ed.). *Victorian military campaigns* (London: Hutchinson, 1967).
Dated but still useful narratives of British colonial campaigns.
Bradford, J.C. (ed.) *The military and the conflict between cultures: soldiers at the interface* (College Station, Tex.: Texas A & M University Press, 1997).
Brave attempt to broaden new front in "New Military History".
Carman, W.Y. *A history of firearms from earliest times to 1914* (London: Routledge, 1955).
Cohen, W.B. *The French encounter with Africans: white response to blacks, 1530–1880* (Bloomington, Indiana: Indiana University Press, 1980).
French are not as colour-blind as they claim.
Curtin, P.D. *Death by migration: Europe's encounter with the tropical world in the nineteenth century* (Cambridge: Cambridge University Press, 1990).
Why West Africa was the "white man's grave".
Earle, E.M. (ed.). *Makers of modern strategy: military thought from Machiavelli to Hitler* (Princeton: Princeton University Press, 1943).
See chapter by Gottmann on French colonial warfare.
Headrick, D.R. *The tools of empire: technology and European imperialism in the nineteenth century* (New York: Oxford University Press, 1981).
Technological determinists' bible; authoritative.
Headrick, D.R. *The tentacles of progress: technology transfer in the age of imperialism* (New York: Oxford University Press, 1988).
Technological trickle-down from West to rest.

242

Killingray, D. Colonial warfare in West Africa, 1870–1914. See De Moor & Wesseling (eds), 146–67, 1989.

To be read in conjunction with Crowder's *West African Resistance*.

Paret, P. (ed.). *Makers of modern strategy: from Machiavelli to the nuclear age* (Princeton: Princeton University Press, 1986).

New version of Earle; Porch's chapter on French colonial warfare updates Gottmann.

Ralston, D.B. [1990]. *Importing the European army: the introduction of European military techniques and institutions into the extra-European world, 1600–1914* (Chicago: University of Chicago Press, 1996).

Technological-determinist; Egypt only African country treated.

Strachan, H. *European armies and the conduct of war* (London: Allen & Unwin, 1983).

Contains useful chapter on colonial warfare.

van Creveld, M.L. *Technology and war: from 2000 B.C. to the present* (London: Collier Macmillan, 1989).

Technology seldom determines victory in war.

France

Aldrich, R. *Greater France: a history of French overseas expansion* (New York: St. Martin's, 1996).

Thematic approach; up-to-date bibliography.

Anon. *Les troupes de marine, 1622–1984* (Paris-Limoges: H. Charles-Lavauzelle, 1986).

Heavily illustrated, breezy, but sweeping and informative.

Béaudza, L. *La formation de l'armée coloniale* (Paris: Librairie Militaire L. Fournier, 1939).

Old, but still an essential book on its subject.

Betts, R. *Tricouleur: the French overseas empire* (London: Gordon & Cremonesi, 1978).

Graceful retrospective.

Brisac, General. Les polytechniciens de l'armée d'Afrique et les grands coloniaux. *Revue historique de l'armée* **10**(2), pp. 19–28, 1954.

Highlights extraordinary role of *École Polytechnique* in servicing French imperialism.

Brunschwig, H. *French colonialism, 1871–1914: myths and realities* (New York: Praeger, 1966).

France sought colonies for prestige, not profit.

Cohen, W.B. Malaria and French imperialism. *Journal of African History* **24**, pp. 23–36, 1983.

Frémeaux, J. *L'Afrique à l'ombre des épées* [2 vols] (Vincennes: Service historique de l'armée de terre, 1995–6).

Doctoral thesis; insights on "military imperialism".

Ganiage, J. *L'expansion coloniale de la France sous la Troisième République (1871–1914)* (Paris: Payot, 1968).

Rather uncritical survey.

Girardet, R. *L'idée coloniale en France de 1871 à 1962* (Paris: Le Table Ronde, 1972).

Girardet, R. *La société militaire dans la France contemporaine, 1815–1939* (Paris: Plon, 1953).

Best book on its subject.

Jauffret, J.-C. *Parlement, gouvernement, commandement: l'armée de métier sous la 3e République, 1871–1914* [2 vols] (Vincennes: Service historique de l'armée de terre, 1987).

Essential for French debate on volunteer colonial army.

Johnson, G.W. (ed.). *Double impact: France and Africa in the age of imperialism* (Westport, Conn.: Greenwood Press, 1985).

See essays by Balesi and Barrows.

Murphy, A. *Ideology of French imperialism, 1871–1881* (Washington, D.C.: Catholic University Press, 1948).

Imperial thought in France on eve of Scramble.

Newbury, C.W. & A.S. Kanya-Forstner. French policy and the origins of the Scramble for West Africa. *Journal of African History* **10**, pp. 253–76, 1969.

Contests Robinson-Gallagher thesis on origins of Scramble.

Person, Y. French military imperialism. *Journal of African History* **13**, pp. 507–10, 1972.

Mild corrective of Kanya-Forstner thesis.

Porch, D. *The march to the Marne: the French army, 1871–1914* (Cambridge: Cambridge University Press, 1981).

Good chapter on colonial army.

Porch, D. *The French Foreign Legion. A complete history of the legendary fighting force* (New York: HarperCollins, 1991).

Chapter on Dahomey war in 1890s, Legion's only venture into sub-Saharan Africa.

Schneider, W.H. *An empire for the masses: the French popular image of Africa, 1870–1900* (Westport, Conn.: Greenwood, 1982).

Attempt to show that France, too, had its popular imperialist phase.

Vansina, J., C.H. Perrot, R. Austen, Y. Person et al. (eds). *Etudes africaines offertes à Henri Brunschwig* (Paris: Editions de l'école des hautes études en sciences sociales, 1983).

See essay by Pasquier on Algerian roots of colonial policy in Senegal.

Britain

Bailes, H. Technology and imperialism: a case study of the Victorian army in Africa. *Victorian Studies* **24**(1), pp. 82–104, 1980.

British colonial army was not blind to technical progress.

Bolt, C. *Victorian attitudes to race* (London: Routledge & Kegan Paul, 1971).

Clayton, A. & D. Killingray (eds). *Khaki and Blue: military and police in British colonial Africa* (Athens, Ohio: Ohio University Press, 1989).

Clowes, W.L. *The Royal Navy: a history from the earliest times to the death of Queen Victoria* [7 vols] (London: Sampson, Low, Marston, 1903).

Still very useful; mine of information on African campaigns.

Dawson, G. *Soldier heroes and adventure narratives* (New York: Routledge, 1994).

Eldridge, C.C. *England's mission: the imperial idea in the age of Gladstone and Disraeli, 1868–1880* (Chapel Hill, North Carolina: University of North Carolina Press, 1974).

Another view of era of "imperialism of free trade".

Faber, R. *The vision and the need: late Victorian imperialist aims* (London: Faber & Faber, 1966).

Farwell, B. *Queen Victoria's little wars* (New York: Harper & Row, 1972).

The old military history but a good read.

Field, C. *Britain's sea soldiers. A history of the Royal Marines and their predecessors and of their services in action, ashore and afloat, and upon sundry other occasions of moment* [2 vols] (Liverpool: Lyceum Press, 1924).

Fraser, E. & L.G. Carr-Laughton. *The Royal Marine Artillery, 1804–1923* [2 vols] (London: Royal United Service Institution, 1930).

Gann, L.H. & P. Duignan (eds). *The rulers of British Africa, 1870–1914* (Stanford: Stanford University Press, 1978).

Contains useful information but a bit too jolly.

Harries-Jenkins, G. *The army in Victorian society* (London: Routledge, 1977).

See entry for Skelley below.

Haywood, A. & F.A.S. Clarke. *The history of the Royal West African Frontier Force* (Aldershot: Polden, 1969).

Compares unfavourably with Moyse-Bartlett's history of KAR.

Judd, D. *Radical Joe: a life of Joseph Chamberlain* (London: Hamilton, 1977).

Political face of popular imperialism.

Kennedy, P.M. *The rise and fall of British naval mastery* (London: A. Lane, 1976).

Kennedy, P.M. *The rise of the Anglo-German antagonism, 1860–1914* (London: Allen & Unwin, 1980).

Lorimer, D.A. *Colour, class and the Victorians: English attitudes to the Negro in the mid-nineteenth century* (Leicester: Leicester University Press, 1978).

Lugard, F.D. [1893]. *The rise of our East African empire: early efforts in Nyasaland and Uganda* (London: Cass, 1968).

Lugard's first bow on imperial stage in Africa.

MacKenzie, J.M. (ed.). *Popular imperialism and the military, 1850–1950* (Manchester: Manchester University Press, 1992).

Good chapters on heroic myths and war correspondents.

Mangan, J.A. *The games ethic and imperialism: aspects of the diffusion of an idea* (Harmondsworth: Viking, 1986).

Meinertzhagen, R. *Kenya diary, 1902–1906* (London: Oliver and Boyd, 1957).

Diary of an unabashed war lover.

Morris, J. *Heaven's command: an imperial progress* (San Diego, Calif.: Harcourt Brace Jovanovich, 1973).

James/Jan Morris's volumes are essential first reading for novice students of British imperialism.

Morris, J. *Pax Britannica: the climax of an empire* (San Diego, Calif.: Harcourt Brace Jovanovich, 1968).

Moyse-Bartlett, H. *The King's African Rifles, a study in the military history of East and Central Africa* (Aldershot: Gale & Polden, 1956).

One of the more scholarly regimental histories; useful.

Perham, M. *Lugard. The years of adventure, 1858–1898* (London: Collins, 1956).

Too admiring, but one of the best biographies extant of an imperial proconsul.

Porter, B. *The lion's share: a short history of British imperialism* (Harlow: Longman, 1975).

Next essential reading after Morris.

Rich, P. *Race and empire in British politics* (Cambridge: Cambridge University Press, 1986).

Schreuder, D.M. *The Scramble for Southern Africa, 1877–1895* (Cambridge: Cambridge University Press, 1980).

To be read along with Axelson and Katzenellebogen.

Skelley, A.R. *The Victorian army at home* (London: Croom Helm, 1977).

Early 'army and society' study but still important.

Spiers, E.M. *The [British] army and society, 1815–1914* (Harlow: Longman, 1980).

Seminal; very helpful on Cardwell reforms.

Uzoigwe, G.N. *Britain and the conquest of Africa* (Ann Arbor, Michigan: University of Michigan Press, 1975).
African specialist on military history.

Germany

Hiery, H.J. *The neglected war: the German South Pacific and the influence of World War I* (Honolulu: University of Hawai'i Press, 1995).
Useful for comparative purposes.
Knoll, A.J. & L.H. Gann (eds). *Germans in the tropics: essays in German colonial history* (Westport, Conn.: Greenwood Press, 1987).
Pogge von Strandmann, H. Domestic origins of Germany's colonial expansion under Bismarck. *Past and Present* **42**, pp. 140–59, 1969.
'Peripheral flux' didn't pull Germans into Africa.
Pogge von Strandmann, H. The German role in Africa and German imperialism: a review article. *African Affairs* **69**, pp. 381–9, 1970.
Dated now German unification has opened Potsdam archives to all comers.
Rudin, H. *Germans in the Cameroons, 1884–1914: a case study in modern imperialism* (New Haven: Yale University Press, 1938).
Generally favourable picture.
Schnee, H. [1926]. *German colonization past and future: the truth about the German colonies* (New York: Kennikat Press, 1970).
Attempt to dispel 'Black Legend' of German colonialism.
Smith, W.D. *The German colonial empire* (Chapel Hill, North Carolina: University of North Carolina Press, 1978).
Best survey in English.
Stoecker, Helmuth (ed.). *German imperialism in Africa: from the beginnings until the Second World War* (London: C. Hurst, 1986).
East German essays.

Congo Free State

Ascherson, N. *The king incorporated: Leopold II in the age of trusts* (London: Allen & Unwin, 1963).
Colourful journalist's life of the king.
Gann, L.H. (ed.). *Rulers of Belgian Africa, 1884–1914* (Princeton: Princeton University Press, 1979).
Slimmest of "Rulers of . . ." series; weak on military side.
Slade, R.M. *King Leopold's Congo: aspects of the development of race relations in the Congo Independent State* (London: Oxford University Press, 1962).
Stanley, H.M. *The Congo and the founding of its Free State* [2 vols] (New York: Harper & Bros, 1885).
Personal account by "founding father" of Free State.

Stengers, J. (ed.). *Textes inédits d'Emile Banning* (Brussels: Académie royale des sciences d'outre-mer, 1955).

Banning was Leopold's advisor on colonial affairs.

Vansina, J. *Kingdoms of the savanna* (Madison: University of Wisconsin Press, 1966).

Classic use of oral history to fill in gaps in history of African pre-colonial states, in this case kingdoms of southern Congo.

Italy

Battaglia, R. *La prima guerra d'Africa* (Turin: Einaudi, 1958).

First major non-fascist account of first Ethiopian war; breakthrough to revisionist history of Italian imperialism.

Baratieri, O. *Pagine d'Africa (1875–1901)*. N. Labanca (ed.) (Trento: Museo del Risorgimento e della lotta per la libertà, 1994).

Focus is on Baratieri before Adowa.

Bosworth, R.J.B. *Italy, the least of the Great Powers: Italian foreign policy before the First World War* (London: Cambridge University Press, 1979).

Useful on pro-imperial lobbying in nineteenth century Italy.

Clark, M. *Modern Italy, 1871–1982* (Harlow: Longman, 1984).

One of the best histories of contemporary Italy in English.

Del Boca, A. *Gli italiani in Africa orientale* [4 vols] (Rome-Bari: Laterza, 1976–9).

Masterwork of Italian revisionist imperial history; engagingly written.

Giolitti, G. *Memoirs of my life* (New York: Fertig, 1973).

Some pages on Libyan war; not entirely trustworthy.

Gooch, J. *Army, state and society in Italy, 1870–1915* (New York: St. Martin's, 1989).

Pithy chapter on Italy's African wars.

Labanca, N. *Storia dell'Italia coloniale* (Milan: Fenice 2000, 1994).

Survey written for undergraduates.

Labanca, N. *In marcia verso Adua* (Turin: Einaudi, 1993).

Classic; sets Italian colonial army firmly in Italian & African socio-political contexts.

Miège, J.-L. *L'impérialisme colonial italien de 1870 à nos jours* (Paris: S.E.D.E.S, 1968).

Survey stressing demographic factor in Italian imperialism.

Pescolido, G. Il dibattito coloniale nella stampa italiana e la battaglia di Adua. *Storia contemporanea* **4**, pp. 675–711, 1973.

How the Italian press reacted to the Adowa debacle.

Rainero, R. *L'anticolonialismo italiano da Assab ad Adua (1869–1896)* (Milan: Edizioni di Comunità, 1971).

The Italian anti-imperialist tradition before Adowa.

Rainero, R. Les études italiennes sur l'Afrique de la fin de la deuxième guerre mondiale à nos jours. *Afrique contemporaine* (May–June), pp. 16–21, 1980.

Charts early days of revisionist writing on Italian imperialism.

Rochat, G. *Il colonialismo italiano* (Turin: Loescher Editore, 1972).

Documents; major emphasis is on twentieth century.

Rochat, G. & G. Massobrio. *Breve storia dell'esercito italiano dal 1861 al 1943* (Turin: Einaudi, 1978).

Outline history of Italian army in national era.

Rochat, G. *L'esercito italiano in pace e in guerra. Studi di storia militare* (Milan: RARA, 1991).

Contains helpful essays on nineteenth century Italian army.

Seton-Watson, C. *Italy from liberalism to fascism, 1870–1925* (New York: Barnes & Noble, 1967).

Now somewhat dated, but still useful.

Whittam, J. *The politics of the Italian army, 1861–1918* (London: Croom Helm, 1977).

Only book of its kind in English; a bit schematic.

Portugal

Axelson, E. *Portugal and the Scramble for Africa, 1875–1891* (Johannesburg: Witwatersrand University Press, 1967).

When Powers coveted Portuguese domains.

Clarence-Smith, G. *The third Portuguese empire, 1825–1975: a study in economic imperialism* (Manchester: Manchester University Press, 1985).

Hammond (see below) is wrong: Portugal fought to keep her colonies because they were an economic asset.

Duffy, J. *Portuguese Africa* (Cambridge, Mass.: Harvard University Press, 1961).

Old but still best rapid survey around.

Hammond, R.J. *Portugal and Africa, 1815–1910: a study in uneconomic imperialism* (Stanford: Stanford University Press, 1966).

Portugal hung on to her empire for prestige, not profits.

Oliveira Marques, A.H. de. *From empire to corporate state*, vol. 2 of *History of Portugal* (New York: Columbia University Press, 1972).

Good on nineteenth-century Portuguese domestic politics, but uncritical of Portuguese imperial record.

Telo, A.J. *Economia e imperio no Portugal contemporaneo* (Lisbon: Edições Cosmos, 1994).

See Preface.

Chapter Three: The shifting balance, 1830–1880

Algeria

Abun-Nasr, J.M. *A history of the Maghrib* (Cambridge: Cambridge University Press, 1971).

Good on Algeria before French arrived.

Ageron, C.-R. *Modern Algeria: a history from 1830 to the present* (Trenton, New Jersey: Africa World Press, 1991).

Survey by leading French specialist on area.

Bois, J.-P. *Bugeaud* (Paris: Fayard, 1997).

Up-to-date, massive, painstakingly-researched; sympathetic.

Danziger, R. *Abd-al-Qadir and the Algerians* (New York: Holmes & Meier, 1977).

Questions effectiveness of Algerian resistance.

Guiral, P. L'opinion marseillaise et les débuts de l'entreprise algérienne (1830–1841). *Revue historique* **154**, pp. 9–34, 1955.

Economic dimension of French occupation of Algiers.

Julien, C.-A. *Histoire de l'Algérie contemporaine: la conquête et les débuts de la colonisation* (Paris: Presses universitaires de France, 1964).

The indispensable source on French conquest of Algeria.

Naylor, P.C. & A. Heggoy (eds). *Historical dictionary of Algeria* (Metuchen, New Jersey: Scarecrow Press, 1994).

Useful compendium of background information.

Perkins, K.J. *Qaids, captains, and colons: French military administration in the colonial Maghrib, 1844–1934* (New York: Africana, 1980).

French army/indigenous "interface" during colonial occupation.

Ruedy, J. *Modern Algeria: the origins and development of a nation* (Bloomington: Indiana University Press, 1992).

Sees 1840s resistance to French as proto-nationalist movement.

Sullivan, A.T. *Thomas-Robert Bugeaud, France and Algeria, 1784–1849: politics, power and the good society* (Hamden, Conn.: Archon, 1983).

Best book in English on Bugeaud; useful on his impact on French style of colonial warfare.

Valensi, L. *On the eve of colonialism: North Africa before the French conquest* (New York: Africana, 1977).

Senegal

Barrows, L. The merchants and General Faidherbe. Aspects of French expansion in the 1850s. *Revue française d'histoire d'outre-mer* **61**, 223, pp. 236–83, 1974.

Faidherbe as tool of commercial interests.

Charles, E. *Precolonial Senegal: The Jolof kingdom, 1800 to 1890* (Boston: African Studies Center, 1977).

Delavignette, R. Faidherbe. See Julien (1946), pp. 75–92, 1946.

Some interesting insights, but uncritical.

Faidherbe, L.L.C. *Le Sénégal. La France dans l'Afrique occidentale*. Paris: Hachette, 1889.

Self-serving, but a mine of information.

Hardy, G. *Faidherbe* (Paris: Editions de l'Encyclopédie de l'Empire Français, 1947).

Still the best life; helpful but too admiring.

Klein, M.A. *Islam and imperialism in Senegal: Siné-Saloum, 1847–1914* (Stanford, Cal.: Stanford University Press, 1969).

Conflict and accomodation in a difficult relationship.

McLane, M.O. Commercial rivalries and French policy on the Senegal river, 1831–1858. *African Economic History* **15**, pp. 39–67, 1987.

More on Faidherbe and the merchants.

Oloruntimehin, B.O. *The Segu Tukulor empire* (New York: Humanities Press, 1972).

Good corrective to more laudatory treatments of al-Hajj Umar.

Pasquier, R. L'Influence de l'expérience algérienne sur la politique de la France au Sénégal (1842–1869), in *Perspectives nouvelles sur le passé de l'Afrique noire et de Madagascar. Mélanges offerts à Hubert Deschamps*, C.-A. Julien (ed.), 263–84 (Paris: Publications de la Sorbonne, 1974).

Faidherbe l'Algérien.

Robinson, D. *The holy war of Umar Tal* (Oxford: Clarendon, 1985).

Fine interpretive study of al-Hajj Umar's jihad from a politico–military perspective.

Willis, J.R. *In the path of Allah: the passion of al-Hajj Umar: an essay into the nature of charisma in Islam* (London: Cass, 1989).

More theological than Robinson, but also helpful.

Ashanti

Arhin, K. Asante military institutions. *Journal of African Studies* **7**, pp. 22–31, 1980.

Disappointing.

Brackenbury, H. *Ashanti war* [2 vols] (London: Blackwood, 1874).

Insider's account; author was Wolseley's military secretary.

Edgerton, R.B. *The fall of the Asante Empire: the hundred-year war for Africa's Gold Coast* (New York: Free Press, 1995).

Zulus on dust jacket; sensationalism within.

Fynn, J.K. Ghana-Asante (Ashanti). See Crowder (1971), pp. 19–52, 1971.

Some insights on Ashanti army but generally uncritical.

Keegan, J. The Ashanti campaign, 1873–4. See Bond (ed.) 1967, pp. 161–198, 1968.

Good on decision to send British troops into "white man's grave".

Lehmann, J.H. *All Sir Garnet: a life of Field-Marshal Lord Wolseley* (London: Jonathan Cape, 1964).

Admiring, perhaps more revealing than author intended.

Lloyd, A. *The drums of Kumasi: the story of the Ashanti wars* (Harlow: Longman, 1964).

Anecdotal, without scholarly apparatus, but evocative.

Maurice, F. *Life of Lord Wolseley* (London: Heinemann, 1924).

Another insider; Wolseley's private secretary 1873–4.

Maxwell, L. *The Ashanti Ring: Sir Garnet Wolseley's campaigns, 1870–1882* (London: Leo Cooper, 1985).

Popular account of heyday of Wolseley's coterie.

McCaskie, T.C. *State and society in pre-colonial Asante* (Cambridge: Cambridge University Press, 1995).

Helpful, but does not replace Wilks' older study.

McIntyre, W.D. *The imperial frontier in the tropics, 1865–75: a study of British colonial policy in West Africa, Malaya and the South Pacific in the age of Gladstone and Disraeli* (London: Macmillan, 1967).

Illuminating on evolution of Britain's Ashanti policy.

Myatt, F. *The Golden Stool: an account of the Ashanti War of 1900* (London: William Kimber, 1966).

Hardboiled but informative soldier's treatment of Ashantis' last stand.

Reynolds, E. *Trade and economic change on the Gold Coast, 1807–1874* (Harlow: Longman, 1974).

Useful for economic background to 1873–4 Ashanti war.

Stanley, H.M. *Coomassie and Magdala: the story of two British campaigns in Africa* (New York: Harper, 1874).
Ebullient eyewitness account by one of era's leading journalists.
Tordoff, W. *Ashanti under the Prempehs, 1888–1935* (London: Oxford University Press, 1965).
Traces disintegration of Ashanti kingdom following 1873–4 war.
Wilks, I. *Asante in the nineteenth century: the structure and evolution of a political order* (London: Cambridge University Press, 1975).
Massive, difficult to use, but the one really indispensable book on the Ashanti side of the conflict.

Zulu War

Delius, P. *The land belongs to us: the Pedi polity, the Boers, and the British in nineteenth-century Transvaal* (Berkeley: University of California Press, 1984).
How the Pedi kept the Boers at bay down into our century.
Duminy, A. & C. Ballard (eds). *The Anglo-Zulu War: new perspectives* (Pietermaritzburg: University of Natal Press, 1981).
Essays on debate over British culpability in coming of war.
Edgerton, R.B. *Like lions they fought: the Zulu War and the last black empire in South Africa* (New York: Free Press, 1988).
Good social analysis of British and Zulu armies.
Emery, F. *The red soldier: letters from the Zulu War, 1879* (London: Hodder & Stoughton, 1977).
What Tommy thought of his Zulu enemies.
Gump, J.O. *The dust rose like smoke: the subjugation of the Zulu and the Sioux* (Lincoln, Nebraska: University of Nebraska Press, 1994).
Stimulating cross-cultural study; popular with students.
Gump, J. *The formation of the Zulu kingdom in South Africa, 1750–1840* (Lewiston, New York: Edwin Mellen Press, 1991).
Background to *Mfecane* and creation of Zulu empire.
Guy, J. A note on firearms in the Zulu kingdom with special reference to the Anglo-Zulu War, 1879. *Journal of African History* **12**, pp. 557–70, 1971.
Why Zulus never took up the gun.
Guy, J. *The destruction of the Zulu kingdom: the civil war in Zululand, 1879–1884* (Harlow: Longman, 1979).
Wolseley destroyed the Zulu empire, not Chelmsford.
Knight, I. *The anatomy of the Zulu army: from Shaka to Cetshwayo, 1818–1879* (London: Greenhill, 1995).
Study of "how the Zulu army actually worked"; basic.
Laband, J. *Kingdom in crisis: the Zulu response to the British invasion of 1879* (Manchester: Manchester University Press, 1992).
Perhaps best politico-military account of events of 1879.
Lock, R. *Blood on the Painted Mountain: Zulu victory and defeat, Hlobane and Kambula, 1879* (London: Greenhill, 1995).
Popular account of Hlubane, the "other" Zulu triumph.

Morris, D. [1965]. *The washing of the spears: a history of the rise of the Zulu nation under Shaka and its fall in the Zulu War of 1879* (New York: Simon & Schuster, 1972).
First big book on Zulus, dated but still influential.

Mostert, N. *Frontiers: the epic tragedy of South Africa's creation and the tragedy of the Xhosa people* (New York: Knopf, 1992).
Grinding down of Nelson Mandela's people in nine frontier wars.

Ritter, E.A. *Shaka Zulu: the rise of the Zulu Empire* (London: Longmans, Green, 1955).
Partially rooted in oral history, contemporary accounts.

Chapter Four: Flood tide, 1880–1898

Western Sudan

Andrew, C.M. & A.S. Kanya-Forstner. The French "Colonial Party": its composition, aims and influence, 1885–1914. *The Historical Journal* **14**(1), pp. 99–128, 1971.
Rise of powerful pro-imperial lobby.

Balesi, C. *From adversaries to comrades-in-arms: West Africans and the French military, 1885–1918* (Waltham, Mass.: Crossroads Books, 1979).
Too willing to overlook French beastliness to African soldiers, but very useful study.

Cooke, J.J. *New French imperialism 1880–1910: the Third Republic and colonial expansion* (Hamden, Conn.: Archon Books, 1973).

Davis, S.C. *Reservoirs of men: a history of the black troops of French West Africa* (Geneva: Chambéry Press of the University of Geneva, 1934).
Background to the *Force noire*.

Echenburg, M. Late nineteenth-century military technology in Upper Volta. *Journal of African History* **12**, pp. 241–54, 1971.

Echenberg, M. *Colonial conscripts: The Tirailleurs Sénégalais in French West Africa, 1857–1960* (Portsmouth, New Hampshire: Heinemann, 1991).

Fugelstad, F. *A history of Niger, 1850–1960* (Cambridge: Cambridge University Press, 1983).
To be read along with Porch's *Conquest of the Sahara*.

Harrison, C. *France and Islam in West Africa, 1860–1960* (Cambridge: Cambridge University Press, 1988).
Mostly on twentieth-century affairs.

Kanya-Forstner, A.S. *The conquest of the western Sudan: a study in French military imperialism* (Cambridge: Cambridge University Press, 1969).
The essential book on French "military imperialism".

Kanya-Forstner, A.S. The French marines and the conquest of the Western Sudan, 1880–1899. See De Moor & Wesseling (eds), pp. 121–45, 1989.
Covers period of Scramble: wars against Ahmadu Seku and Samori.

Kanya-Forstner, A.S. Mali-Tukolor. See Crowder (1971), pp. 53–79, 1971.
The wars of al-Hajj Umar and Ahmadu Seku.

Legassick, M. Firearms, horses and Samorian army organization, 1870–1898. *Journal of African History* **7**(1), pp. 95–115, 1966.
Insightful attempt at explaining how Samori's army worked.

Michel, Marc. Un mythe: la "Force Noire" avant 1914. *Relations internationales* **2**, pp. 83–90, 1974.

Persell, S.M. *The French colonial lobby, 1889–1938* (Stanford: Hoover Institution Press, 1983). Superseded by research of Andrew and Kanya-Forstner.

Person, Y. Samori and resistance to the French. See Rotberg & Mazrui (eds), pp. 80–112, 1970.
Useful but heavy going; Person assumes a great deal from readers.

Porch, D. *The conquest of the Sahara* (New York: Knopf, 1984).
The ignominious Chad campaign, among others.

Power, T.F. *Jules Ferry and the renaissance of French imperialism* (New York: King's Crown Press, 1944).
Old but still useful study of leading French imperialist.

Weiskel, T.S. *French colonial rule and the Baulé peoples* (Oxford: Oxford University Press, 1980).
One of few studies of resistance of "stateless peoples" to European conquest.

Congo Free State

Brode, H. *Tippoo Tib: the story of his career in Central Africa, narrated from his own accounts* (Chicago: Afro-Am Press, 1969).
Useful corrective to Leopoldine demonologies.

Ceulemans, P. *La question arabe et le congo, 1883–1892* (Brussels: Académie royale des sciences coloniales, 1959).
Major revisionist account of Arab wars; perhaps leans too far in opposite direction.

Cornevin, R. *Histoire du Congo, Léopoldville-Kinshasha* (Paris: Berger-Levrault, 1970).
Rapid overview.

Force Publique. *La Force Publique de sa naissance à 1914: participation des militaires à l'histoire des premières années du Congo* (Brussels: Institut Royal Colonial Belge, 1952).
Self-serving, but extremely helpful if used critically.

Hinde, S. *The fall of the Congo Arabs* (New York: Negro Universities Press, 1969).
British doctor in *Force Publique*; interesting on Arab wars.

Hochschild, A. Mr. Kurtz, I presume? *The New Yorker* (April), pp. 40–47, 1997.
Search for "real" Kurtz of Conrad's *Heart of darkness*; good on "interface" between *Force Publique* and indigenous population.

Portuguese wars of occupation

Enes, A. [1899]. *A guerra de Africa em 1895*, 2nd edn (Lisbon: Edições Gama, 1945).
Best source on 1895 war; gives political as well as military dimension; author was High Commissioner in Mozambique.

Enes, A. [1893]. *Moçambique: Relatorio apresentado ao governo*, 3rd edn (Lisbon: Agencia Geral das Colonias, 1946).
What's wrong with the colony; what must be done.

Isaacman, A. & B. Isaacman. *The tradition of resistance in Mozambique: the Zambesi Valley, 1850–1921* (Berkeley: University of California Press, 1976).

Best source on resistance in Zambesi area; good bibliography.

Isaacman, A. & B. Isaacman. *Mozambique: from colonialism to revolution, 1900–1982* (Boulder, Colorado: Westview Press, 1983).

Chapters 2,3,4 on pre-1914 era.

Katzenellenbogen, S.E. *South Africa and southern Mozambique: labour, railways and trade in the making of a relationship* (Manchester: University of Manchester Press, 1982).

How South Africa shaped future of Mozambique.

Newitt, M.D.D. *A history of Mozambique* (Bloomington: Indiana University Press, 1995).

Massive, comprehensive; good on nineteenth century.

Pélissier, R. *Les guerres grises. Résistance et révoltes en Angola (1845–1941)* (Orgeval, France: Pélissier, 1977).

Endless wars in Portugal's most important colony.

Pélissier, R. *Naissance du Mozambique: résistance et révoltes anticoloniales (1854–1918)* [2 vols] (Orgeval, France: Pélissier, 1984).

Exhaustive and exhausting; crucial to understanding colonial warfare in Mozambique in 1890s.

Pélissier, R. *Naissance de la Guiné: Portugais et africains en Sénégambie (1841–1936)* (Orgeval, France: Pélissier, 1989).

Can be read for own sake or as introduction to later struggle of Amilcar Cabral in Guinea-Bissau.

Texeira Botelho, J.J. *Historia militar e politica dos Portugueses em Moçambique de 1833 aos nossos dias*, 2nd edn (Lisbon: Centro Tip. Colonial, 1936).

Comprehensive military history of Portugal's colonial wars.

Vail, L. Mozambique's chartered companies: the rule of the feeble. *Journal of African History* **19**, pp. 239–63, 1978.

1895 war opens up Mozambique to inefficient private monopolies.

Warhurst, P.R. *Anglo-Portuguese relations in South-Central Africa, 1890–1900* (Harlow: Longman, 1962).

From conflict to accomodation.

Wheeler, D.L. Gungunhana. See Bennett, pp. 167–220, 1968.

Biography of Gaza Nguni king in Mozambique.

Wheeler, D.L. Gungunyane the negotiator: a study in African diplomacy. *Journal of African History* **9**, pp. 585–602, 1968.

King's vain attempt to preserve his realm through diplomacy.

Wheeler, D.L. Joaquim Mousinho de Albuquerque (1855–1902). See Gann & Duignan (eds), *African proconsuls*, pp. 427–44, 1979.

Portrait of feudal knight errant who became a fascist hero.

Wheeler, D.L. & R. Pélissier. *Angola* (New York: Praeger, 1971).

First part, by Wheeler, covers nineteenth century.

Ethiopia

Aquarone, A. La politica coloniale italiana dopo Adua: Ferdinando Martini governatore in Eritrea. *Rassegna storia del Risorgimento* **62**, pp. 449–83, 1975.

Damage control.

Baratieri, O. *Mémoires d'Afrique (1892–1896)* (Paris: H. Lavauzelle, 1899).

His side of the story; useful detail.

Caulk, R.A. Armies as predators: soldiers and peasants in Ethiopia. *International Journal of African Studies* **11**, pp. 457–93, 1978.

Chandler, D.G. The expedition to Abyssinia, 1867–8. See Bond (ed.), pp. 105–159, 1967.

Crummey, D. Tewodros as reformer and modernizer. *Journal of African History* **10**, pp. 457–69, 1969.

Darkwah, R.H.K. *Shewa, Menelik and the Ethiopian empire* (London: Heinemann, 1975).

Background to rise of Menelik.

Dunn, J. " 'For God, Emperor, country!' The evolution of Ethiopia's nineteenth-century army", *War in History* **7**(3), pp. 278–99, 1994.

Ehrlich, H. *Ethiopia and Eritrea during the Scramble for Africa: a political biography of Ras Alula, 1875–1897* (East Lansing, Michigan: African Studies Center, Michigan State University, 1982).

Emperor Yohannes's great general; victor over Italians at Dogali.

Hess, R.L. The "Mad Mullah" and Northern Somalia. *Journal of African History* **5**, pp. 415–34, 1964.

One of Africa's great guerrilla leaders.

Hess, R.L. Italian imperialism in its Ethiopian context. *The International Journal of African Historical Studies* **6**(1), pp. 94–109, 1973.

Jaenen, C. Theodore II and British intervention in Ethiopia. *Canadian Journal of History/ Annales canadiennes d'histoire* **1**(2), pp. 27–56, 1966.

Jaenen, C. *Ethiopia before the Congo: a proposed Belgian colony in Ethiopia, 1838–1856* (Ottawa, Canada: Institute for International Co-operation, 1974).

Loring, W.W. *A Confederate soldier in Egypt* (New York: Dodd, Mead, 1884).

Marcus, H.G. The black men who turned white: European attitudes towards Ethiopians, 1850–1900. *Archiv Orientalni* **39**, pp. 155–66, 1971.

Marcus, H.G. *The life and times of Menelik II: Ethiopia, 1844–1914* (Oxford: Clarendon, 1975).

Marcus, H.G. *A history of Ethiopia* (Berkeley: University of California Press, 1994).

Best modern account in English.

Myatt, F. *The march to Magdala: the Abyssinian war of 1868* (London: Leo Cooper, 1970).

More hardboiled narrative from Myatt.

Prouty, C. *Empress Taytu and Menilek II: Ethiopia, 1883–1910* (London: Ravens Educational & Development Service, 1986).

Fascinating life and times study of Menelik's fiery, nationalist consort.

Prouty, C. *Historical dictionary of Ethiopia and Eritrea* (Metuchen, New Jersey: Scarecrow Press, 1994).

Useful for background data.

Rubenson, S. Adwa 1896: the resounding protest. See Rotberg & Mazrui (eds), pp. 113–42, 1970.

Significance of Ethiopian victory.

Rubenson, S. *The survival of Ethiopian independence* (London: Heinemann, 1976).

Why and how Ethiopia avoided the common African fate.

Taddesse B., T. Taddesse & R. Pankhurst (eds). *The centenary of Dogali: proceedings of the International Symposium, Addis Ababa-Asmara, January 24–25, 1987* (Addis Ababa: Institute of Ethiopian Studies, 1988).

Essays on first major Ethiopian victory over Italians.

Wylde, A.B. *Modern Abyssinia* (London: Methuen, 1900).

Knowledgeable British diplomat.

Zewde B. *A history of modern Ethiopia, 1855–1974* (London: James Currey, 1991).

Outline history by Ethiopian historian.

Zewde G.-S. *Yohannes IV of Ethiopia: a political biography* (Oxford: Clarendon, 1975).

The Mahdiyya

Bjorkels, A. *Prelude to the Mahdiyya* (New York: Cambridge University Press, 1988).

Brown, L.C. The Sudanese Mahdiya. See Rotberg & Mazrui (eds), pp. 145–68, 1970.

Sees Sudanese Mahdism as typical product of "Muslim fringe area".

David, P. Le Soudan et l'état mahdiste sous le khalifa 'Abdullahi (1885–1899). *Revue française d'histoire d'outre-mer* **75**(280), pp. 273–307, 1988.

Useful focus on Mahdist state in Sudan after death of Mahdi.

Elton, G.E. *Gordon of Khartoum; the life of General Charles George Gordon* (New York: Knopf, 1954).

Hill, R. & P. Hogg. *A black corps d'elite: an Egyptian Sudanese conscript battalion with the French Army in Mexico, 1863–1867, and its survivors in subsequent African history* (East Lansing: Michigan State University Press, 1995).

Far-flung adventures of one of Africa's "martial races".

Holt, P.M. & M.W. Daly. *History of the the Sudan*, 4th edn (Harlow: Longman, 1988).

Holt, P.M. *Mahdist state in the Sudan*, 2nd edn (Oxford: Clarendon Press, 1970).

The classic account of Mahdist politics. Indispensable.

Keown-Boyd, H. *A good dusting: a centenary review of the Sudan campaigns 1883–1899* (London: Leo Cooper, 1986).

Lavish, large-format account of Sudan wars which shows how little some people have learned in a hundred years.

Magnus, P. *Kitchener: portrait of an imperialist* (London: Murray, 1958).

A life badly in need of updating; weak on Sudan episode.

Robson, B. *Fuzzy Wuzzy: the campaigns in the Eastern Sudan, 1884–85* (Tunbridge Wells, Englang: Spellmount, 1993).

Conventional military history of "forgotten years" of Sudan warfare between death of Gordon and advent of Kitchener.

Shaked, H. *The life of the Sudanese Mahdi* (New Brunswick, New Jersey: Transaction Books, 1978).

Theobald, A.B. *The Mahdiyya: a history of the Anglo-Egyptian Sudan, 1881–1899* (Harlow: Longman, 1957).

Old, but still useful on military dimension of Mahdism.

Vatikiotis, P.J. *A modern history of Egypt* (New York: Praeger, 1969).

Good on Egypt's involvement in Sudan in nineteenth century.

Zulfo, I.H. *Karari: the Sudanese account of the battle of Omdurman* (London: Zed Press, 1980).

Important corrective to "Four Feathers" version of battle of Omdurman.

Chapter Five: Ominous portents, 1898–1914

Boer Wars

Amery, L.S. *The Times history of the War in South Africa, 1899–1902* (London: S. Low, Marston, 1900–9).

Influential account which lionized Roberts at expense of Wolseley and Buller.

Bond, B. The South African War, 1880–1. See Bond (1967), pp. 199–240, 1967.

Sheds much light on one of more obscure British colonial wars.

De Kiewiet, C.W. *The imperial factor in South Africa* (Cambridge: Cambridge University Press, 1966).

Denoon, D. *Settler capitalism: the dynamics of independent development in the Southern Hemisphere* (Oxford: Clarendon, 1983).

Farwell, B. *The great Anglo-Boer war* (New York: Harper & Row, 1976).

By one of the great practicioners of "guns and drums" military history; eminently readable.

Hamilton, I. *Listening for the drums* (London: Faber, 1944).

The Cardwell reforms cost Britain the First Boer War.

Kruger, R. *Goodbye, Dolly Gray: the story of the Boer War* (Philadelphia: Lippincott, 1960).

Highly readable popular account.

Nasson, B. *Abraham Esau's war . . . 1899–1902* (Cambridge: Cambridge University Press, 1991).

An African's Second Boer War.

Pakenham, T. *The Boer war* (New York: Random House, 1979).

Massive like all of Pakenham's books; notable for attempt to salvage reputation of Redvers Buller.

Porter, A.N. *The origins of the South African war: Joseph Chamberlain and the diplomacy of imperialism, 1895–99* (Manchester: Manchester University Press, 1980).

Ransford, O. *The battle of Majuba Hill; the first Boer War* (New York: Crowell, 1967).

Old style military history.

Stone, J. & E. Schmidl. *The Boer War and military reforms* (Lanham, Maryland: University Press of America, 1988).

Warwick, P. *Black people and the South African War 1899–1902* (Cambridge: Cambridge University Press, 1983).

Explodes myth of black non-involvement in 1899–1902 war.

Northern Nigeria

Adeleye, R.A. Mahdist triumph and British revenge in northern Nigeria: Satiru 1906. *Journal of the Historical Society of Nigeria* 6(2), pp. 193–214, 1972.

Backwell, H.F. (ed.). *The occupation of Hausaland, 1900–1904* (London: Cass, 1969).

Reprint of contemporary account.

Dusgate, R.H. *The conquest of Northern Nigeria* (London: Frank Cass, 1985).

Cryptic, nuts-and-bolts military history.

Fisher, H.J. & V. Rowland. Firearms in the Central Sudan. *Journal of African History* 12, pp. 215–239, 1971.

Ikime, O. *The fall of Nigeria* (London: Heinemann, 1977).
Nigerian perspective on conquest of Northern Nigeria.
Muffett, D.J.M. *Concerning brave captains: being a history of the British occupation of Kano and Sokoto and of the last stand of the Fulani forces* (London: André Deutsch, 1964).
Best book on the Northern Nigeria campaign.
Perham, M. & M. Bull (eds). *Nigeria, 1894–5 and 1898*, vol. 4 of *The diaries of Lord Lugard* (London: Faber & Faber, 1963).
Lugard in employ of Sir George Goldie.

South West Africa (& Maji-Maji rebellion)

Adas, M. [1979]. *Prophets of rebellion: millenarian protest movements against the European colonial order* (Cambridge: Cambridge University Press, 1987).
Some insightful pages on Maji-Maji rebellion.
Bridgman, J. *The revolt of the Hereros* (Berkeley: University of California Press, 1981).
Standard account in English.
Drechsler, H. *Let us die fighting. The struggle of the Herero and Nama against German imperialism (1884–1915)* (London: Zed Press, 1980).
Translation from German; more detail than Bridgman but also more polemic.
Gann, L.H. & P. Duignan (eds). *The rulers of German Africa, 1884–1914* (Stanford, Cal.: Stanford University Press, 1977).
Useful like all "Rulers of..." books, but too unreflective.
Gugelberger, G.M. (ed.). *Nama/Namibia: diary and letters of Nama chief Hendrik Witbooi, 1884–1894* (Boston: Boston University African Studies Center, 1984).
Another of Africa's great guerrilla leaders.
Iliffe, J. *A modern history of Tanganyika* (Cambridge: Cambridge University Press, 1979).
Puts Maji-Maji rebellion in context of modern history of Tanzania.
Iliffe, J. Organization of the Maji-Maji Rebellion. *Journal of African History* **8**(3), pp. 495–512, 1967.
Jackson, R.D. Resistance to the German invasion of the Tanganyikan coast, 1888–1891. See Rotberg & Mazrui (eds) pp. 37–79, 1970.
First revolt against Germans in Tanganyika.
Poewe, Karla. *The Namibian Herero: a history of their psychological disintegration and survival* (Lewiston, New York: Edwin Mellen Press, 1985).
Narrow escape from genocide.

Morocco

Andrew, C. & S. Kanya-Forstner. *The Great War and the climax of French imperial expansion* (London: Thames & Hudson, 1981).
The Moroccan conquest set in the context of continued French imperial expansion during the era of the First World War.
Burke, Edmund. Pan-Islam and Moroccan resistance to French colonial penetration, 1900–1912. *Journal of African History* **13**, pp. 97–118, 1972.

French feared that Moroccan resistance was part of pan-Islamic movement.

Dunn, R.E. *Resistance in the desert: Moroccan responses to French imperialism, 1881–1912* (London: Croom Helm, 1977).

Study of resistance in one region of Morocco.

Hoisington, W.A. *Lyautey and the French conquest of Morocco* (New York: St. Martin's, 1995).

Most recent biography in English; nicely nuanced.

Lyautey, H. *Paroles d'action* (Paris: Imprimérie Nationale, 1995).

The great man's views on colonial policy.

Maurois, A. *Marshal Lyautey* (London: John Lane & The Bodley Head, 1931).

Admiring biography.

Porch, D. *Conquest of Morocco* (New York: Knopf, 1983).

Good corrective to laudatory treatments of Lyautey.

Libya

Askew, W.C. *Europe and Italy's acquisition of Libya, 1911–1912* (Durham, North Carolina: Duke University Press, 1942).

The diplomatic dimension.

Beehler, W.H. *The history of the Italian-Turkish war, September 29, 1911, to October 18, 1912* (Annapolis, Maryland: Advertiser-Republican, 1913).

Report of an American observer.

Childs, T.W. *Italo-Turkish diplomacy and war over Libya, 1911–1912* (Leiden: Brill, 1990).

Del Boca, A. *Tripoli bel suol d'amore 1860–1922*, vol. 2 of *Gli italiani in Libia* (Rome-Bari: Laterza, 1968).

The authoritative history.

Griffin, E.H. *Adventures in Tripoli: a doctor in the desert* (London: P. Allan, 1924).

Herrmann, D.G. The paralysis of Italian strategy in the Italian-Turkish War, 1911–1912. *English Historical Review* **104**(411), pp. 332–56, 1989.

Impact of war on Italian military preparedness.

Malgeri, F. *La guerra libica* (Rome: Edizioni di Storia e Letteratura, 1970).

Next best account to Romano.

Romano, S. *La quarta sponda: la guerra di Libia, 1911/1912* (Milan: Bompiani, 1977).

Good account of opening phase of Libyan war.

Segrè, C.G. *Fourth Shore: the Italian colonization of Libya* (Chicago: Chicago University Press, 1974).

Colonization of Libya as a response to demographic pressure at home.

Chapter Six: Legacies

Imperial rivalry

Bates, D. *The Fashoda incident of 1898: encounter on the Nile* (New York: Oxford University Press, 1984).

Giffen, M.B. *Fashoda: the incident and its diplomatic setting* (Chicago: University of Chicago Press, 1930).

Lewis, D.L. *The race to Fashoda: European colonialism and African resistance in the scramble for Africa* (New York: Weidenfeld & Nicolson, 1987).

Michel, M. *La mission Marchand, 1895–99* (Paris: Mouton, 1972).

Much more than just the French version of the Fashoda story.

Stengers, J. Une facette de la question du haut-nil: le mirage soudanais. *Journal of African History* **10**, pp. 599–622, 1969.

Impact on military theory & practice

Hoyt, E. *Guerrilla: Colonel von Lettow-Vorbeck and Germany's East African empire* (London: Collier Macmillan, 1981).

Popular biography of Great War's premier guerrilla leader.

Miller, C. *Battle for the Bundu: the First World War in East Africa* (New York: Macmillan, 1974).

Best book on First World War in East Africa.

Paret, P. *French revolutionary warfare from Indochina to Algeria: the analysis of a political and military doctrine* (New York: Praeger, 1964).

Links between French art of colonial warfare and later counter-revolutionary war theory.

Ranger, T.O. *Peasant consciousness and guerrilla war in Zimbabwe: a comparative study* (London: James Currey, 1985).

Popular participation in 1890s Shona-Ndebele revolt and 1970s liberation war in Rhodesia compared.

Weigert, S. *Traditional religion and guerrilla warfare in modern Africa* (London: Macmillan, 1996).

African traditional faiths are still powerful mobilizing factor.

Impact upon the imperial powers

Betts, R. *France and decolonization, 1900–1960* (New York: St. Martin's, 1991).

Bristow, J. *Empire boys: adventures in a man's world* (London: Unwin Hyman, 1991).

Castle, K. *Britannia's children: reading colonialism through children's books and magazines* (Manchester: Manchester University Press, 1996).

Eynikel, H. *Congo belge: portrait d'une société coloniale* (Paris-Gembloux: Duculot, 1984).

Guttmann, A. *Games and empires: modern sports and cultural imperialism* (New York: Columbia University Press, 1996).

Haupt, G. & M. Rébérioux (eds). *La Deuxième Internationale et l'Orient* (Paris: Editions Cujas, 1967).

Perhaps surprisingly, socialists also were divided over virtues of empire.

MacDonald, R.H. *Sons of the empire: the frontier and the Boy Scout movement, 1890–1918* (Toronto: University of Toronto Press, 1993).

Rochat, G. *Guerre italiane in Libia e in Etiopia. Studi militari 1921–1939* (Paese: Pagus Edizioni, 1991).

Revenge for Adowa under Mussolini; also in French edition.

Thornton, A.P. *The imperial idea and its enemies* (London: Macmillan, 1959).

Classic study of anti-imperialism in Anglo-Saxon world.

Impact upon Africa

Anstey, R. *King Leopold's legacy* (London: Oxford University Press, 1966).

Arlinghaus, B. & P.H. Baker (eds). *African armies, evolution and capabilities* (Boulder, Colorado: Westview, 1986).

Asiwaju, A.I. (ed.). *Partitioned Africans: ethnic relations across Africa's international boundaries, 1884–1984* (New York: St. Martin's, 1985).

Useful collection of essays on a major African post-independence problem.

Ayittey, G.B.N. *Africa betrayed* (New York: St. Martin's, 1992).

Birmingham, D. *The decolonization of Africa* (London: UCL Press, 1996).

Clear, concise survey.

Cope, N. *To bind the nation: Solomon kaDinuzulu and Zulu nationalism, 1913–1933* (Pietermaritzburg: University of Natal Press, 1993).

Cox, T.S. *Civil-military relations in Sierra Leone: a case study of soldiers in politics* (Cambridge, Mass.: Harvard University Press, 1976).

Crowder, M. *West Africa under colonial rule* (Evanston, Illinois: Northwestern University Press, 1968).

Davidson, B. *The liberation of Guinea: aspects of an African revolution* (Harmondsworth: Penguin, 1969).

Davidson, B. *The people's cause, a history of guerrillas in Africa* (Harlow: Longman, 1981).

Decalo, S. *Coups and army rule in Africa: motivations and constraints*, 2nd edn (New Haven: Yale University Press, 1990).

Fanon, F. [1961]. *The wretched of the earth* (New York: Grove Press, 1996).

One of most important books of post-1945 era.

First, R. *The barrel of a gun: power in Africa* (New York: Pantheon, 1970).

Troubled history of military in post-independence Africa.

Griffiths, I.L. *The African inheritance* (London: Routledge, 1995).

Grundy, K.W. *Guerrilla struggle in Africa: an analysis and preview* (New York: Grossman, 1971).

Grundy, K.W. *Soldiers without politics: blacks in the South African armed forces* (Berkeley: University of California Press, 1983).

Iyob, R. *The Eritrean struggle for independence, 1941–1993* (Cambridge: Cambridge University Press, 1995).

Killingray, D. The "Rod of Empire": the debate over corporal punishment in the British African colonial forces, 1888–1946. *Journal of African History* **35**, pp. 201–16, 1994.

Lan, D. *Guns and rain: guerrillas and spirit mediums in Zimbabwe* (London: James Currey, 1985).

Continuing role for traditional religion in African warfare.

Lawler, N.E. *Soldiers of misfortune: Ivorien Tirailleurs of World War II* (Athens, Ohio: Ohio University Press, 1992).

Lee, J.M. *African armies and civil order* (New York: Praeger, 1969).

Clearly written exposé of difficulties of adaptation of colonial militaries to post-independence regimes.

Lonsdale, J. Some origins of nationalism in East Africa. *Journal of African History* **9**, pp. 119–46, 1968.

Mazrui, A.A. (ed.). *The warrior tradition in modern Africa* (Leiden: E.J. Brill, 1977).

Argues, among other things, that colonial regimes "emasculated" African males who did not do military service.

Omara-Otunnu, A. *Politics and the military in Uganda, 1890–1985* (New York: St. Martin's, 1987).

Model study of impact of colonial military recruitment policies on contemporary African politics.

Seegers, A. *The military and the making of modern South Africa* (New York: St. Martin's, 1995).

Useful on historically-conditioned Boer preference for military solutions to difficulties with African population.

Throup, D.W. *Economic and social origins of the Mau Mau, 1945–1952* (London: James Currey, 1988).

Welch, C. *Military role and rule: perspectives on civil-military relations* (North Scituate, Mass.: Duxbury Press, 1974).

Welch, C. *Civilian control of the military: theory and cases from developing countries* (Albany, New York: State University Press of New York, 1976).

Some African case studies.

Welch, C. *No farewell to arms? Military disengagement from politics in Africa and Latin America* (Boulder, Colorado: Westview, 1986).

Welch, C. (ed.). *Soldier and state in Africa: a comparative analysis of military intervention and political change* (Evanston, Illinois: Northwestern University Press, 1970).

Comparative

Axtell, J. *The invasion within: the contest of cultures in colonial North America* (New York: Oxford University Press, 1985).

Balesi, C. *The time of the French in the heart of North America, 1673–1818* (Chicago: Alliance Française, 1992).

Bearce, G. *British attitudes towards India, 1784–1858* (Oxford: Oxford University Press, 1961).

Belich, J. *The New Zealand wars and the Victorian interpretation of racial conflict* (Auckland, New Zealand: Auckland University Press, 1986).

Blakely, A. *Blacks in the Dutch world: the evolution of racial imagery in a modern society* (Bloomington: Indiana University Press, 1993).

Cady, J.F. *The roots of French imperialism in eastern Asia* (Ithaca, New York: Cornell University Press, 1954).

Calloway, C. *Crown and calumet: British-Indian relations, 1783–1815* (Norman: University of Oklahoma Press, 1987).

Caplan, L. *Warrior gentlemen: "Gurkhas" in the Western imagination* (Oxford: Berghahn Books, 1995).

Hagan, K.J. *American gunboat diplomacy and the Old Navy, 1877–1889* (Westport, Conn.: Greenwood Press, 1973).

Healy, D. *Drive to hegemony: the United States in the Caribbean, 1898–1917* (Madison, Wisconsin: University of Wisconsin Press, 1988).

Heathcote, T.A. *The military in British India: the development of British land forces in South Asia, 1600–1947* (Manchester: Manchester University Press, 1995).

Horsman, R. *Race and Manifest Destiny: the origin of American racial Anglo-Saxonism* (Cambridge, Mass.: Harvard University Press, 1981).

Ion, A.H. & E.J. Errington (eds). *Great powers and little wars: the limits of power* (Westport, Conn.: Praeger, 1993).

Jaenen, C.J. *Friend and foe: aspects of French-Amerindian cultural contact in the sixteenth and seventeenth centuries* (New York: Columbia University Press, 1976).

Jennings, F. *Empire of fortune: crowns, colonies, and tribes in the Seven Years' War in America* (New York: Norton, 1988).

Jennings, F. *The invasion of America: Indians, colonialism, and the cant of conquest* (New York: Norton, 1976).

Kuitenbrouwer, M. *The Netherlands and the rise of modern imperialism: colonies and foreign policy, 1870–1902* (Oxford: Berg, 1991).

Lezcano, V.M. *El colonialismo Hispanofrances en Marruecos (1898–1927)* (Madrid: Siglo Veintiuno de España, 1976).

Limerick, P. *The legacy of conquest: the unbroken past of the American West* (New York: Norton, 1988).

Linn, B.M. *The U.S. Army and counterinsurgency in the Philippine War* (Chapel Hill, North Carolina: University of North Carolina Press, 1989).

Metcalf, T.R. *Ideologies of the Raj* (Cambridge: Cambridge University Press, 1994).

Miller, S.C. *"Benevolent Assimilation": the American conquest of the Philippines, 1899–1903* (New Haven: Yale University Press, 1982).

Munholland, K. Admiral Jauréguiberry and the French scramble for Tonkin, 1879–83. *French Historical Studies* **16**(2), pp. 81–107, 1979.

Omissi, D. *The sepoy and the Raj: the Indian Army, 1860–1940* (London: Macmillan, 1994).

Peers, D. *Between Mars and Mammon: colonial armies and the garrison state in India, 1819–1835* (London: Tauris, 1995).

Rickey, D. *Forty miles a day on beans and hay: the enlisted soldier fighting the [USA] Indian wars* (Norman, Oklahoma: University of Oklahoma Press, 1963).

Ricklefs, M.C. *A history of modern Indonesia since c. 1300* (Stanford: Stanford University Press, 1993).

Scammell, G.V. *The first imperial age: European overseas expansion c. 1400–1715*, 2nd edn (London: HarperCollins, 1992).

Schulten, C.M. Tactics of the Dutch colonial army in the Netherlands East Indies. *Revue internationale d'histoire militaire* **70**, pp. 59–67, 1988.

Sinha, M. *Colonial masculinity: the "manly Englishman" and the "effeminate Bengali" in the late nineteenth century* (Manchester: Manchester University Press, 1995).

Steele, I.K. *Warpaths: invasions of North America* (New York: Oxford University Press, 1994).

Stokes, E. Traditional resistance movements and Afro-Asian nationalism: the context of the 1857 Mutiny Rebellion in India. *Past & Present* **48**, pp. 100–118, 1970.

Index

265